Kate Taylor

GOING HUNGRY

Kate Taylor is a culture reporter at *The New York
Sun*; her writing has also appeared in *Slate* and
The New Yorker. She graduated from Harvard
and lives in New York.

GOING HUNGRY

*Writers on Desire, Self-denial,
and Overcoming Anorexia*

EDITED BY

Kate Taylor

Anchor Books
A Division of Random House, Inc.
New York

AN ANCHOR BOOKS ORIGINAL, SEPTEMBER 2008

Library of Congress Cataloging-in-Publication Data
Going hungry : writers on desire, self-denial, and overcoming
anorexia / edited by Kate Taylor.
p. cm.
Includes bibliographical references and index.
ISBN: 978-0-307-27834-0
1. Anorexia nervosa. I. Taylor, Kate.
RC552.A5G65 2008
616.85'262—dc22
2008021642

Book design by Rebecca Aidlin

www.anchorbooks.com

Printed in the United States of America
10 9 8 7 6 5 4 3 2

To all my parents

CONTENTS

INTRODUCTION

_____

For several years, I carried in my wallet a folded piece of paper with one sentence on it:

Tomorrow there will be no more bullshit.

I wrote this when I was eleven, on the night that I decided to put all of my willpower into fighting my anorexia. The charm worked, or seemed to: I started resisting my fears and superstitions about food and, almost magically, I gained weight and became sane again. At least that's how I saw my recovery for a long time. It would be many years, and a serious relapse, before I stopped seeing anorexia as "bullshit" and began to understand what it was really about.

The first seeds of this book were planted on the day I entered the hospital, in the spring of my junior year in college. I had strongly resisted going to the hospital, because I thought I knew what the other patients would be like: pathetic, passive, probably former ballerinas with nothing more important on their minds than how many calories are in a carrot stick or a slice of diet bread.

I didn't want to imagine that I was like them. I believed, for reasons I will explain, that my weight loss was the result of a series of rational acts, which had nothing to do with wanting to be thin. Rather, I had simply found that I loved being hungry. Hunger made me feel alive and creative, emotionally sensitive and intellectually sharp. Naturally, I didn't want to give up this belief that I was rational and in control, despite overwhelming evidence to the contrary.

But meeting the other patients in the hospital, whom I had so dreaded encountering, changed my perspective. From observing them and hearing their stories, I formed a view of anorexia very different from the one I had previously held, and the one that most books about eating disorders present.

To begin with, the other patients defied all the stereotypes. Very few were young, rich white girls. At that first treatment unit outside Boston and in a later program in New York, I met anorexics who were middle-aged, who were mothers, who were African American, Latino, Orthodox Jewish, even male.

Furthermore, while I had always pictured anorexics as leading shallow and sheltered lives, these individuals had faced challenges that I could hardly imagine. Some had alcoholic or drug-addicted parents. Some had been sexually abused. Some were totally cut off from their families. I was astonished. From my reading of the literature about anorexia, which emphasizes overprotective mothers and "perfect little girls," it had never occurred to me that the illness could be the outcome of such serious problems as poverty, addiction, and abandonment. In an odd way, it was a relief, because it made being anorexic seem less silly and perverse. In some circumstances, it was the only available outlet for distress.

It also became clear to me that, despite our differences, we had something particular in common, which explained why we had ended up together in this room, at this moment in time.

The stereotypes I'd absorbed prepared me to see anorexics primarily as anxious and frightened—of growing up, of being criticized, of not being perfect. While this wasn't wholly untrue, the more I got to know the other patients, what emerged from under the layers of anxiety was the intensity of our desires and ambitions—our *hunger.* In our different ways, we were all animated by dreams of the future, of who we would be and what we would do. Like most people, we wanted love and security and feared their absence. But we also yearned for accomplishment, recognition, and a sense that our lives were meaningful.

I decided, after I finished treatment, that if listening to my fellow patients' stories had been so helpful and illuminating for me, it could be for others, too. I hope that this book will break through the stereotypes and the widespread confusion about anorexia. Many people justifiably find this illness very hard to understand. It appears at once so conventional and so strange: After all, many women wish they were thinner or worry about getting fat, but very few would starve themselves to the point of severe discomfort or death. This paradox between the conventional and the exceptional aspects of anorexia—or, one might say, between the negative (fear of being fat) and the positive (a desire *for* something)—remains when examined more closely. We exhibit a strange combination of fear of the world and hunger for it.

In my effort to put anorexia into the proper context, I compared it with other diseases that, similarly, emerged at a particular cultural moment, and later disappeared. The obvious connection is to hysteria and neurasthenia, psychosomatic diseases that were widely diagnosed in Europe and the United States in the late nineteenth century. Like anorexia, hysteria was believed primarily to affect women. Neurasthenia, symptoms of which included fatigue, depression, and impotence, was more commonly diagnosed in men.

Historians have pointed out that these illnesses simultaneously mimicked and violated the era's social conventions, in which men were supposed to be powerful and industrious, while women were expected to be delicate and refined. Men who were diagnosed with neurasthenia were described as having pushed themselves too hard professionally, until they collapsed and were reduced to total ineffectuality. Hysterics, with their emotional outbursts, flouted standards of ladylike decorum and restraint. Yet in being weak and physically helpless, they were also a sort of caricature of the ideal woman.

One interpretation of these two illnesses is that they resulted from internal conflicts, in which individuals were torn between obeying and transgressing contemporary social standards. In the words of the historian Nathan Hale, hysterical women and neurasthenic men were people with "intensely strong drives and equally intense consciences." Because of this, they "could not fulfill social norms, yet, because they had internalized them, could not consciously reject them."

When I read this description, I felt a sense of recognition: This was me. Hadn't I always felt different, yet tried to fit in? Wasn't I driven by passionate desires, yet hobbled by inhibition? Ambitious and independent, yet painfully sensitive to criticism?

———

The idea of anorexia as "bullshit" was not something I came up with on my own. It came from a talk I had with my stepdad during a family camping trip, when I was at the worst point of my childhood anorexia. My stepdad took a more detached view of my illness than my mother or father did, which meant that he often stepped in to mediate between my mom and me in our constant fights about food. Because he was a doctor, and because his manner was tough and impassive, I trusted him. This particular afternoon, on a hike, he and I walked ahead of my mom and started talking about my continuing failure to gain weight. I must have said something about wishing my food-related anxieties would just disappear, or could somehow be cut out of my brain. My stepdad said, "Look, what you've got to understand is that your brain is diseased. It's feeding you all this bullshit. What you have to do is ignore it."

It sounds facile in retrospect, but at the time I found this very inspiring. It was simple and tough. It appealed to the part of me—the willful, ambitious part—that had made me so dangerously good at dieting in the first place. Soon after this conversation, I wrote that note to myself and started getting better.

At least that was how I saw my recovery during the years that I carried the note around in my wallet. I thought I'd gotten better by making a single, brave decision. I had confronted my phobias and, in doing so, proved that they were illusions, like the ghosts I had once imagined lurking at the dark end of the hall, which vanished when I turned on the light. Once released from the spell, over time I completely forgot what it felt like to be anorexic. I became scornful of anorexics. I saw them as weak and cowardly. I was ashamed of myself for having given in to the disease for so long, and sad and angry that my two years of severe malnutrition had suppressed my growth and delayed puberty, so that I was stuck in what felt like a child's body— five feet tall and small-breasted. But I was confident that the experience gave me one thing: I was way too smart to ever become anorexic again.

Right.

I started losing weight in the spring of my freshman year in college, but in some miracle of denial, I didn't initially see it as a problem. Nor did I see it as intentional; it was merely a side effect of discovering how much I loved being hungry. In fact, it was a little more complicated.

To begin with, I happened to make this discovery during the three weeks of rehearsal for a play in which I would spend most of my time onstage in panties and a bra. Since I was going to be so prominently on display, I thought it couldn't hurt to eat a little less and go to the gym more often for a few weeks. Once we were performing, I planned my days so that I didn't eat for several hours before the show, making my stomach as empty and flat as possible. The play, a farce by Joe Orton called *What the Butler Saw,* was incredibly fun, and the fact that I was always starving by the end only enhanced the rush of performing. After the show, when I finally ate, I was amazed to notice how great food tasted.

I didn't even notice I'd lost weight until it was pointed out to me by my roommate's boyfriend, Brian, who went to college in another state and was visiting for his spring break. "Really?" I said. And then, as though it were the most reasonable question in the world, I asked, "So do I look better this way, or did I look better before?" I thought I would simply stop or reverse my weight loss if I dropped below whatever degree of slimness was most attractive. Brian was too smart to answer.

In any case, I continued my new eating habits, which involved fasting until I was light-headed and then rewarding myself with a big meal. In my view, I didn't really eat less than other people, just differently. But I continued to lose weight.

During the next year and a half, I learned that prolonged hunger offered many perks. I used it like a drug, the way some people take Ritalin or Adderall. Being hungry kept me awake, alert, and focused. It also made me feel unusually imaginative and empathetic. Indeed, looking back, it's hard to fully separate the intellectual excitement of my college years from the effects of starvation. My body's wildly fluctuating energy levels often heightened my response to literature: I got the flu when I began reading *Madame Bovary* and lay on the floor for the next twenty hours while I finished it, feeling as if I, too, had been poisoned by the small-mindedness of provincial bourgeois life. I read many Henry James novels and remember being particularly haunted by *The Wings of the Dove*, in which the young American heiress, Milly Theale, wrestles psychologically with her impending death from tuberculosis. Was my response sharpened by some unconscious awareness of my body's own fight to keep functioning in the face of diminishing resources?

My mood grew darker as time went on, but for a while, I enjoyed enough highs to be protective of my strange eating habits. Like a lot of people addicted to a drug, I liked the person I was when I was hungry. She was intense, creative, dramatic: the opposite of the pale, subdued little girl I had been at eleven, and different, too, from the shy, inhibited teenager I had been ever since. So, while a part of me worried that I was slipping into dangerous territory, I continued to assure myself that this couldn't possibly be anorexia. Its effect was too different from my earlier experience.

By the end of my sophomore year, though, I could no longer convince myself I was okay. The telltale symptom was back: namely, that even when I knew I should eat more, I often couldn't make myself do it. I didn't talk about it to anyone—not to my boyfriend, whom I didn't want to start monitoring my eating, and definitely not to my parents. But when I saw them that June at a family friend's graduation in Chicago, they were horrified. My father sat me down in our hotel room and told me, with pain in his voice, how frail I looked and how, based on past experience, if I lost any more weight, I would soon be beyond the point of no return. Rather than being relieved that someone had noticed and was about to intervene, I was only ashamed. How could I be back here again? I wanted to sink through the floor and be magically transported back to Boston and my oblivious boyfriend.

Through my shame, I tried to reassure my parents. I said I knew I had a problem, and I promised to find a therapist and start getting weighed regularly at the university health center. But I claimed that I still had basic control over the situation. By exerting my will, I said, I could gain weight and be out of the danger zone quickly. And I believed this. I wasn't like other anorexics, I thought. I wasn't viscerally afraid of food: If I decided to eat, I could do it. Plus—and this was something I believed passionately—I didn't actually care about being thin.

For the next nine months, I gained a few pounds, lost a few, gained a few, lost more. The therapist my parents found pressed me to go to the hospital, but I dug my heels in. My last shred of dignity depended on proving that I could get better on my own, and therefore that I hadn't really been anorexic. Going to the hospital would prove the opposite. Beyond that, the idea of being cooped up with other anorexics was frightening and repugnant.

My insistence that I would gain weight on my own delayed things by several months, but the end result was inevitable. By April of my junior year, my promises were no longer credible. One Friday, after another big weight loss—and the discovery by the nurse at the health center that I had been "water loading," that is, consuming large amounts of water (in my case, hot tea) before my weigh-ins—my therapist called to tell me that she had contacted a nearby hospital with an eating-disorders unit, and there would be a bed for me starting on Monday. I cried hysterically, but there was nothing more I could say. I wrote down the phone number she gave me to call for directions and agreed that I would go.

"You've tried to do it on your own," my roommate said when I came crying to her. "Maybe it's time to get some help."

My experience with the hospital program began inauspiciously. When I called for directions, I was horrified to learn that I wouldn't be permitted to bring my laptop. In fact, I was expected to neglect my schoolwork completely while I was there. The nurse told me that bringing a computer would "create inequality among the patients"; plus, she added, I would have very little free time, and, when I did, I would be discouraged from spending it alone in my room. This fit my idea of the hospital exactly: a flock of girls who couldn't be left alone with their crazy thoughts. Well, if they thought I was going to sit around all day doing puzzles, they were sorely mistaken. I packed a bag with a dozen back issues of *The New York Review of Books* and vowed to spend as much time in my room as possible.

As far as eating went, I was determined to be the perfect patient, always a step ahead of the hospital staff. But on the first night, when I dictated my menu choices for the next day with bright enthusiasm, the nurse gave me a skeptical, even suspicious look. Over the following days, the other nurses also seemed suspicious, as though they saw my good behavior as a front. They seemed to be hunting for some hidden obsession or deviancy. Was I washing my hands too often? Was I water loading again? Granted, they had some reason to suspect me on that count. Only I knew how spotlessly virtuous and truthful I wanted to be from here on out, how exhausted I'd been by my chain of deceptions. Still, it felt unfair that my very conscientiousness seemed to provoke mistrust.

After a few days of trying to respond to their inquisitions calmly, my patience evaporated, and I finally let myself start acting like a patient. I talked back. I complained about the rules. I screamed and cried when, a few days in, my case manager threatened not to let me go back to school for just one evening, to attend a dinner I'd been looking forward to all year.

As clichéd as it sounds, allowing myself to admit that I was resistant, that I wasn't really on their side, was the first important step toward letting go of my anorexia. I continued saying that I wanted to leave the hospital, because it seemed weak to give in completely. But, increasingly, my struggle was mere show. In truth, it was very comforting to be there and to have other people dictate the rhythm of my day. Being told what to eat was a huge relief. I was amazed to realize that life could stop when I needed it to, and grateful to be forced, at least briefly, to quit pretending that I could carry on as a normal college student. I also wanted to stay because contrary to my expectations, I found it was impossible to be lonely in the hospital. I was with the other patients all day long. And, to my surprise, I was starting to like them.

Listening to their stories, for the first time I felt that I understood why anorexics resist getting better. It wasn't because we were psychologically weak; it was because anorexia gave us something real. It was a source of comfort; a means of escaping from intolerable situations; a language, if a garbled one, in which to express our anger and unhappiness. It did something a little different for each person I met. While in treatment, I finally began to think about what anorexia had done for me, and to admit that I was afraid of giving it up. I tried to imagine what my daily existence would be like without those feelings— the constant struggle against fatigue, the determined holding out to the next meal—that had given my life rhythm and texture, and at least an appearance of meaning. I saw a blank expanse of time, a frightening purposelessness.

Shortly before the point where I really let go, I remember talking to my therapist on the phone and insisting that I was ready to leave the hospital and go back to school. Things were on the right track now, I said; I would be fine. Her response, while cheesy, was immensely helpful to me, as helpful as my stepdad's be-tough-and-ignore-the-bullshit advice had once been, although what she said was in some ways the opposite. "That's the strong, tough Kate talking," she said of my assertion that I was ready to leave. "She always gets to make the decisions. But I have to be here to listen to the other Kate, who doesn't talk as loudly."

The idea that there was another Kate—a layer of feelings and needs that I was ignoring, and that only my anorexia was in touch with and expressed—changed my understanding of what I had to do to get better. Far from simply suppressing my anorexia, I had to start looking at it with respect, because it knew something about me that I didn't. I had to find out what that silenced thing was and incorporate it into the rest of my life. I had to learn new ways of understanding and meeting the other Kate's needs. In that sense, recovery wasn't just a matter of relinquishing my anorexia, but of finding and reintegrating a part of myself.

———

Anorexia was formalized as a diagnosis in the late nineteenth century, by the same school of physicians who were simultaneously elaborating the theory of hysteria. In the over a hundred years since its official recognition, anorexia has been subject to interpretation by many disciplines and has been viewed alternately as a psychological disorder and a physiological illness. Since the late 1960s, the dominant paradigm has described anorexia as resulting from a combination of psychological conflicts, social pressures, and the physical effects of starvation. The last decade has also witnessed an effort to identify the source of anorexia in our genes.

I have come to view anorexia, like hysteria, as a deeply ambivalent response to social expectations. Naturally, the expectations today are very different from what they were in the late nineteenth century. At that time, they revolved around Victorian morality: the repression of sexual desire and the separation of men and women into distinct spheres, one of worldly power and the other of domestic virtue. Today, women in Western society are free to pursue both sex and success. From an early age, we have a new set of imperatives: academic and professional achievement on the one hand, physical attractiveness on the other.

But to start at the beginning: In 1873 two doctors, an

English physician named William Gull and a French neurologist named Charles Lasègue, both claimed credit for discovering a new disease. Both Gull and Lasègue had observed
young women who, without appearing to have any physical illness, refused to eat and wasted away. In naming the disease,
they chose the word *anorexia*—the general medical term for loss
of appetite—and added a qualifier to suggest that the condition was psychological, or at least psychosomatic. Lasègue called
it *anorexie hystérique*. Gull chose the name *anorexia nervosa*, or
nervous lack of appetite.

These men saw anorexia as essentially similar to hysteria:
a set of irrational symptoms produced by upheavals in the
bodies and minds of developing girls. There is little evidence that either man was very curious or skeptical about the
ways in which anorexics rationalized their self-starvation: if
a girl claimed she couldn't eat because her stomach hurt,
they took this at face value, as the description of a real psychosomatic symptom. Few nineteenth-century experts linked
anorexia to a desire to be thin. Only Jean-Martin Charcot, the
doctor famous for presenting staged exhibitions of his hysteric
patients, made the connection between anorexia and the
contemporary obsession with physical delicacy. He described
discovering that one of his anorexic patients kept a pink ribbon tied around her stomach, beneath her clothes. She said
it was to make sure that her waist never got bigger than its
circumference.

Some aspects of the nineteenth-century interpretation of
anorexia correspond to our views today. Lasègue was interested
in the role of the family and of a young woman's desire for
autonomy. The typical bourgeois home of the period was intimate and somewhat claustrophobic; daughters were sheltered
and had little privacy. In Lasègue's view, the anorexic's refusal to

eat was both a means of asserting her will against her parents and a reflection of her anxiety about the future—specifically, the prospect of sexual development, courtship, and marriage. Like academic and professional success today, the necessity of attracting the right husband was hardly a trivial concern for a middle-class adolescent girl in the nineteenth century. Not only her personal happiness but her economic and social status depended on it.

After the turn of the century, Gull and Lasègue's view of anorexia was eclipsed by new medical discoveries on the one hand, and by Freudian theory on the other. Early twentieth-century doctors considered the psychological interpretation of anorexia to be unscientific. Excited by advances in endocrinology, they began to look for physiological causes of the disease. In 1913 a German physician named Morris Simmonds autopsied a woman who had died of emaciation and found that she had a shrunken pituitary gland. He generalized from this that *all* women who mysteriously wasted away did so because they suffered from a pituitary deficiency. Doctors started injecting anorexics with pituitary extract and, soon, with other hormones. Physicians at the Mayo Clinic treated anorexic patients with thyroid hormone. Others gave them insulin or estrogen. All of these treatments were completely ineffective, and decisively by 1940, the idea that anorexia was an endocrine disease had been rejected.

Freudian analysts also tried to reduce the illness to a simple, although very different, cause. In a 1939 paper, a Rhode Island analyst named George H. Alexander described an anorexic girl who had apparently started dieting after two of her classmates became pregnant. After he elicited a confession that the patient herself was irrationally afraid of becoming pregnant, Alexander extrapolated his own new theory of anorexia: that it represented a fantasy in which fat was pregnancy, and food the impregnating agent. This bizarre idea was taken seriously for at least two decades, during which physicians commonly referred their anorexic patients to psychoanalysts.

It was not until the 1960s and '70s, decades of radical changes in opportunities and expectations for women, that anorexia emerged as a major social phenomenon. This is no coincidence. In the late 1960s the standard of feminine beauty started to change, along with clothing, sexual mores, and attitudes about health and nutrition. Between Marilyn Monroe and Twiggy, the ideal feminine figure went from soft and voluptuous to stick-thin and nearly prepubescent. Clothing became skimpier and less structured. A combination of vanity and health concerns led members of both sexes to transform their diets and take up previously unknown activities like jogging. Historians have suggested that this shift toward valuing thinness was a product of industrialization, which resulted in an increasingly abundant and inexpensive food supply. While previously it was the poor who were fated to be thin, and plumpness was a sign of wealth and leisure, by the late twentieth century the identifying physiques of rich and poor, and hence the social status of each, were reversed.

In the same period that these social changes were under way, a handful of doctors developed a more sophisticated theory of anorexia, which acknowledged how anorexics themselves experienced the illness and what they felt they gained from it. These doctors, who included Mara Selvini Palazzoli in Italy and Hilde Bruch in the United States, saw anorexia as a young woman's attempt to assert her identity. They also linked it to the new value placed on thinness and dieting. Palazzoli suggested that many anorexic girls started dieting out of a straightforward desire to be slimmer, often they even had their parents' encouragement. But then girls lost too much weight, and their parents became frightened or angry. At that point, the girls realized the emotional power they'd gained and, not wanting to give it up, kept starving themselves.

This new theory quite soon began to attract attention. Bruch was interviewed in *Family Circle* in 1972, the year before her first book on anorexia, *Eating Disorders: Obesity, Anorexia Nervosa, and the Person Within,* was published. In the book, she described anorexia as being very rare. She noted, however, that it tended to attract medical interest "quite out of proportion to its infrequent occurrence," perhaps because the spectacle of a young person starving herself was so shocking and alien. "The continued fascination with this rare condition," she wrote, "is probably evoked by the tragedy of seeing a young person, in the bloom of youth, seeking [a] solution to life's problems through this bizarre method of voluntary starvation, something that runs counter to all human experience."

Within a couple of years, this way of describing anorexia—"rare," "bizarre," "counter to all human experience"—would be obsolete, replaced with terms like "epidemic." In fact, as anorexia began to attract attention in the press, the whole image of the disease changed. It transformed from something strange and freakish into a kind of runaway fad.

Beginning around 1974, articles about anorexia appeared with increasing frequency in general-interest and women's magazines. The authors of these articles described anorexia as a once-rare disease whose incidence was now rapidly rising. Although they almost never offered any statistics to back up this claim, their assertions shaped the popular view of anorexia, which by the late 1970s was a household word.

Most likely, anorexia's explosion into the popular culture

resulted from a combination of three factors: a gradual increase in the number of new cases; interest in the new psychological theories about anorexia; and, as time went on, feminist interest in anorexia as a symbol of the pernicious effects of the media on women and girls.

How much the actual incidence of anorexia increased in this period is very hard to know, considering the shortage of statistics and the enormous increase in awareness of the disease. The Web site of the Academy for Eating Disorders, a professional organization, states that it is "generally agreed that the prevalence of eating disorders has increased over the last 30–40 years." In any case, even today, anorexia remains very rare. According to the AED, approximately 0.5–1 percent of late-adolescent and adult women in this country meet criteria for the diagnosis for anorexia, while 1–2 percent meet criteria for the diagnosis of bulimia. (However, 10 percent of women report some symptoms of eating disorders, such as excessive concern about their weight or occasional bingeing and purging.)

As with any popular or journalistic trend, what really drove the spread of information about anorexia was the way in which stories about it dovetailed with other topics on the social agenda, such as girls' self-esteem; or, alternately, the way these stories pandered to sexist clichés and old-fashioned stereotypes about women and mental illness. A 1974 article in *The New York Times Magazine*, for example, described anorexic patients in a hospital as "gorgeous waifs [whose] grooming is generally impeccable . . . even while dying." The article added that anorexics, while "incapable of real relationships," are "experts in eliciting love and sympathy. People want to take care of them."

At the other end of the spectrum, anorexia and bulimia

became favorite topics for feminist writers. They starkly dramatized women's dissatisfaction with their bodies, which feminists blamed on a patriarchal culture and the media's propagation of unrealistic images. In 1977 *Ms.* magazine devoted a section to "Why Women Dislike Their Bodies." In 1980 it devoted another such section to "Why Women Love/Hate Food." Ten years before Naomi Wolf wrote *The Beauty Myth*, Kim Chernin, in *The Obsession: Reflections on the Tyranny of Slenderness* (1981), linked women's preoccupation with dieting to society's supposed need to undermine their power.

By the early 1980s, the popularization of anorexia was complete. In 1981 ABC aired the first television movie about the disease, *The Best Little Girl in the World*, starring Jennifer Jason Leigh. In 1983 the singer Karen Carpenter died of heart failure, caused by long-term anorexia, and became the disease's most famous casualty.

Bruch, whose ideas contributed greatly to popular awareness of the disease, nonetheless noted anorexia's rise to fame with ambivalence. In a letter to a friend in 1983, she wrote, "I'm glad you have sympathy for my problem with the runaway popularity of anorexia nervosa, 'bulimia,' and all other eating disorders. It looks as if my habit to get interested in unpopular topics nearly produces a boom." Now, "everybody wants to jump on the bandwagon," she continued. With so many authors writing about anorexia, "the concept is being stretched so that practically everybody who puts some food into her mouth and then worries about it is considered anorexic."

———

Bruch felt that the popularization of anorexia was changing the illness. In the preface to her second (and very popular) book about anorexia, *The Golden Cage* (1978), she noted that, until recently, none of her patients had heard of anorexia before they saw her; each one was "an original inventor of this misguided road to independence." Now, most had heard or read about it, and some knew other anorexics at their schools. "The illness used to be the accomplishment of an isolated girl who felt she had found her own way to salvation," she said. "Now it is more a group reaction."

This idea—that anorexia is no longer a solitary experience, but a group activity—has continued to shape people's view of anorexia through the present. A friend of mine who attended an elite girls' school in Manhattan says the widespread view of parents, teachers, and students at her school was that anorexia was a contagious illness, spread by one alpha dieter to her impressionable friends. "There was a group of girls, led by J., who would eat broccoli and mustard for lunch," my friend remembers. (J., the ringleader, was eventually hospitalized.)

Several essays in this book take up variations on the theme of anorexia as a group experience: Jennifer Egan says she was inspired to lose weight by reading a magazine article about an anorexic. "I remember her picture: somber, willowy, standing on a bathroom scale, her shoulder blades jutting out like wings," Egan writes. "I looked at her and felt my whole being contract into a single strand of longing."

Clara Elliot first learned about purging from her older sister. Sarah Haight wanted to imitate the eating habits of the dancer who lived across the hall from her at Barnard. A half century earlier, Francine du Plessix Gray was introduced to dieting by the models and socialites who attended her parents' cocktail parties. Other writers remember the comments that triggered their initial diets, or the compliments they received when they started losing weight.

But for the most part, these essays portray an experience more along the lines of the isolated girl seeking salvation. Ilana Kurshan remembers how her anorexia alienated her from her family. Priscilla Becker describes becoming increasingly reclusive: cutting school, hiding in closets, and dreading the social situations she couldn't avoid.

Particularly interesting in this respect is Louise Glück's essay, written in 1981, about her experience being anorexic in the late 1950s. She distances herself from younger, more recent anorexics, who she imagines experiencing the illness as a shared generational phenomenon. She notes that she had never heard of anorexia at the time she became sick, nor was she aware of any books about it. If she had been, "I'd have been stymied," she writes. "To have a disease so common, so typical, would have obliged me to devise some entirely different gestures to prove my uniqueness."

Fairly or not, what I take from this remark is pretty much the opposite of what Glück intends. To me, her attempt to differentiate herself from later generations of anorexics—just as I tried to differentiate myself from my image of the girls in the hospital—reveals not how much anorexia has changed, but how much it has remained the same, even as awareness of it has increased. In my view, the two aspects of the disease that Bruch commented on—the isolation and desire to set oneself apart on the one hand, and the instinct for conformity on the other—did not succeed each other, but exist in a constant tension.

For this reason, it is not surprising that anorexia has developed a life on the Internet, in "pro-anorexia" Web sites and "thinspiration" or "thinspo" videos; more than any other medium, the Internet is conducive to behaviors that are simultaneously secretive and shared with a community of similarly isolated peers.

The kind of person who develops anorexia is driven equally by a desire to be accepted and a desire to feel special and distinct, a hunger for praise and a hunger for self-expression. Anorexia seems to offer a quick and dirty means of having it both ways: thinness buys you social acceptance, while the psychological experience of starvation isolates you and appears to draw you closer to your true self.

This conflict between internal drives and external expectations is expressed in some form in all of the essays in this book. Glück describes how, when she was a child, writing satisfied both her desire to assert her identity and her need for her mother's approval. As she became an adolescent, these impulses were increasingly at odds, a tension that eventually resulted in her anorexia.

This is a dynamic I know well. I grew up proud of my ability to think independently, yet also extremely dependent on approval. Like Glück's parents, mine encouraged me to express myself creatively. But I also received conflicting messages from them about the importance of being liked and accepted—of being "normal." In my father and stepmother's house, this seemed to be pretty important, although the cues were mostly implicit. Both of them worked hard to stay slim, eating a low-fat diet and exercising daily. This lifestyle was partly motivated by my father's fear of dying young, as his father had, but their health consciousness overlapped neatly with an attention to appearance. They dressed nicely; my father rarely appeared in anything more casual than khakis, and my stepmom always wore makeup. Theirs was the house where I was taught manners: Don't talk with food in your mouth; don't rest your elbows on the table.

Such a lesson would have been impossible at my mom and stepdad's house, because there wasn't a table, at least not for family dinners. My stepdad prefered to eat on the floor, reclining like a pasha, so that is what we did. My mother never wore makeup; my stepdad hardly ever wore shoes—or other clothing, for that matter, if he could help it. Everything in that house was a little bit more extreme, from the rich, intensely flavored food to my mother's emotional displays, which included great outpourings of love and affection, but also reasonably frequent anger and tears.

If I were to psychoanalyze my parents, I would observe that both my mom and my stepdad grew up feeling—for reasons of poverty, parental stinginess, and domestic disorder—different from other people. Having suffered but survived, they are happy to be unconventional, and they even look down a little on people who are too straight. My dad and my stepmom, by contrast, grew up fitting in and have continued to do so. As a child and adolescent, I was caught between these two worldviews, struggling with the messages I absorbed: It's good to stand out for being smart, but you only know you're smart if your teachers and parents tell you so. It's good to be creative and express yourself, but it's bad to be an outsider.

Part of maturity is learning how to balance our desire for admiration with our desire for integrity and fulfillment. When you're young, to do so is hard, if not impossible. In adolescence, the conflict can become overwhelming, particularly in areas like academic achievement and physical attractiveness, where both external expectations and personal desires are most intense. At this crucial moment, anorexia seems to offer a means of solving the conflict: a way to meet others' demands while staying true to ourselves.

———

Understanding anorexia as the product of an internal conflict also helps explain the anorexic's complicated relationship to her body. When the subject of anorexia comes up, people often ask: "Is it really about being thin?" Well, it is, and it isn't. When it comes to her body, as in many aspects of her life, the anorexic wants both to satisfy social expectations and to escape them.

While I was anorexic, I believed that I saw myself accurately and that I knew I was too thin. I could see my bony wrists and the sad way that my jeans sagged where my butt should have been. But I observed these physical details with detachment. I would stand in front of the mirror and say out loud to my reflection, "You look terrible!" In my mind, it was as though the girl in the mirror were another person, who persisted in her illness without my real, rational self having anything to do with it.

This sense of disconnection from my body was no doubt exaggerated by my anorexia, but it predated it—or, rather, it went back as far as my previous bout with the illness. And I think that, along with my conflicts over how much to submit to social pressure, it was a major factor in my weight loss. I didn't think of my body in sexual terms, so I was oblivious when the crucial aspects of my sexual attractiveness, my softness and curves, disappeared.

Around the age of ten, I suddenly became physically inhibited. It had at least partly to do with a need to separate from my mother. I had been a happy child, fond of affection and cuddling, but at this point I began to withdraw and stiffen when she tried to hug or kiss me. Other factors added to my frustration with my body. I switched in fourth grade to a school where sports were very important. Since being unathletic was a social liability, I started exercising and losing weight.

I may also have been ambivalent about puberty, though I wasn't aware of being so at the time. Certainly, as a result of my anorexia, I didn't go through a normal puberty: After a promising start, it was cut short, and proceeded later in a protracted and anticlimactic fashion. I finally got my period at sixteen (only to lose it again two years later), but I never experienced the surges of hormones that my healthy friends describe. I didn't lie in bed filled with physical longings; I had romantic longings, of course, but that's a different thing. I didn't masturbate and, to be honest, it never occurred to me that anyone did, outside of literature or movies, until I was sixteen and making out with my first boyfriend. And my inhibition wasn't only sexual. Even with friends, I had difficulty giving or receiving physical affection, although I secretly craved it.

In college, I still had little interest in sex, but I did want badly to be noticed by guys. Partly through the influence of a roommate who was my equal in narcissism, I became obsessed with clothes. Wearing cute clothes attracted compliments and gave me social confidence, but it didn't make me any more comfortable in my skin. Instead, I felt like I was cut off from the world: physically restricted and enclosed in a shell that I had to be careful not to damage. The more I cultivated my appearance, the more I worried that it was a barrier to people truly seeing or knowing me.

My relationship to clothes itself had some of the features of an eating disorder: anxiety, compulsiveness, an inability to decide that kept me trying on outfits in front of the mirror for up to an hour. But I actually got some relief from this obsession when I was at my thinnest. There were only a few things that fit me, so deciding what to wear wasn't hard. And even those things that fit looked baggy and odd, so I had to engage in a kind of denial, ignoring how ill I looked and pretending that other people didn't notice, either. I behaved almost as though I were invisible.

It is not uncommon for anorexics to feel that extreme thinness offers an escape from social pressures about appearance. In our society, many people are preoccupied with their weight. Bruch coined a wonderful term, *thin fat people,* to describe people who are of normal weight, but are neurotically worried about becoming fat. She included in this category people in professions that demand thinness, such as modeling and ballet. She also included people who, for whatever reason, decide that they are most attractive at a weight that is somewhere below their bodies' most comfortable one and who must therefore exercise constant vigilance and self-denial to stay there.

The full-fledged anorexic, on the other hand, has discovered a powerful trick, which is that becoming habituated to behaviors that keep you thin actually allows you not to think about your weight. An accomplished writer, who has been anorexic off and on since high school and who is very thin, told me, when I asked about her eating habits, that she doesn't like to eat real meals and that she writes better without them. But she also said, with total sincerity, that she thinks about food and her weight "much less than other women do." From her tone, it was clear that she thought this preoccupation with weight was silly, and she was glad her mind was free for more important thoughts.

I recognized her feeling of superiority, because I once felt that way. It was only after I had physically recovered that I realized I, too, was capable of feeling silly, conventional concerns about my body—in other words, that I did care about being thin. My senior year I came back to school at a healthy size for the first time in two years. For the most part, I was happy. I had energy. I felt like going to parties and meeting people. I'd bought new clothes, and I thought I looked good in them. But every so often, when I looked in the mirror, I was startled by what I feared was a very typical female pang: My clothes were too tight, and I looked pudgy, shapeless, childish.

The thought was doubly painful. In the first place, I looked fat. But, almost worse, now I had to acknowledge that I was the type of woman who could look in the mirror and think that! I wasn't superior; I'd simply been living with a twenty-pound buffer between me and such worries. Without it, would I just become accustomed to these stings of shame and self-criticism? Was that what normal, healthy girls did?

It's a psychological cliché that, when an anorexic says, "I feel fat," she is really trying to express something else: that she feels sad, or lonely, or angry. Although it's a cliché, it expresses something real, which is that anorexics' ideas about their bodies are as much psychological and intellectual as they are physical.

Several months before I went into the hospital, I attended an eating-disorders support group at the campus health center. The first time I went, I remember one girl, who later became a close friend, coming in twenty minutes late, sobbing. The others kept talking for a while, as she continued crying and sniffling. Finally, one of the psychologists running the group asked her what was going on. She explained that today was the one-year anniversary of her entrance into the hospital, where she ultimately gained thirty pounds. (She was still very slim; thirty pounds lighter, she must have been at death's door.) Instead of being grateful to be healthy again, today, at least, she was in mourning. "I just feel so huge," she sobbed. "I feel like I'm taking up the whole room." This stuck with me, because it expressed something much deeper than a physical self-image—something about her right to exist in the world, and how she shared space with the people around her.

Some anorexics have very intellectualized ideas of what thinness means. Ilana Kurshan describes being drawn to images of slenderness in her old art history textbooks: Degas' little bronze ballerinas, Ionic columns. She imagines anorexia itself personified as "a snow white princess who glided along in a winter fairyland, leaving no footprints"—a beautiful waif, who takes up no space and leaves no mark.

One former anorexic I know described her physical ideal as a woman who was beautiful without makeup or fancy clothes—someone with an otherworldly beauty, austere, almost saintly, as one pictures Dorothea Brooke in *Middlemarch*. Indeed, some anorexics have a compulsion to keep their appearance very plain. In her biography of the philosopher (and anorexic) Simone Weil, Francine du Plessix Gray notes that as a teenager, Weil adopted the severe look that she would maintain throughout her life: uncombed hair and large glasses, a long skirt and a huge, dark cape obscuring her tiny body.

In many cases, embedded in the anorexic's physical or aesthetic ideal is the idea of sacrifice in service of a higher goal. Simone Weil probably believed that her physical frailty and plain appearance would make her a better conduit for intellectual insight and for God's will. The track-and-field star believes that being thinner will make her faster. The ballerina believes that her insubstantiality makes her a more perfect vehicle for the music and the aesthetic lines of the dance.

When Amanda Fortini lost an enormous amount of weight

in her twenties—not from intentionally depriving herself, but because she'd picked up a parasite in Belize—the high of semi-starvation, and of moving around in an almost prepubescent body, carried her back to the sense memories of her rigorous ballet training as a child.

In *Winter Season: A Dancer's Journal,* the former ballerina Toni Bentley wrote about going without food and needing "artistic sustenance only." The novelist Sigrid Nunez, also a former dancer, remembers: "To see how long I could go without solid food (up to five days) was a favorite game. How beautiful the hollowed gut, the jutting bones. To be light as a feather, light as a soul—'a feather on the breath of God.' "

———

Although I was not a dancer, I was a student, and one of my conscious motives in eating strangely was that I believed it helped me work. Being weak with hunger helped me sit still through long hours of reading, and the mood and energy swings I experienced became part of the rhythms of writing.

Because I always wanted to produce something brilliant, my process of writing papers was intensely labored. I would lie on my couch for days making notes, considering topics and rejecting them, alternating between elation and despair. One of my roommates later told me that it was painful to watch. It was also just plain painful: I felt at the mercy of a capricious and ultimately mysterious mechanism of inspiration, of which the results could only be judged by my professor's praise or criticism in the margin.

My relationship to hunger became entwined with this masochistic cycle; perhaps it reassured me that this was what creative work should feel like. To me, the rhythm of hunger imitated the rhythm of working: the adrenaline and euphoria when my stomach was empty, and the letdown of exhaustion and relief when it was full. (It has been pointed out to me that this is also the pattern of sexual arousal, which was not something I experienced, or perhaps allowed myself to experience, at that stage of my life. So perhaps there were many kinds of frustrated energy that hunger allowed me to release.)

In 1978 Hilde Bruch linked the rising incidence of anorexia with women's entrance into the professional world. "Growing girls can experience this liberation as a demand and feel that they *have to* do something outstanding," she wrote. "Many of my patients expressed the feeling that they are overwhelmed by the vast number of potential opportunities available to them which they 'ought' to fulfill, that there were too many choices and they had been afraid of not choosing correctly." In this environment of seemingly boundless options, anorexia offers a focus and a sense of purpose, however narrow and self-destructive.

I have been fascinated to read the various accounts of ambition in these essays. Louise Glück, whose essay is primarily about her formation as a poet, describes how her ambition intensified as she reached adolescence, and, as a result, her accomplishments rarely reached the level of her own expectations. "I wrote and painted, but these activities were hardly the famous release of such pressure they are contended to be," she recalls. "I cared too much about the quality of what I made."

Lisa Halliday describes her anorexia beginning with her recognition of the limitations of her high school environment. With her growing awareness of literature and art, she no longer trusted the judgment of her teachers. Having no way to measure her talents, she sought relief in something she could measure: her weight.

Anorexia often develops in adolescence, when one's ambitions are vast but undirected. Several former anorexics have expressed to me the feeling that their youthful ambitions were grandiose. "My hopes at that time were more like dreams, or fantasies, really, in which I was a famous musician," Priscilla Becker writes in her essay. "I had no plan to bring this about, although by high school I was a fairly accomplished violinist."

Assuming that the anorexic recovers, with time and maturity she will learn how to channel her energies and become capable of making her mark on the world. At twenty-eight, I am still learning, but I am much further along than I was at twenty. Today I'm a reporter at a newspaper, covering news in the art world. It's challenging and often exhausting, but it has been the perfect corrective for my anxieties and bad habits. I can't obsess, because I have tight deadlines. I know clearly what my task is. And, at least in the reporting part, accomplishment is generally proportional to effort, which was not always the case in my academic work.

Perhaps not coincidentally, as I've gained professional confidence, I have also become more comfortable in my body. I get more sexual attention at my current weight than I did even a few years ago, when I was ten pounds lighter and my body was more boyish, and I enjoy that attention in a way that my younger self wasn't prepared to do.

Best of all, these days I have a very close and strong relationship to my family. There is a stereotype that anorexia is all the mother's fault. This is not true, of course, although several essays in this book do reveal the importance of the mother's role. She is the first source of nourishment, after all, and the source of our flesh itself. I used my anorexia to push myself out of the nest, and for years, even after I had technically recovered, I couldn't really relax around my parents; I was still both too dependent on their approval and too anxious about proving my self-sufficiency.

I can't say just when this stopped being so important, but it did. Today I take pleasure in those parts of myself—my hunger for intimacy, my desire to mother and be mothered—that I was trying to shut off while I was anorexic. When I think of how I have changed in the years since I recovered, I picture an outline of a body being filled in. And the more solid I become, the more confident in my ability to meet my own needs, the more I can enjoy returning to the bosom of my family, without worrying that my facade of independence will be shattered.

———

Despite my ambitions when I began it, no book can capture every facet of a phenomenon as complex as anorexia. As images idealizing thinness and sensationalizing eating disorders are spread by tabloid magazines, television shows, and the Internet we are seeing more and more young women, with various problems, turn to extreme dieting as an outlet for their distress. Does my explanation of how anorexia develops apply to them all? Probably not.

The composition of this book reflects anorexia's spread, in recent years, into populations once considered invulnerable to it. If this were a different kind of book—a collection of interviews or a work of sociology—I would have liked to explore this further. Exactly how much anorexia has spread beyond its "core" population of white, middle-class girls, and why it has done so, remain unanswered and important questions.

Even today, the type of anorexia I have described involves conventionally middle-class beliefs: in unlimited individual potential, for instance, and the importance of self-knowledge and self-expression. And it is mostly privileged kids who experience their array of opportunities as a kind of pressure to choose the "right" option—the right school, the right career. (Since for many of the writers, their anorexia developed when they were in their late teens, the subject of college comes up frequently; it may also contribute to existing stereotypes about anorexics that several of them went to Ivy League schools.)

But, just because anorexia results from typically middle-class problems, that doesn't mean it only affects people in the middle class. Young people who want to move up, who seek more opportunities, adopt middle-class values that can make them more vulnerable to anorexia. Recent studies conducted in Curaçao and Fiji have shown that disordered eating among women in these societies is often triggered by a belief that being thin allows for greater upward mobility. In the United States, this could explain why the incidence of eating disorders among different racial groups seems to have converged in recent years, as racism has become more subtle and more based on social-class markers.

The two African American writers in this book, Latria Graham and Maya Browne, both grew up in upper-middle-class homes. Racial issues seem to have played a relatively small role in the development of their eating disorders—smaller, for instance, than family conflict and their own strong drive to distinguish themselves. Rudy Ruiz, who grew up on the U.S.-Mexico border in Texas, the son of an immigrant and a first-generation American, believes that the different attitudes toward food and weight in the cultures he straddled contributed to his eating problems.

In some cases, race plays a significant role in how a community responds to someone who is struggling with an eating disorder. A young woman recently responded to an article I had published about anorexia, saying that she identified closely with what I described, but that she had never been able to talk about her eating disorder openly. She couldn't talk about it to her friends, who were mostly, as she was, African-American. Her friends thought of eating problems as something only white girls had, and they responded to her increasing thinness almost as an insult. At the same time, she couldn't talk about it to her family, because in their West Indian immigrant community, thin women were very admired. To them, the idea that being thin could be a health problem was unimaginable. If nothing else, her experience belied the common assumption that women of color are immune to eating disorders, because they all worship the curvy physiques of J.Lo and Beyoncé, rather than—just for example—Thandie Newton's bony beauty.

I wish that this book could have included this story and many others. But for several people, writing their stories to share them with the world was too painful or too revealing. My closest friend in the treatment program I attended in New York was a young woman who was born in the Dominican Republic and moved to Washington Heights when she was twelve years old. Although very talented—she attended a liberal arts college and earned an MFA in creative writing—she is dogged by severe depression and anxiety. She considered writing an essay but was ultimately unable to do so, which was the case with a half dozen others who at one point were meant to be a part of this book. For some, telling the full story would have required admitting that they had been raped or sexually abused. For others, it would have meant exposing their families in a way that they were not willing to do.

Even some of those who did contribute remained ambivalent about sharing these experiences. One of the male contribtors chose to use a pseudonym, and others considered it. There seems to be a stereotype about writers of memoir—particularly those who are women, and those of either gender whose stories fall into the "recovery" genre—that they have a great desire to spill their guts to the world. I can't emphasize how much the opposite is true for most of the contributors to this book. And so, while I miss the stories that aren't here, I am grateful for the courage of the writers who agreed to tell theirs.

I hope that this book will offer support, insight, and hope to those struggling with anorexia or watching their loved ones struggle with it. Anorexia is horrible and time wasting and, at the extreme, life threatening, but it can also be seen as the expression of impulses—toward ambitious activity and toward emotional connection—that need to be drawn out and turned in a positive direction. If I could, I would go back to my eleven-year-old self and say: "Look, what you *think* will improve your life—eating 'healthily,' running—actually won't. Let's figure out how to find what you really need, which is friendship and outlets for creativity."

The stories in this book offer proof that one can learn to listen to one's needs and satisfy them in a healthy and productive way, including through the activity of writing. Those who would like to share their own stories, including friends and relatives, are encouraged to do so at www.goinghungry.com, which also includes basic information about seeking treatment for anorexia and a link to e-mail me with responses to the essays in this book.

I hope you find these essays helpful and illuminating.

Kate Taylor
2008

GOING HUNGRY

HUNGER STRIKING

Maura Kelly

———

For a few weeks during the summer before high school, I resembled one of the catwalkers from the pages of *The New York Times*'s style supplement, which covered my bedroom wall in a Scotch Tape collage. It wasn't my face that was like theirs, or my clothes. (My usual look was a pocket T-shirt and cutoff jeans shorts, while the glossy girls wore kimono dresses, peacock-feather hats, and short pointy boots like white cockatoos.) It was my body. My stomach had caved in. My hip bones flared like wings. My legs met only at the knees and ankles: There was a teardrop-shaped gap between my thighs, and another between my calves. Knobby bones protruded dangerously from my wrists and elbows. My arms seemed longer, and from the ends of them, my enormous hands flopped, awkward as a marionette's. I was barely thirteen, five feet and five inches tall, and down to 90 pounds from 110.

My transformation thrilled me.

Still, I wasn't quite thin enough. So I kept going, and the changes became even more exciting. The colored hairbands I kept around my wrist got so loose that I could easily slide them up to my elbow. If I pressed my hand around the part of my arm where the shoulder met the biceps, I could touch my thumb with the pad of my ring finger. I could also put both hands around my thigh and touch thumb to thumb, pinky to pinky. I'd measure myself like that again and again when no one was watching, usually in the bathroom stall at school; it reassured me that I hadn't somehow gotten fatter in the hours since I'd been on the scale that morning. My ribs became so visible that I could count them not only from the front but also, if I used two mirrors, from the back as they curved out from the knotted rope of my spine.

I began to resemble someone else tacked up in my room: Jesus Christ.

Now *there* was an icon. There was a guy who knew something about style: the original long-haired, emaciated, rockstar type. But it wasn't just Jesus' body that I admired; it was his suffering, too, and the way it made people love him. Jesus had been my first role model, and I still respected the guy, even if I was a full-fledged nonbeliever by then. As he hung from the crucifix my dead mother had positioned over my dresser, Jesus inspired me—with his skeleton hanging out of his skin, his blood dripping from his crown of thorns, and his face turned imploringly upward in the moment before his death as he said, "My God, my Father, why have you forsaken me?"

———

I knew how Jesus felt, asking that question. When my mother died of cancer the summer I turned eight, I felt pretty forsaken myself. I had no idea she was dying. I knew she was sick, of course, but my parents told my sister and me that she just had a very bad cold, kind of like chicken pox, except the bumps were inside.

Her illness replaced me—the baby—and became the most important thing in my mother's life. Before she'd gotten sick, she loved everything I did, whether it was the Little Tea-pot dance, or one of my typically opinionated comments ("I don't want to grow up to be like you, Mommy, always driving my kids around"), or just burying my face in her neck to cry. But after she was diagnosed, I wasn't as easy to love; at least, it was harder to get her full attention. For the last four years of her life, she spent one week out of every month in the hospital getting chemotherapy—a word I could say but not define—and when she was home, she spent a lot of time in bed with the curtains drawn. She didn't like it when I was loud, and sometimes she was too weak to even kiss me back after I pressed my lips against her cheek. Her head would just stay on the pillow.

Whenever she wasn't feeling well, I tried to leave her alone. I tried not to need anything from her. I became self-conscious: worried about what effect my actions would have, and aware of my own presence in a room.

Everyone—my parents, my other relatives, and the priests and nuns we knew, including my uncle Father Jimmy—told me that my mother might get better if I was a very good girl and asked God to help us. I would have done anything to get my mother back the way she used to be, so I *prayed.* I also sang at church with my family on Sunday mornings, as loudly and clearly as I could, because the pastor said singing was praising God twice. (I just hoped that Juan-Juan Santiago, who sat across the aisle from us with his parents and little brother, wouldn't notice what a geek I was.) One of my favorite hymns was in praise of lasagna—or so I thought, till my mother caught on to what I was saying, and explained that the word was actually *hosana,* which means, roughly, "God is great." And to show the devil I hated him, I'd jump up and down in the grass—as close to Hell as I could get—until I'd exhausted myself. Then I'd lie on the ground, blowing kisses up to the angels. Everyone said God was always watching over me, which was nice, especially since my mother wasn't anymore. My growing love for God, and His for me, was helping to fill the hole my mother was making. I'd picture Him with the big white beard, in a white robe, in a white throne that floated on the clouds, smiling down at me, and I'd smile back.

It wasn't just through physical actions that I tried to make myself God's favorite; there were also the things I'd do in my head. During Mass, I'd recite the Penitential Rite with the rest of the congregation: "I have sinned through my own fault, in my thoughts and in my words, in what I have done, and in what I have failed to do." I'd feel gravely sorry about all my transgressions: how I'd once again stuffed myself with chocolate-chip cookies and marshmallows in the morning, before my parents woke up; how I'd punched my sister in the rear end; how I'd stuck my tongue out at my father when he wasn't watching. I'd pinch myself once on the thigh for each sin, and resolve to become a better person. I knew how important it was to God that my head be as pure as my actions, so whenever I had bad thoughts—like how much I hated the new Indian kid in our class, Raj, because he smelled funny and was hairy—I'd start to pray, trying to push the evil away. I was trying so hard and God loomed so large in my mind (even larger than Juan-Juan) that I was confident I was one of His favorites.

But I started to wonder if that was true after my mother died that August, twenty days after my birthday. I was so unprepared that when my father first told me I laughed. "Really, when can we pick her up from the hospital?" I said. "Tell me."

He only stared at me. "*Tell* me," I insisted. Still, he didn't speak, and my sister, sitting in his lap, started to cry. That unsettled me enough that I went to get a closer look at my father. When tears started coming down his face, too, I was terrified. Something had to be seriously wrong, but I was too young—or too shocked—to really understand what was going on.

I didn't give up the hope that my mother might somehow pop out of her coffin until I first saw her in the wooden box at the wake. That's when I started to appreciate what being dead meant. The rosy blush my mother usually wore had been replaced by two heavy circles of red on her cheeks; instead of her favorite mauve lipstick, there was a brown smear on her mouth. I could see the pores on her face as clearly as if they'd been made with a pencil. Her skin was thick and hard and unyielding under my fingertips, like football leather. I realized there was no way *that* body was going to sit up and say "Surprise!" and then reach out to tickle me under the arms. I climbed up on the kneeler and kissed her, maybe because I still had fairy-tale hopes about what that could do for a dead person. But it didn't make any difference. Those rubber lips took away any doubt I had left—about her death, anyway.

But suddenly, everything else in my life was thrown into question. It wasn't only my mother who was gone: It was my understanding of the universe, of myself, of God, and even of my own father. Overwhelmed by his grief, bills, and the responsibility of trying to raise two girls alone, he became a stranger to me: moody, unpredictable, and frightening—the big villain in my life. Suddenly, we were shouting at each other so much that I believed it when the first nanny we had after my mother died, a young woman from northern Ireland named Marie, told me again and again my father didn't love me. Every night, I waited for him to come home with the worst longing and the most terrible fear, wondering if he would prove Marie right one more time.

I couldn't count on my so-called Heavenly Father anymore, either, considering I was convinced that He'd killed my mother to punish me. (He couldn't have had it out for anyone else in my family, I figured, since my connection to Him was more intense than theirs, for better and for worse.) What I couldn't figure out was *why* God was so angry with me. In what way had I offended Him? I kept going over and over everything that I'd done and thought in the weeks leading up to my mother's death, the way a guilty lover will after a suicide, and though there were all the usual little bad things—sneaking cookies, punching my sister, hating Raj—there wasn't anything new and outstandingly wicked that would explain God's act of vengeance against me. Also, I was nowhere near as bad as some of the other kids in my town, especially not the ones from the public middle school, who smoked cigarettes on the railroad tracks behind my house, or had sex in the old band shell at Memorial Park, or did drugs in their cars in the Burger King parking lot.

Since it seemed obvious I couldn't have *done* anything to bring on the wrath of God, I figured there must be something inherently wrong with me. Did He hate me because I wasn't as good in my heart as I'd thought? Probably. And maybe my mother hadn't really loved me, either. Why else would she have left without even saying good-bye, or that she'd miss me?

Those kinds of questions were hard to face, so eventually I convinced myself, as best as I could, that the problem wasn't with me but with Catholicism. I'd tried so hard to follow the rules, in my actions and my thoughts, and what had it got- ten me but a dead mother? I didn't want to live that way anymore. But I did want something to believe in—a system that was more transparent and would yield visible results. I wanted proof that I was good.

———

Dieting eventually became a replacement religion for me, with its own set of commandments and rituals. It became a way for me to be my own god and my own creation—Pygmalion and Galatea in the same human body. It became a perverse method for mothering myself: I structured my meals, my days, and my thoughts around it. Dieting became my internal compass. It became the new thing for me to be the best at. I was so devoted that I was practically ready to give up my life for it.

But when I first started losing weight, toward the end of eighth grade, I had no idea I would become a fanatic. It was far more simple than that. All I wanted was to look like I had at the beginning of the school year, before my abdomen began to protrude under the band of my Hanes underwear. Though I realize now it was just an early sign of puberty, that curve disgusted me. I felt like a dog in heat, with it poking out of me. I had to be out of control if I'd let my body turn into *that*. And I figured if I lost five pounds—just five—my stomach would be flat again. But as it turned out, I had to drop closer to fifteen pounds before the curve disappeared, and once I got that far, I couldn't stop. I was addicted to losing.

Part of the appeal was how much dieting simplified my life. Nothing else mattered but the numbers: how many calories I'd eaten that day; how many pounds I'd lost in the last week, or month; how many leg lifts or push-ups I'd do that night. I'd add, subtract, and double-check constantly. I felt like I was moving toward some great new salvation. Instead of praying when I felt scared or guilty or lonely, I'd turn to the numbers, like my grandmother to her wooden rosary beads, and they'd calm me down.

My head became so full of equations and plans about what I would eat and what exercises I would do that I didn't have room for much else. I stopped worrying about not having any boobs even though every other girl in my class had them. I stopped caring about how all the boys, including Juan-Juan, had a crush on my best friend, Catherine McMurtry. I stopped feeling guilty about all the games of Truth or Dare and Seven Minutes in Heaven I'd played, and how it made me feel weird and gross but also excited whenever there was a boy's tongue in my mouth. I stopped thinking about all those times Marie had told me that my father didn't love me. My calculations not only filled up all the empty spaces in my head; they also helped me determine the value of my self. On any day that I'd eaten less, worked out longer, or lost more, it didn't mean I was *good*, but at least I wasn't bad.

The most important number, though, was one I had no idea how to determine: the weight I'd have to be to let myself stop, the weight that would mean I was finally good enough. In the very beginning, I thought it would be 105. Then it became one hundred. Ninety-five. Ninety. By the time I weighed eighty-five, I started to wonder if I'd ever be able to predict what the right weight was. Maybe I wouldn't know until I reached it.

————

That summer before high school, when the dieting fever really started to take hold, I was fighting more than ever with my father, an Irish immigrant who made his living paving people's driveways and laying concrete. Maybe part of the problem was that there was no other adult in the house to help keep us in our corners: My father hadn't (and still hasn't) remarried, and we were between housekeepers at that point. He hired and fired sixteen different women before I got to college, but never before I got attached to them; each one of them seemed like some kind of mother to me.

Our door started to revolve after he kicked out Marie, who'd been with us for four years. She'd become slowly obsessed with my father, and eventually demanded that he marry her, though they'd never been romantically involved. She pleaded with him, saying that she was already acting like a mother to my sister and me; why not make her role official?

My father turned her down. One night shortly after the rejection, Marie pulled a huge knife out of the kitchen drawer and threatened to kill herself with it. I grabbed the cleaver away from her; my father ordered her out of the house, and we never saw her again, though for years she prank-called our house and one time even phoned Catherine McMurtry's house, looking for me.

It wasn't a coincidence that my obsession with dieting started soon after my father fired Marie. Screwed up as she was, she'd been a temporary stay against the confusion that ensued after my mother was gone. In the four years that she'd been with us, I'd come to depend on her, especially because I didn't feel like I could depend on my father anymore. It never occurred to me to ask him if Marie was right all those times she said he didn't love me; it seemed obvious he didn't. After all, I apparently had a special talent for saying things that would infuriate him so much that he'd give me the silent treatment for days, even weeks. During those periods, he'd do everything he could to avoid looking at me, even keeping his head down if we were in the kitchen together.

Often our arguments would start over things in the news. My father was a conservative then, despite the fact that he also subscribed to *The New York Times,* whereas I was a born liberal, despite the fact that I'd represented Ronald Reagan in some faux presidential debate we'd had at school. I would read the Week in Review section every Sunday so I'd have ammunition when my father started in about something.

That summer, abortion made the headlines. (JUSTICES UPHOLD RIGHTS BY NARROW VOTE, *The New York Times* said, after the Supreme Court ruled against a Pennsylvania anti-abortion law.) The topic was big in our kitchen, too. We'd get into it after my father arrived home, as the three of us were sitting down to a dinner I'd made. I always volunteered to cook whenever no one was on the payroll. My sister wasn't any good at it—she'd once tried to boil spaghetti without put-ting any water in the pot. Besides, I thought my father would like me better if I took on some adult responsibilities. Because the weather was warm and we didn't have air-conditioning, my father would preside at the head of the table wearing only his tar-blackened jeans and his mustard yellow work boots, in all his muscled bulk, smelling of sour sweat. His huge biceps always looked flexed even when they weren't, and though his pecs had gotten slightly flaccid with middle age, they were still powerful. His torso and arms were evenly burned the same leathery brown color—no "farmer's tan" for him—because he liked to take his shirt off in the sun when he was working.

Who knows exactly how our "discussions" would start, but soon enough, I'd swallow the instant rice I had in my mouth so

I could say, "I just think a woman should be able to do whatever she wants with her body, is all. It seems pretty obvious to me."

My father would raise his caterpillar eyebrows at me, and his face would twist from disbelief to disparagement to rage, and I knew things were about to get absurd.

" 'Whatever she wants with her body'—oh yeah?" He'd pound his Heineken bottle on the table. "So if you wanted to jump off a bridge, I should let you do that?"

"Wait—what?" Realizing my paper napkin had fallen to the floor, I'd grab another out of the wooden holder in the middle of the table so I could have something to hold on to. "I didn't say anything about jumping off a bridge. Besides, suicide is totally different from abortion. There's no law against it, I don't think. I mean, no one really cares what you do to yourself—"

"So what are you saying? I should let you kill yourself?"

I felt outrage like a stab in my chest. "What?" I'd glance over at my sister, hoping she would at least roll her eyes at me—that she would give me *some* sign I wasn't losing my mind—but she would refuse to look up from the wilted heap of green beans on her plate.

"You heard me," he said.

"Of course you shouldn't let me kill myself."

My father would point his knife at me. "But it's okay to kill babies?"

"This is crazy. First of all, we don't even know when they become alive!" I'd slam my own fist on the table, and the milk in my glass would jump.

My father would drop his utensils onto his plate with a clatter and glare at me. "You just watch your step now. Just watch your step."

I'd try to calm down. "All right, look. All I'm saying is a woman shouldn't be forced to ruin her life just because—"

"*Ruin her life?* Well, isn't that something. Isn't that something. What if your mother thought *you* were going to ruin her life—did that ever occur to you?"

"That's totally different. Isn't it? It's not like you guys were so poor you didn't want to have me. Right? Right?"

He wouldn't answer me directly. "Did you know that when your sister was born, they weren't going to let me take her or your mother out of the hospital? I had no insurance. I didn't have the money to pay the bill. I told them, 'You goddamn better let me take them out—that's my wife and my baby daughter we're talking about.' Did you know that?"

I did know. He'd told me a thousand times. But I wished he'd get back to my question.

Instead, he'd go on. "Where would *you* be now if your mother had gotten an abortion? You ever think of that?"

"That's beside the point. All I'm saying is, it seems really stupid for people who can't be decent parents to have kids."

"Oh, now I get it. Now I'm stupid."

"What?" I'd look across the table to my sister again, but she'd be pushing her chair back, on her way to the fridge to pour herself another glass of milk. "No, Dad. I didn't—"

"You know, if only you were a boy, I'd be able to teach you something about having such a smart mouth."

He'd go back to eating after that, and I'd stare down at my white thighs, then squeeze my fingernails into them till it killed. I'd wish that I was a boy, too, because at least then there would be a chance I might become more powerful than my father someday.

More unsettling than those debates were the other kind of

fights we had—the ones that erupted out of what I could've sworn were perfectly innocent sentences. That summer, the thing that seemed to set my father off most was asking how his day had been. Though I'd ask as soon as he came in from work, he'd ignore the question until after he'd gotten his beer out of the fridge, taken a seat at the table, and started stabbing at the chicken breast on his plate. Once the anticipation had become unbearable, he'd finally answer. "What do *you* care how my day was?" he'd say. "That is one phony question if I ever heard one."

"No, it's not." My eyes would widen. "I *do* care."

"Do you have any idea how hot it was out there today?"

"Maybe ninety-nine degrees?"

"That's right. And do you know what it feels like to be raking hot asphalt with the sun beating down on you when it's ninety-nine degrees?"

All I knew was that it couldn't feel too great, not when I'd been uncomfortable reading a book in the shade under the big tree in our front yard.

He went on. "But I go out there and bust my tail every day so I can provide for you guys. And you don't *care*! What do you ever do for me?"

"We do stuff," I'd say.

He'd laugh. "Oh yeah? Like what?"

I'd mention that I'd made dinner.

He'd laugh again. "And who paid for the food?"

He had, of course. His point seemed to be that nothing I did would have any meaning without him.

Things would degenerate from there, and as we kept quibbling, everything I thought I knew at the beginning of the conversation became uncertain. *Did* I really care about him? Did

I really want to hear how his day had been? Maybe I didn't—
not if it meant him flipping out like this. So, I probably *didn't*
care about him. Let's face it: I hated him. No wonder he didn't
love me.

"Oh, now here we go," my father would say, waving a hand
in my direction. "As if I don't have enough problems. Now she's
crying."

"I am *not* crying," I'd say, even though I was. I'd clench my
teeth and tense all my muscles, trying to control myself.

"I'd like to cry, too," my father would say. "But what would
happen if *I* cried? If I let myself fall apart, what would happen
to you guys?"

I'd never have much interest in finishing my food after that.

———

That fall, after I became a freshman at an all-girls' Catholic
high school, I kept chiseling away at myself, trying to purify
myself more, and to need less. The skinnier I got, though, the
tougher it became to stick to my self-improvement plan. The
problem wasn't that starving had become physical torture,
although it had. I was down to three hundred calories a day by
then: a tiny serving of Special K with watered-down skim milk
and a blue packet of Equal for breakfast; a green apple for
lunch; a rice cake or two later in the afternoon; and some vegetables and canned tuna for dinner. Exercising had become
painful, too. Somehow, I'd made it onto the varsity soccer
team, and our workouts were far more intense than anything
I'd been doing on my own—yet I refused to stop doing a
nightly calisthenics routine in the secrecy of my room. I was
chronically exhausted and chronically freezing, without any
body fat to keep me warm. But despite how bad my body felt,

my mind felt better than ever—even if it didn't exactly feel *good.*

No, the real obstacle was that the adults around me had started to notice what I was doing. My new teachers wanted to know if I'd always been so thin. My father kept saying he didn't think it was normal for a girl my age to be so skinny. I knew they'd all try to stop me if they found out the truth, so I did everything I could to hide myself. I didn't want to go back to a life without dieting to give it shape and meaning. So I'd spend my lunch hour in the library with my books open in front of me, too hungry to concentrate, watching Sister Concepta in her white habit and black veil as she watered the plants. To make myself look heavier, I'd wear an undershirt and long underwear beneath my blue oxford blouse, and a pair of boxer shorts below my plaid wool skirt. As a bonus, all the extra padding helped me stay warm. Instead of changing into my soccer clothes in the locker room with everyone else, I'd do it in the handicapped bathroom downstairs, making sure to keep my underlayers on and to stuff my thick shin guards into my socks before anyone saw me. At home I wore huge clothes (ones that used to fit perfectly) to cover myself up, but they didn't do much to calm my father's suspicions. Eventually he and I started to battle over a new topic: how much I'd eaten that day. I always lied, saying I'd stuffed my face before he came home, or that our coach had gotten us pizza after practice again (not that she ever had). I think my father wanted to believe me instead of finding out there was another worry to add to his list. And it was easy to evade him, since my soccer schedule had made it tough for me to remain family chef; we were fending for ourselves when it came to dinner by then.

Though he would still yell at me, my father also began to cajole. "Please eat," he would say. "For me? A little food's not going to hurt you." As satisfying as it was to hear him plead, the better pleasure was knowing that my body was finally doing what I wanted it to do. It had been a long time since anything he said had been able to make me cry; I thought maybe he'd never be able to do it again. I was finally beating my father at our ongoing battle of wills—and I'd done it not by getting bigger, but by getting smaller.

———

By late October, things started happening that I couldn't cover up with clothes or lies. My sister and I were walking to the bus one rainy morning when, seeing me struggle under the weight of my backpack, she tried to help me by pushing up the bottom, thinking she would hold it for a while. But I was so rickety that the shift threw me off balance and I fell backward, cracking my tailbone against the sidewalk. I would have lain there forever, staring up at the gray sky, but my sister could see the bus coming, so she pulled me up and tried to get me to run. The strange tingling pain I felt at the bottom of my spine, like the kind you feel after you whack your funny bone, made me limp for the rest of the day.

During soccer practice that afternoon, my coach, Miss Sawyer, called me off the field. "What the heck happened to you?" she said. Miss Sawyer was a boyish, fortysomething woman who wore khakis with V-neck sweaters and boat shoes; her blond hair was short and her legs were as bowed as a jockey's. On the day she posted the list of people who'd made the cut for the team, I stopped by her office and asked why she'd chosen me. Because she'd never seen anyone with more heart, she said, which sounded strange: I didn't feel like I had one left. I went straight into the bathroom after that and sobbed, because the only way I'd gotten through the excruciating tryouts was by telling myself it would all end soon; I was sure I'd never get picked.

Now she was waiting for me to answer her. I shrugged. "I fell this morning, and I'm a little sore. But I'll be fine."

"Why don't you take a break till you feel better?"

"No, no," I said, trying to sound calm. Ditching practice was not an option: If I didn't burn those calories, I'd despise myself. Plus, I'd have to stay up late in my room, doing more sit-ups and push-ups and leg lifts to make up for it, and I was too tired for that. "I'll be fine. Really. Just let me practice. I don't want everyone to totally lose respect for me. I'm already the worst on the team. Please let me practice, Miss Sawyer, please?"

She gave in. "But I'm keeping an eye on you, skinny," she said. "You haven't been looking so good lately."

A few days later, foot sores that had been coming on slowly made me more of a cripple than I'd been after the wipeout. My bony feet had been rubbing dangerously against my cleats for weeks by then, eroding the skin and forming holes—my stigmata—that slowly got deeper around both my ankles. For a while, the pain was barely noticeable if I covered the wounds with Band-Aids, then wrapped Ace bandages around them and wore an extra pair of socks. But one afternoon I hit my saturation point, and after tying my laces, I could barely hobble from the bathroom to the field.

Practice that day started with wind sprints, and I felt my spikes cutting into me with every step. Miss Sawyer called me over before I'd even finished the first leg. "You look terrible out there! Like a drunk with two broken feet." She forced a laugh, but there was uneasiness in it. "What's going on?"

I shook my head. "I guess it still hurts from when I fell before. I don't know. Probably nothing. Once I warm up, I'll be fine."

I didn't quite believe myself, and apparently neither did Miss Sawyer. She squinted at me. "You're sitting out today."

"But Miss Sawyer—"

"No buts! Except yours on that bench. Enough is enough. Get one of your books if you want to study. Otherwise, sit and watch."

When I got home later that day, Miss Sawyer had left a message for my father on our answering machine.

"Could you please call me as soon as you can?" her recorded voice said.

I erased it, but my time was running out. The next morning, I was in Spanish class with Sister Carol—a tall, athletic nun with curly silver-brown hair; a tough teacher, but fair. I was sitting in the front row of desk chairs, near the windows and the sputtering white radiators, and had one of my legs wrapped tightly around the other for warmth. As we translated sentences from our book, my head kept nodding with exhaustion; every time it bounced to the end of my neck, I snapped it back and tried to shake myself awake. Finally, the bell rang and we all prepared to leave, rustling our graded quizzes and packing our bags. When I was ready, I tried to stand, but my left leg collapsed under me.

"Are you okay?" a chorus of girls murmured. "What happened?"

I had no idea. I was sprawled on the cold marble floor; that was all I knew. Had I slipped? I must have. Embarrassed, I tried to get up, but as soon as I put weight on my foot, it collapsed again and I was back to the floor.

"Oh my God," someone behind me whispered. "What's wrong with her?"

Sister Carol seemed to think I was trying to be a clown. She put her hands on her hips and said, *"¿Cuál es el problema?"*

I wanted to tell her I didn't think this was any time for practicing *mi español.* "My leg," I answered stubbornly, in English.

"Un dolor?" she said. (A pain?)

"No," I said, my voice cracking. "More like . . . I can't feel anything. Like it went to sleep, but it's not waking up." I was panicking then, realizing the truth of what I was saying.

Sister Carol asked the girl behind me to help her right me, and once they had me in a standing position, Sister Carol asked if I thought I could walk on my own. I shook my head.

"Try," she said. "We'll help you."

Using the two of them as crutches, I teetered up the aisle, toward the door, floundering, taking panicked shallow breaths before I figured out that even though my left leg didn't seem to be working from the knee down, I could more or less get it to function by dragging it forward and pivoting off it.

Some seniors who'd filed in for the next class were staring at me.

"I think I'm okay now," I whispered to Sister Carol. We were near the chalkboard.

Sister Carol's lips were pursed. "Try going to the podium and back on your own."

Using my new method, I was able to shuffle up and down that catwalk, but I knew it didn't look pretty.

Once I returned to Sister Carol, she wiped the tears off my cheek with a hard thumb and, motioning at the other girl, said,

"She's going to take you up to the nurse's office. I'd do it myself, but I need to teach this class."

Our school was small, and I remember everything, so it's funny that I can't remember that girl's name or even her face. All I can remember was that I didn't think she was that cool, and yet, once we got out in the hall, she walked a few steps ahead of me. I knew why: She was embarrassed to be seen with me. She didn't want anyone to think she was friends with the sniffling, broken-down weirdo. I understood how she felt.

———

The next day my leg was still paralyzed, and my father took me to see the pediatrician who'd been treating me for as long as I could remember. In his beige office, with wall-to-wall carpeting and a framed picture of a train on the wall, old Dr. Newton said he couldn't be sure what had happened to me, but that a nerve had probably gotten pinched between the bones of one knee and the other when I had them crossed. Until the nerve relaxed again, I wouldn't have sensation.

"This never would've happened except that you're so emaciated," he said. "And your leg isn't going to heal unless you put on some weight. Your body is shutting itself down to conserve energy, sweetheart." The familiar lull of his voice had always soothed me before—through the chicken pox, through endless cases of strep throat, and a few sprained ankles—but that day it was getting on my nerves.

"I'm not going to be paralyzed forever, though, am I?"

"I don't think so, not as long as you eat better, although I'm going to recommend to your father that you see a neurologist for a second opinion."

Everything Dr. Newton was saying sounded so vague and

unscientific that I suspected he was just trying to scare me into getting fat.

"Do you understand?" Dr. Newton continued. His eyes bulged out from behind his convex square glasses; the frames seemed to be made out of the same kind of wire that lay combed over in thin strands across his head.

I shrugged.

"You've lost nearly forty pounds since the last time I saw you. And you didn't have any to spare in the first place. So come on. I know you're a good girl. You don't want to worry your poor father any more. You start eating better now, all right?"

Dr. Newton forbade me to exercise, and said that if I didn't gain at least one pound by the following week, he'd have to recommend more drastic measures.

———

When my father and I drove home in his red pickup later that night, he cried in front of me for the first time since my mother's funeral. He recounted a story I'd heard before, about how he watched his six-year-old brother die of lockjaw on Christmas Day, less than a week after he'd stepped on a rusty nail. The accident had devastated my father's parents so much that his mother had barely gotten out of bed for a year. She was always whispering to him that he should watch out for my grandfather; she was worried he'd drown himself in the tide off the west coast of Ireland, where they lived. "I'm not sure I'd be able to live with it if I lost you," my father told me. "So please, will you eat? For me?"

I mumbled something about trying, but the way he'd phrased his question infuriated me. One of the things I wanted out of my hunger strike was for my father to realize that he wasn't the only one with a shitty life. But it seemed like I still hadn't gotten my point across, that my suffering was significant only because it was making *him* suffer more.

Later that night, my sister and I sat at the top of the stairway near our bedrooms, eavesdropping on my father. He was on the phone in the living room downstairs, talking about what was wrong with me. Maybe the person on the other end was the parish priest; or my aunt, who was a private nurse; or Winnie Nee's father, who delivered babies at Columbia Presbyterian Hospital.

"What can I do to help her?" my father was saying.

As he listened to the answer, it got quiet, and my sister said, "Why are you doing this to Dad?"

"I'm doing it to *myself*," I said. "But I just can't stop."

"Don't you know you're already way too skinny?"

I said it was more complicated than that.

"But can't you see how you look?" she said.

I shrugged. "I guess. But I like it."

She stretched out her hand, and it was a normal girl's hand; the skin was soft, pink, and perfectly smooth except for the joint lines along her fingers.

"Now let me see yours," she said.

Mine was a chicken's foot: the five tendons poked out against the yellow-gray skin in hard steel lines from my wrist to my fingers, and curling blue veins crisscrossed over them. Looking at it, my sister started to cry. We hugged each other and I buried my face in her shoulder so she wouldn't see that I was grinning.

———

Within a couple of weeks—after I failed Dr. Newton's first test and a similar second one—my father and I were sitting in the Upper West Side office of an eating disorders specialist, Joseph Silverman, M.D.: a bald man with a skeletal head, reading glasses balanced on the tip of his nose, and a maroon silk bow tie that bloomed at the top of his lab coat. His rich cologne was as thick in my throat as frankincense in a church. I felt underdressed in my school uniform, and embarrassed by my father in his work boots, jeans, and flannel shirt. Sun was spilling in through the long bars on the two windows behind Silverman, and the same square of light that reflected off his skull also appeared on the black-and-white parquet marble floor, the polished wooden desk.

"Today, you weigh sixty-seven pounds," Silverman was informing me.

I nodded and crossed my arms over my chest, hoping he wouldn't notice how pleased with myself I was.

"Your resting heart rate is only thirty-six beats per minute."

"Is that bad?" I asked coyly.

"Between sixty and one hundred is normal. Your body temperature and blood pressure are precariously low. Frankly, you're in terrible shape. I've seen a lot of bad patients before, but never anyone whose leg has gone out like yours."

I bit down on my lip, thrilled to be that uniquely bad, and focused my eyes on the huge knuckles popping out of Silverman's folded hands. His fingers were icy cold, I knew; I'd jumped the first few times he'd touched me during the examination. He began drumming them on the desk, like two daddy longlegs coming toward me.

"I'm sure you're happy to hear you're one of the worst cases I've seen," he said. "But can it feel good to know that you've made yourself a cripple?"

A wave of heat burned through me. "Dr. Newton said it's not permanent. Right?"

"If you gain weight, it will probably get better. Probably. But you're lucky it's only your leg. Keep it up and more important parts of your body will give out on you." He started counting organs off on those fingers. "Your kidneys. Your pancreas. Your liver. Your heart. And you're a smart girl. I don't have to tell you what happens to people whose hearts stop."

"What—you mean they have heart attacks?"

With a flash of his shiny head, Silverman nodded. "Exactly."

Heart attacks had always been abstract to me—things that happened to old people—and I suppose it was partly because they seemed so unreal that I wondered idly if having one might finally prove I was thin enough.

"And some of them die," Silverman continued.

When he said that, I realized that death was exactly what some part of me had been gunning for all along. Of course, the idea of not being alive was terrifying; but at the same time, I wasn't sure I could go on living without proof that I deserved to. I wanted to be sure I was enough of *something*—skinny enough or important enough or smart enough or powerful enough—to deserve a life. I suppose what I wanted to know was if I was lovable enough.

Fat, salty tears started curling down my face.

Silverman pushed a box of tissues toward me. "Your father is here today because he thinks I can save you," he said.

"I would like *someone* to save me," I said.

I could feel my father staring at me; then he pulled himself forward on the edge of the desk. "I'd give up my life for her, Doctor. I'll find a way to pay you. Whatever it takes. All that matters to me now is her and her sister. On her deathbed, my wife said, 'Just take care of my two girls.' And that's all I want to do."

I thought I *was* going to die then, of embarrassment.

Silverman turned back to me. "The thing is, Maura, I've found that girls who don't want my help are incurable in the long run. So I have to know: Do you want to get better, or don't you?"

It took a while before I could answer. "I used to like what was happening to me. But now I'm scared I'll never be able to stop until . . ." The rest of that thought was too squalid to make it explicit. "I want to feel happy again for once. I don't really want to die. So, yes, could you please save me? Please?" I was begging him.

"Not exactly," Silverman answered. "But I can help you save yourself."

———

Four months later, I was discharged from the children's ward of Columbia Presbyterian, where Silverman treated all his patients. My body was a lot healthier by then: I weighed one hundred pounds, and my leg had improved so much that you'd never notice my limp unless you were looking for it. But I started fooling around with bulimia right after I was released, and it wasn't until my midtwenties that I began dealing with food in a way that felt more or less normal. It also took about ten years before all the numbness in my foot went away. And I'm still waiting to regain *feelings*. Losing weight was a way for me to reshape myself psychologically as well as physically: an attempt to starve off my emotions before they killed me. It helped me exorcise the ghosts of all the people I'd lost, like my mother and the sixteen house-keepers, by depleting me to the point where I didn't have the mental energy to care about them or hope for their return. I also stopped worrying about whether my father hated me, and whether he would disappear, too, like everyone else did. I felt like I was making myself stronger by surviving on less and less—not only nutritionally, but in terms of human interaction.

At the same time, though, I was subconsciously hoping for some human intervention: I wanted my father to rescue me. Becoming a walking skeleton was my way of going out to the middle of that bridge he liked to mention in our arguments, and daring him to stop me from taking a leap. And he did: Although his talk of how he'd do anything for me sometimes seemed cheap, all the money he spent on medical bills and psychotherapy over the years was as good as tangible proof that he believed I deserved to live. (My hospital stay alone was roughly equivalent to the cost of four years' tuition at a private college.) I doubt I'd have made it through without him.

But our relationship still isn't easy for me. No intimate relationship ever has been. Since I stopped depending on my father for the basics, I haven't truly depended on anyone else for anything—not financially, emotionally, or psychologically. There's still part of me that refuses to get close to anyone I might end up loving and losing. I haven't overcome the idea that the best way to protect myself is by remaining a self-contained unit. I can't stay with anyone for much more than three months. And while I'm ashamed that I can't commit to someone, some deeper shame prevents me from doing it.

I don't hide what I eat anymore, but there's still so much I want to conceal from everyone around me. These days, I use the novel I've been working on as my excuse to remain withdrawn from the world. It seems like there's still so far to go before I become "normal" that I often wonder if I'll ever really be happy. Most of the time I doubt that I will ever be *something* enough—attractive enough, smart enough, successful enough—for someone to love me.

Finally, though, I do feel thin enough.

TO POISON AN IDEAL

Ilana Kurshan

Ever since I moved to Jerusalem, I have done almost all of my food shopping in the *shuk,* the open-air market where vendors hawk their wares at all hours of the day. I wander amid the stands teeming with bloodred pomegranates, bright yellow melons, dried fruit and nuts of every variety, and warm cinnamon pastries hot out of the oven. I follow my nose and eyes, enticed by the pungent-smelling cheeses and the cardamom-flavored Turkish coffee. As I jostle my fellow bag-laden shoppers in the narrow, crowded aisles, I choose the juiciest tomatoes, the spiciest olives, the warmest and crispiest potato *burekas.* On my walk home, I reach into my bag and take out a pita so hot that the plastic bag encasing it has become clouded with steam, and savor each bite as I cross over the streets and yards of my neighborhood. I think about what I have purchased and what I will prepare in my kitchen that week, humming happily to the rhythm of my strides. I inhabit the present moment entirely; only rarely do I remember that less than ten years ago, I never would have been able to rejoice in such bounty.

It was during the summer after my sophomore year in college that I first discovered the power of self-denial. I was working as a science writer for a pharmaceutical company in New York City. My task, which I found disappointingly boring and mindless, was to summarize the pharmacological literature on Zoloft and Prozac—two of the drugs that my doctors would later recommend after I was diagnosed with an eating disorder. At that time, though, I was wholly unaware of anything unusual about my eating or my lifestyle. I used to sleep on the train from my parents' home in the suburbs into the city and then wake myself up by walking the thirty blocks from the train station to my office, hoping to arrive at work alert and invigorated. During the day, while I sat at my desk for hour after empty hour, I searched for something to keep my mind occupied. Lacking the challenge and stimulation that school had always provided, I thought up a new project to keep myself busy: I would exercise and watch my diet in an effort to become as healthy as possible. Ironically, that summer marked the beginning of the most dangerously unhealthy period of my life.

As I focused more and more on becoming "healthier," my desires and appetites slowly began to shift. After a few weeks of turning down my mother's chocolate cake, I soon convinced myself that I really didn't like chocolate cake anymore. Fat— both the fat in foods and the fat on my body—soon became in my mind associated with sloth, evil, and sin. First I simply avoided fattening foods, and then, after a while, I stopped thinking of ice cream and cake as food at all. Desserts became, to my mind, inedible; I considered them in the same category as the ham and cheeseburgers forbidden by Jewish law. That summer, incidentally, I also began studying Masechet Brachot, the section of the Talmud that deals with the blessings for various foods. I began reciting blessings before I ate, and as I did so, my eating became increasingly ritualized and belabored. I remember savoring every bite of my sugar-free, nonfat yogurt on the train rides home from work. I'd eat it with a fork, only dusting the tip of each prong with that milky white sweetness. It would take me almost thirty minutes to get through the entire container, and when I was finished, I would scrape the bottom with a plastic spoon and then lick the rim with my tongue, desperately craving every last trace. I would then keep the container in my bag until I got home and make a big show of throwing it out in the kitchen garbage when my family was around, both as sin offering (oh! the sin of having eaten and enjoyed) and as evidence at dinnertime that indeed, I had *already eaten.*

Since my commute took over an hour, I often returned from work so late that my family did not wait for me for dinner. As the weeks went by, I began to feel more and more distant from my parents and siblings, who laughed around the table together while I counted calories alone. The rift between us finally culminated in an explosive encounter during our family vacation at the Jersey shore at the end of August. I remember how nervous I felt about appearing in a bathing suit beside my two beautiful younger sisters. I convinced myself that no matter how hard I tried, I would never be able to measure up to them—and I felt all the more ashamed because I was the oldest, and so I should be the most sophisticated of us all. But if I couldn't ever be as beautiful, I told myself, at least I would be the thinnest. And so when my mother passed around a bag of potato chips while we all sat together on a beach blanket, I politely declined, telling myself that since I'd never be pretty, I had to make myself thin. One evening, when we were sitting as a family in an ice-cream parlor, I found myself utterly unable to take a bite of the chocolate cone in my hand, and my mother lost her temper. "What has gotten into you? Why can't you just eat like the rest of us? Who do you think you are?" Ashamed and embarrassed, I did not even try to defend myself. I hung my head and walked out of the ice-cream parlor, sheltering my melting ice cream, with tears already brimming in my eyes.

What had gotten into me? Who did I think I was? My mother, in her questioning, implied that I acted as if I were superior to everyone else because I was the master of my own desires. In some ways this was true: I was proud that I didn't need to indulge in "unhealthy" foods and that I could discipline myself to go running early every morning. But underlying this very superficial veneer of superiority was a deep sense of inferiority and insecurity. I believed that I did not deserve to eat as much as everyone else; I was not as beautiful or as talented as my sisters and friends, and hence I could not justify consuming any extra calories. I didn't think anyone could ever find me worthy or attractive unless I looked still thinner, so I turned down chocolate cake and ice cream and the people who loved me most.

The thinner I became that summer, the thinner I wanted to become. Being thin no longer meant simply being healthy; I convinced myself that thinness signified strength, self-control, and perfection. I mused on the phonetic similarity between *ascetic* and *aesthetic,* believing that through self-denial, I could achieve a sort of delicate beauty. I was drawn to the images of Degas' bronze ballerinas and to the narrow proportions of the Ionic columns in my old art history textbooks. Even words such as *svelte* and *petite* began to assume, in my mind, a positive valence. All too soon, I would begin to think of *anorexia* in this way as well, conjuring a snow white princess who glided along in a winter fairyland, leaving no footprints. At this point, though, I never thought of myself as an anorexic or as a person with eating "issues"; it wasn't until I returned to college that fall that anyone suggested I might actually have a problem.

I remember my first day back, when I wore a pair of jeans I had borrowed from my younger sister, and a friend stopped me to tell me how great I looked. I actually felt beautiful, and for the first time in a long while I carried my body with pride and confidence. That semester, energized and highly motivated, I decided to take an especially difficult course load, adding a fifth class to the standard four required of all undergraduates. I began waking up earlier than ever before, determined to fit as much into each day as possible. Each morning I'd arrive at the gym just as it opened and claim my treadmill; although I preferred to run outside, I could study on the exercise machines and thus be twice as efficient. I planned my whole day so that I'd never waste a moment: I called my parents while I got dressed in the morning, ate breakfast during my first class, jogged back to my dorm for lunch, and ate dinner at my desk while checking my e-mail. I was proud of my ability to squeeze so many activities into my day, much as I squeezed my body into smaller clothing sizes with each passing week.

Although I never stopped eating three meals a day, I severely restricted my diet and the range of foods I would eat. As the number of calories I ate decreased with each passing week, food assumed more and more of a central role in my life. I drove myself to extremes of hunger so that during class, I'd find myself fantasizing about a green apple in my backpack, counting down the minutes until the lecture would end and I could savor that first juicy bite. Late at night I'd push myself to stay awake until I was so hungry that I could not bear it anymore, whereupon I would surrender to sleep. One night, I remember that I had to stay up unusually late to finish a paper due the next morning, but I was so hungry that I could barely sit upright at my desk. To help push me through the night, I lined up a row of Cheerios next to my keyboard and told myself that for each paragraph I wrote, I could eat one Cheerio. Ten Cheerios later, I collapsed into bed, vowing that I would skip breakfast the next morning to punish myself for having indulged.

As September cooled to October and October chilled to November, I became increasingly manic. Intense hunger acted on me like a double espresso; I was wired, energized, alert, and intensely charged. I found myself unable to ever stand still: I'd run to and from my classes instead of shuffling along with the crowds; stretch my legs in the back of the synagogue instead of sitting among the congregation during morning prayers; and often walk out of my way just so that I wouldn't have to wait at a street corner. I no longer enjoyed relaxing with friends in the student lounge or attending dorm room parties; I always had to be doing, moving, and checking things off some crazy mental list. It was as if I had become so uncomfortable with myself that I could never rest in my body. I was afraid of having the time or the mental space to reflect or digest my experiences.

By November, I had lost so much weight that I had to wear four layers of clothing to stay warm, and my roommates and friends became increasingly concerned. My sister, who was also at school with me, insisted that I schedule regular weigh-ins with a nurse practitioner at the college health services just to make sure things were all right. At the second of those visits, the nurse grew alarmed at my slow pulse and low blood pressure and called in the head doctor, who declared I was on the verge of collapse. As I anxiously glanced at my watch, worried that I might be late for my class presentation, the doctor asked me for my parents' phone number. "Young lady," he announced in a tone that scared me with its severity, "I'm sending you to a hospital."

The rest of the day was a blur. I remember begging the doctor to let me go to class, and his responding that if I left the health services center he would send the police after me. Someone must have contacted my roommates, because they packed a suitcase for me and accompanied me to the airport, where I boarded the next plane home. As I always do before flying, I recited the traditional wayfarer's prayer. When I reached the Hebrew words asking God to return me safely, I panicked for a moment that I might not be free to return when I wanted. But I entertained that fear only briefly before taking a textbook out of my backpack to begin studying for my midterms the following week. Surely I would be back by then.

My plane landed in the early evening and my parents drove me directly to the hospital, where I was placed in a wheelchair, hooked up to an IV, and wheeled to the adolescent ward. I remember muttering as I fell asleep that I had to make sure I got back to school in time for my first exam.

The next morning, I awoke in a strange bed and found a nurse hovering over me to draw blood. "What do you think you are doing?" I asked angrily. "I'm a student, not a patient!" But as much as I cried out to the doctors about the absurdity of the situation and pleaded with my parents on the phone, my resistance was useless. I comforted myself with a grim pun: In the space of a single day, I had been catapulted from the Ivy League to the IV League, with little hope of release.

In the pastel-curtained eating disorders ward, there were five other girls—"skeletons in the closet," as I used to jokingly refer to us. Seven times a day, we'd gather for meals and snacks: 7:00 a.m., 10:00 a.m., noon, 2:00 p.m., 5:00 p.m., 8:00 p.m., and 10:00 p.m. One of the ward nurses would record the amount of food on our trays at the start and end of the meal. In between, she would sit at the head of the table, peering at us quizzically over her spectacles. We never spoke at meals; each bite was chewed silently and painstakingly. We were all conscious of just how many calories we were consuming with each sip of sickly sweet fruit juice and each bite of dry hospital rice. Some of the girls would try to hide food in their napkins or "accidentally" spill juice on the floor, and their cheating infuriated me. But to my shame, I, too, found myself obsessing over who got stuck with the largest serving of broccoli or the extra piece of cheese. In the hospital I felt reduced to a competitive and petty adolescent; I hated the person I had become, but I also felt increasingly estranged from the person I had been in my preanorexia days.

In an attempt to maintain my dignity, I stubbornly refused to act like a typical hospital patient. The mornings were always the worst. When the nurse would come to wake us for the 6:00 a.m. weigh-in, I'd turn over on my stomach and wish I were dead. But once I was up, I insisted on taking a shower, washing my hair, and dressing fully from head to toe. While the other girls remained all day in their hospital gowns and slippers, I wore corduroys and sweaters just as I had at school. During the day, in the free hours between meals, I read the complete works of Jane Austen (including *Sanditon* and *The Watsons*!) and studied for my exams. I even managed to persuade the nurses to let me borrow the hospital computer several times a week so I could work on my final papers. For my History of Physics class, I wrote a comparison of the methodology of Werner Heisenberg and Niels Bohr, using physics books that my sister mailed to me from the university library. I still remember the looks on the doctors' faces when they looked at my window sill and saw stacks of library books about the philosophy of quantum mechanics.

For my final paper in my poetry class, I wrote about A. R. Ammons's "Easter Morning," a poem whose first lines haunt me to this day: "I have a life that did not become, / that turned aside and stopped, / astonished." I felt that my life had stopped abruptly in the hospital, cut short by the cruel hands of the doctors who sent me there and who wouldn't let me return to the normalcy of seminars, cafeterias, and morning runs on the river. In those miserable hospital days, I drew strength from Frank Bidart's "Ellen West," a long poem about a woman's experience with anorexia: "But each compromise, each attempt / to poison an ideal / which often seemed to me sterile and unreal, / heightens my hunger." I memorized a few lines of the poem each day in the hospital, determined that I would secure my release before I reached the final stanzas, in which the woman in the poem dies of starvation.

My commitment to school saved me during my three long weeks in the hospital, and so did my religious faith and practice. Each day I prayed the requisite three times, facing toward the eastern wing of the hospital. I found that the self-imposed structure of prayer was a way of resisting the externally imposed structure of meals, much like Meg Murray's shouting of the multiplication tables to ward off the tyrannical rhythm of IT in *A Wrinkle in Time*. I remember pleading with God to get me *out,* and finding strength in the psalms traditionally recited in time of distress: "From the depths I called to you, God, hear my voice, may your ears be attentive to the call of my pleas." I felt most buried in the depths during my first Shabbat in the hospital, when I tried to perform the ritual activities associated with the day. I requested a cup of grape juice so I could recite the kiddush prayer; but then I realized that before performing the ritual hand washing, I'd have to unplug my IV tube, thereby violating the prohibition against using electricity. I remember standing for a moment and wondering whether I should violate Shabbat by unplugging the IV, or else disregard the hand-washing ritual altogether. Faced with this choice, I burst into tears and buried my head in my hands at the table, as the other girls forged forward into their mounds of mashed potatoes.

Though the hospital was very lonely and isolating, my family and friends reminded me that I was missed. My parents visited every couple of days, coming and leaving with tears in their eyes. On each visit, my mother brought another gift relating to the care of the physical body: vanilla-scented shampoo; warm flannel pajamas; furry pink slippers. I remember that when she gave me the pajamas, I promised myself I wouldn't wear them until I stopped gaining weight. I stashed them beneath the hospital bed, unable to enjoy the warmth and softness of the material against my shamefully flabby body. In between my parents' visits, my friends reminded me with cards and phone calls that they loved me no matter how I looked or what I weighed, and I cherished their heartfelt words. Some of the members of my synagogue sent flowers, which I refused to keep at my bedside in my stubborn refusal to identify as a hospital patient. I would unwrap the flowers, place them neatly in water in one of the hospital vases, and deliver them to another patient in the ward, explaining that I was allergic. Part of me genuinely wanted to deny that I was sick and instead play the role of a Pollyanna spreading good cheer; but another part of me, the part that stashed away the soft pajamas, felt far too fat and disgusting to deserve anything so pretty and fragrant.

Much as I tried to deny that I was undergoing hospitalization for anorexia, the reality was impossible to ignore. After months of running each morning at the crack of dawn, I was now confined to a three-room radius: bedroom, bathroom, and, of course, kitchen. With each day, I had to introduce a new terrifying food into my meal regimen: baked potatoes (I hadn't eaten hot food in weeks!), lasagna, chocolate cake. I felt like Wilbur in *Charlotte's Web,* being fattened for slaughter. The dilemma was overwhelming, distressing, and a constant source of agony: If I ever wanted to get out of the hospital, I'd have to gain weight; if I gained weight, I'd never want to get out of the hospital.

One of the most difficult moments was the very first time I felt full after a meal. I thought something was growing in my stomach; the heaviness felt as unnatural as a malignant growth. Distressed and uncomfortable, I crawled into the corner of a sticky plastic hospital chair and began shrieking in anger and frustration. I clutched desperately at my legs; I twisted the flesh on my arms; I covered my mouth and eyes in shame. I wanted out of the hospital, out of my body, and out of my life, but the bright red EXIT signs all over the ward appeared blurry through my tears and I had no idea where to turn.

Finally, after three and a half weeks of tireless pleading with my doctors and parents, I was released and allowed to return to school. Although I was back in the place where many of my anorexic behavior patterns had become habitual and ingrained, I forced myself to keep up the hospital regimens. I knew I wasn't allowed to run in the morning, but I also feared that if I slept in or lay in bed past 7:00 a.m., I would lose all my hard-earned self-discipline and self-control. So instead of running, I used to wake up at seven, walk down to the river, and sit on a park bench watching the joggers pass. I'd observe how thin and muscular their legs appeared, and clutch my own thighs in fury and frustration. Then I'd shrink back to my dorm room and try to convince myself that even without having exercised, I still deserved to take a shower.

As I battled with the torture of not exercising in the morning, I struggled to complete my final papers before the end of the semester. I have always loved to write, but after the hospital, writing became increasingly agonized, belabored, and fraught with complicated associations. Somehow, I developed an elaborate economic system in which writing and eating were associated with production and consumption, respectively. As in my prehospital, Cheerio-rationing days, I would only let myself eat once I had done some writing each morning, but sometimes I became so hungry that I could no longer concentrate; then I'd eat what felt like too much, and force myself to stare at a blinking cursor for hours until I was able to make words appear on the screen. I felt uncreative, infertile, and empty.

During my first weeks back, many of my friends and professors commented on how much better I looked and how much happier I must be, and I cringed at their every word. I was sure that they were telling me that I was fat, and inevitably I felt only worse. For the next few years, as I very gradually got back to (and beyond) my preanorexia weight, I often felt like the greatest struggle was not against the inner demons but against the endless ways in which I saw myself reflected in the eyes of others. My experience with anorexia has taught me never to make comments about other people's apparent weight gain or loss. I realize that I can never know how my words will be interpreted; in our highly image-conscious world, it seems safest to say nothing at all.

People who know that I was once diagnosed with anorexia often ask me how I managed to recover. It is a hard question to answer, because I still do not feel all better. I can say that the road has mostly been an uphill one, with several tortuous twists and turns. It was a full three years before I could eat a slice of pizza like a normal person, without taking off all the cheese and hiding it beneath the crust, then cutting up the slice with a fork and knife into minuscule pieces. I had to learn to give away pairs of jeans that were too small, which meant letting go of the hope that they would someday fit again. I had to learn to wake up and jump right in the shower, without going for a run and breaking into a sweat. I had to learn to accept my place in my family, and to see the beauty reflected in all those who look at me with love. Perhaps most difficult, I had to relearn how to view food as a source of nourishment and not as part of a complicated system of reward and punishment. For a while, I found it impossible to pray after I ate; I felt that being full ren-dered me an inadequate vessel for the divine spirit, and so the words would die inside me before I could ask God to open my lips in prayer. Even now, I still find that morning prayers come most easily, because I recite them on an empty stomach.

It has been almost a decade since I was hospitalized, and

although I am physically healthy, the body is only one part of the picture. Anorexia rewired my brain and my aesthetic perceptions, and so while I am at a normal weight, my mind's eye is still not completely refocused. To this day, I never feel as beautiful as my sisters, and whenever I am around my family, I have a hard time making the effort to present myself well. At times, I still look in the mirror and wish I were thinner. I can always pick out an anorexic in a crowd, and when I pass a frighteningly skinny jogger in the morning, I turn my head to follow her with my eyes a bit wistfully. And while this is certainly not a sign of illness, it is also no coincidence that, on my annual visits to the Met, I still prefer Degas' dancers to Gauguin's Tahitian nudes.

I have come very far from those terrifyingly manic undergraduate days, but I still feel the constant need to overschedule myself. I wake up at 6:00 a.m. (though I start my day with a class rather than a run), and I rarely get to bed before midnight, feeling like I need to fill every moment to the brim. Here in Jerusalem I have three jobs—literary agent, editor, and writer. I also study Talmud in a rigorous yeshiva program, meet friends regularly in coffee shops to read Hebrew and English poetry, organize a weekly prayer service, swim several kilometers a week, and write limericks about Talmud in the wee hours of the morning.

If anything has been constant throughout my illness and recovery, it is the strength I have found in Jewish tradition and in the sacred rhythm of daily prayer, holidays, and religious rituals. In Judaism, eating is an affirmation of life, and the body is the house of the soul that is meant to do God's work in the world. I don't always know just what that work is, and sometimes I am terrified by not knowing. What am I meant to give to others? For what purpose was I created? I suspect I shall be wrestling with these questions my whole life—as, indeed, most of us do. But even though I don't have it all figured out, at least now I am able to eat a hot dinner and sleep comfortably in warm, soft pajamas.

Jerusalem is a beautiful city in which to wake up. Through the northern window of my apartment, I can see the outline of the moon as it fades into the lightening sky; at the eastern window, the first rays of the sun sparkle on the stone walls and pierce through the green shutters. Most mornings, I wake up hopeful, ready and eager to greet the new day. As I rub the slumber from my eyes, I don't just thank God for restoring my soul to my body, as the traditional prayer book dictates. I also thank God that I have this body: arms that reach out to others, legs that carry me forward, and a mouth to taste and to savor all the goodness that is out there.

DAUGHTERS OF THE DIET REVOLUTION

Jennifer Egan

––––––

My stepsister Marcia and I share an occasional lust for high-grease breakfast foods, and recently, over pancakes and eggs, she told me something interesting. Marcia's daughter, D., was with us—a wily, emphatic little girl who, at four years old, is young enough that we can still spell out words in her presence and just barely elude the clamp of her curiosity. *S-e-x* is a big one, of course. Marcia is careful to spell out the name of her ex-husband, D.'s father, when speaking of him with anything but the warmest affection. I was surprised, though, when Marcia mentioned that she'd been on a *d-i-e-t.*

"Why did you spell it?" I asked.

"Oh, I don't even want her thinking about all that," Marcia said.

We both looked at D., who was smacking her lips over fried eggs and hash browns. I didn't have to ask what Marcia meant by "all that." We are both thirty-four, members of the vanguard generation of disordered eaters. When Marcia and I were children, no one had heard of anorexia; I first encountered the term at age thirteen, in 1976, in a magazine article about a girl who had starved herself for reasons no one understood. I

45

remember her picture: somber, willowy, standing on a bath-room scale, her shoulder blades jutting out like wings. I looked at her and felt my whole being contract into a single strand of longing. I wanted that: *anorexia.* And I got my wish, not in so dire a way that I was hospitalized with feeding tubes—nothing like that. But at fourteen, when I began losing weight precipi-tously, I initiated myself into the cult of food consciousness and its attendant despairs and elations. I joined the ranks of girls and women whose notebook margins are dappled with obscure caloric tabulations—apple, 100; bagel, 200; frozen yogurt, 150—women for whom meals are fraught with the tension of trying to eat less than anyone else, who keep a sec-tion of their closets full of "skinny" clothes that radiate desire and reproach, who cancel doctor appointments because they're afraid of being weighed that day, for whom "You look too thin" is perceived as a shining compliment, and for whom a growling stomach and a light head inspire feelings of triumph. These rit-uals, and many others like them, were to circumscribe my thoughts and behavior for the next eighteen years.

It can be eerie, in light of our presumed uniqueness, to dis-cover how closely the experiences of our contemporaries paral-lel our own. I've heard many women my age say "I wanted to get anorexia," or even, "I taught myself how to throw up," as a prelude to long and desperate struggles with bulimia. A lot of my peers at the University of Pennsylvania were grappling with full-blown eating disorders; at a minimum, we were wary and self-conscious about food. How could we not be? In the women's restrooms at the Wharton School, where I sometimes studied at night, I'd find food containers lying on the restroom floor right next to the toilets: doughnut boxes, ice cream car-tons. This detritus of desperation frightened me the way nightmares do, grotesque distortions of things that are, at bottom, deeply familiar. Here, eating no longer bore any relation to nourishment or even to pleasure: It had been reduced to a brief complication in the process of purgation, of emptying oneself.

My mother, who graduated from Vassar in 1959, finds these stories incomprehensible. "We'd order in plates of french fries and hamburgers, and we'd just eat it all and go to bed," she says. "We were all a little overweight by today's standards, but I don't remember that troubling me in the least." Marilyn Monroe was the beauty who floated in the minds of my mother and her friends: voluptuous, pillowy. "The models in the fashion magazines were skinny, but no one cared about them," my mother says. "They were anonymous."

But attitudes toward food were the least of the differences between my mother's college years and my own. "There were certain people who planned to have careers," she says, "but the rest of us majored in English or something, and the idea was that you would get married. I thought I'd never have to earn a living. I'd be an even more ornamental accessory." This promise—that in exchange for being lovely and well educated, my mother would be taken care of for life—was one of many the world failed to keep. By age twenty-six, she found herself divorced with a two-year-old daughter. It was 1965. Women only five or six years younger than she were studying at universities awash in demands from all quarters—for equality, for opportunities—demands my mother had never thought to make. The world that she and her Vassar friends had been groomed to inhabit had vanished from under their feet.

My fear of being overweight, which began when I was nine or ten, has always been linked, in my mind, to my mother. She is a glamorous woman with excellent taste and a superb wardrobe. Physically, I resemble her to an almost uncanny degree; people have been doing double takes at the sight of us for as long as I can remember. Maybe because she and my father were divorced before I turned three, my sense of my mother and me as a pair, an inseparable duo, feels ancient and inviolable. When I was five, we wore matching two-piece bathing suits.

I regarded my future stepfather as an unwelcome interloper in our small, simple world. "He's just coming over for a bite to eat," my mother would assure me, to which I would reply, "Okay, one bite. And then make him leave." But they married when I was four, and we moved to San Francisco three years later, which took me far from my father, who was still in Chicago. He, too, remarried; as both families began having more children, I struggled (alongside much of my generation) in the role of stepchild, so perilous in fairy tales and in life. My unease made me cleave all the tighter to my mother—the unit of the two of us was the only one in my life that still felt intact.

I was an average little girl: not skinny, not fat, towheaded, with an unrelenting sweet tooth. I remember my mother suggesting at some point that I hold in my stomach when I stood; not only would this look better, she pointed out, but it would strengthen my stomach muscles so that pretty soon, my stomach would stay tucked in of its own accord (I'm still waiting for that part). This communiqué from the world of adults was something I took seriously: I was careful to hold in my stomach from that time on.

"Something odd happened in the sixties," my mother recalls. "Fashions became very childlike. The models all had these knobby legs and patent-leather shoes. . . . Women suddenly wanted to look like prepubescent girls." Considering that many consumers of fashion in the 1960s were women like my mother, bred to inhabit a world that was now in staggering transformation, this yearning to return to puberty—to start over—seems deeply reasonable. My mother was fashionable; she subscribed to *Vogue* and *Harper's Bazaar*, and she followed their leads—followed, too, the ascension of those skinny, anonymous models from the status of clothes hangers to that of stars. If feminine power in the 1950s was measured in overt sexuality, the ability to attract a man (who would take care of you for life), in the '60s a woman's power became vested in her ability to regulate her sexuality: most obviously with birth control, but also by curbing the womanliness that would land her in the kitchen slinging pork chops. And if it was too late to stave off that fate—as it was for my mother—well, at least you could lose some weight.

In the selfishness of childhood, I could not imagine my mother doing anything but serving us, and she never implied that she would have preferred to do otherwise. But I think I sensed her frustration. By the time I was twelve, her marriage to my stepfather was stretched tight over fissures that would ultimately bring about its collapse. He was gone a lot on business; she cooked dinner for my brother and me every night ("Chicken again?" we were forever whining) and did enough laundry to fill an airplane hangar. Recently I asked my mother what she might have done if she hadn't married at age twenty-three, and she mentioned languages, diplomacy, Europe. (She did return to the workplace in her early forties, and became a successful art dealer.) I can't blame her. As a child, I felt a deep aversion for my mother's life. I envisioned my own future as solitary, independent, childless; I fantasized about having a kind of worldly power I had only ever seen in men like my stepfather, who was an investment banker. I wanted to be my mother's opposite. At the same time, my distaste for her life made me guilty—and afraid. I adored my mother. She was all I had.

A heightened consciousness of food first seized our home in the early 1970s, when my mother read Adelle Davis's *Let's Eat Right to Keep Fit* and banished the breakfast cereals Quisp and Lucky Charms forever from our shelves. Hostess Ho Hos and Ding Dongs yielded to Fruit Roll-Ups and Tiger's Milk bars. My brother and I were fed spoonfuls of cod liver oil each morning before we left for school; I spit mine onto the garage floor, where it mingled nicely with the oil stains ("Smells like fish in here," my stepfather would muse, bewildered). And this health consciousness was duly followed by a growing awareness of weight. The flat green scale in my parents' bedroom acquired delphic powers; it revealed whether you had been Good or Bad. My stepfather became a fanatical runner, and when the early antecedents of aerobics came along (before Jane Fonda, who, incidentally, was a college classmate of my mother's), my mother embraced them with fervor. Both she and my stepfather marveled at snapshots of themselves from the 1960s: "Look at that double chin, that flabby stomach"—as if some prior blindness, some naive vulnerability in which they had unwittingly been muffled, had finally burned off.

I took my Fruit Roll-Ups and Tiger's Milk bars to school and traded them for Ho Hos and Twinkies, which I wolfed down like a refugee. And then I worried. My love of food, of sweets in particular, had begun to feel dangerous. I had absorbed the notion of Good and Bad with regard to eating, and knew that I was Bad. Perversely, the more entangled food became with virtue, or my lack thereof, the more tenuous its connection to hunger and its satisfaction; rather than quelling my desire to eat, these ruminations made me crave food constantly—whether or not I was hungry. By age thirteen, I was eating a lot and it was starting to show. Now, mingled with the general wretchedness of adolescence was the specter of fatness, which loomed before me terrifyingly and compounded my sense of unease in the world.

I began to soothe myself with fantasies, visions in which I became popular, irresistible, strong like the models in my mother's fashion magazines (which I devoured); visions in which I was searingly, mightily, unstoppably thin. The article on anorexia, intended as a cautionary tale, functioned for me as a how-to manual. The reformed anorexic spoke of having survived on popcorn, celery, and apples; I adopted these as dietary staples. She recalled drinking glasses of water before every meal to fill up her stomach; I did the same. Further articles provided more tips: I bought a book with a calorie index and began trying to hold my daily intake to a "dangerously" (read: desirably) low eight hundred calories. I jogged rather than take the bus. I drank coffee and Tab to kill my appetite. I smoked.

And to my own astonishment, these steps had a fairly immediate result: My body changed. Over the course of a few months, I lost ten or fifteen pounds that, in my case, were the difference between average and scrawny. I remember the euphoria of finding myself lighter on the bathroom scale, my sense of joyous and secret achievement when the waistbands of my pants hung loose and my ribs became distinct as fingers and people asked my favorite of all questions, "Have you lost weight?" I felt as if I were finally coming into focus, hard and sharp and light, released from the bulky packing of my sadness. If I felt dizzy at times, or physically weak, or just plain *hungry*, these hardships attested to the gravity of my undertaking. Having been at the mercy of circumstances all my life—divorces, remarriages, a move that separated me from my father—the discovery that I could alter my physical self and make people *see me differently* was momentous. I'd never experienced power like that.

Reactions were mixed: My wraithlike appearance made my stepfather apoplectic, but my mother wasn't nearly as troubled by it—not as troubled as she would have been had I *gained* weight. Fat meant sloppy, out of control; thin meant sleek and disciplined. She joined my stepfather's bullying efforts to make me eat, but on a subterranean level, I believed that I sensed her approval and luxuriated in it. Because she herself was quite thin by then, and a chronic dieter, I felt a kinship with my mother, as if losing weight were a rite of passage into the world of adult femininity. And the pride I felt as the author of my own new-found thinness contained a promise so deep that I doubt it was even conscious: I would avoid the life that had ensnared my mother. I would become one of the strong and worldly, rather than the chicken basting and laundry folding. And I felt, in that same buried way, that my mother wanted this for me.

The irony of equating thinness with power is grotesquely clear in the body of a true anorexic: shriveled, weak, married to a project of self-erasure that often ends in death. But for those of us who inhabited anorexia's middle ground; who struggled with an undue consciousness of food and weight without really endangering ourselves; for whom whole swaths of our lives were measured in terms of fatness and thinness; Good and Bad—for us, too, there are ironies. Chief among them is the fact that our route to worldly power involved shrinking the world to match the dimensions of our own small (but never small enough) bodies, and then dominating those bodies. A conspirator against us couldn't have planned it better.

How I (indeed, my generation of women) got caught in this solipsistic trap is something I still don't fully comprehend. Much as I fantasized about worldly strength and independence, I think I was frightened to seek them out. I thought I didn't deserve them; lacked the knowledge or sophistication to bring them off; that, being female, I *just plain wasn't allowed* to seek out real-world power when neither my own mother, nor any mother I knew, had any. I'm sure I felt this way at fourteen because sometimes I still do. And my guess is that I'm not the only one.

So, a solution: By equating my physical self with the world and exerting harsh control over that, I could feel powerful without threatening anyone. Preoccupied, sometimes physically weak, I rarely spoke in class and at times had trouble concentrating. I had excelled in grade school, but by age fifteen I'd become unexceptional, unnoticed by my teachers. Socially, I was hesitant—a follower. I developed scoliosis, which, by the time I was fifteen, required a back brace and eventually surgery; it's hard not to wonder if my wretched eating habits might have exacerbated it. And I'm one of the lucky ones. For every true anorexic (nearly 5 percent of whom die from the disease), there are hundreds, maybe thousands of dabblers who are spared its lethal hooks. How I ended up in this latter category is a mystery; I can only attribute it to some genetic impulse toward health—the same impulse that allowed me to mess with drugs and smoking and heavy drinking without ever getting hooked. In other words, luck.

But there was a price: time. All that thought and worry about when and how to eat, about not eating, about trying to wear my skinny pants, about times when I'd been skinnier, people who were skinnier, how many calories I'd burned versus how many I'd consumed on a given day—all that cogitation, day in, day out, for eighteen years—what a waste! I could have learned Greek or Latin with that time. I could have built a boat and sailed around the world. I could have earned a Ph.D. or, at the very least, become a lot better read than I am. It's a pit of regret that I still fall into sometimes. But what I end up feeling, in the end, is just relief at finally having been released from that tiny box of thought—subtly, almost without my noticing, somewhere around the time I published a novel. I was thirty-two. It was the first time I'd done anything that resonated in the world beyond myself. And it led me to imagine what real power might feel like.

It's hard to believe that eating disorders will go away when the skinny, beautiful models are still with us, mute proselytizers of impossible standards of thinness and beauty as a route to power. But unlike our mothers, who were as blindsided by the arrival of eating disorders as we, I and my generation are veterans. We know exactly what they are. I don't have children yet, but when Marcia spelled out *d-i-e-t*, I made myself a promise: If I ever had a daughter, I would keep the cult of food consciousness outside her range of vision for as long as possible, so that when it found her some other way, as it surely would, she would be fortified against it by years of healthy innocence. And then I could help her fight it. I made that promise as I watched Marcia's little girl finish eating in peace.

1997

ON THIN ICE

Francine du Plessix Gray

———

It's the summer of 1948, I'm seventeen years old, standing on a Long Island beach with my mother. As I wade into the water, I hear her say to one of the fashionable friends at her side, "If she gets any plumper, of course, we'll put her on a rigid diet." Glancing at my hips, my breasts, I suddenly feel repellent, obscenely swollen—above all, unworthy. And even though I recently weighed in at 128 pounds—fine for a five-feet-nine frame, according to our family doctor—this is the moment at which I first say to myself, "I am too fat." That very night, pleading the flu at the family dinner table, limiting myself to a bit of soup, I begin the often violent calorie watching that has plagued most of my life. Since then, I've seldom sat down for a meal without sizing up the portion before me, deciding what fraction of it I deserve to eat and what I must leave uneaten. The ailment now called *anorexia nervosa,* a term barely known to the public until the 1960s and seldom diagnosed in my generation of young women, is inevitably marked by self-deprecation and by complex filial bonds.

I don't remember which of my mother's gauntly chic friends she was talking to that day, and I don't believe it matters. It could have been one of the several meticulously thin fashion models who attended my parents' parties that decade, or else one of the society beauties—Babe Paley, Gloria Guinness—who were equally part of their world. What does matter is that my ambitious, driven parents were high priests of that rite which every teenager wants to master above all others—seduction; and that they lived at the heart of the sexual-industrial complex that instructed millions of women on how to lure men through the wile of a tiny waistline or a perfectly painted face. My stepfather, Alexander Liberman, was a star of the Condé Nast publishing empire—*Vogue, Glamour,* and so on—and would soon rise to be its editorial director. My flamboyant, Russian-born mother, the hat designer "Tatiana of Saks Fifth Avenue," whose clientele included such celebrities as Marlene Dietrich, Claudette Colbert, and Estée Lauder, was looked on as one of New York's leading fashion arbiters. A majestic war goddess of a woman ever adorned with blazing costume jewelry, she stared at herself in every mirror she passed, and she did not so much converse as proclaim her opinion on anything under the sun, including my appearance: "Dostoyevsky is a terrible writer"; "Your face is too wide for straight hair"; "Your cheeks are too plump for pink lipstick." The brutally critical gaze with which she scrutinized any human surface, particularly mine, had thrust me into panic ever since I could remember. And my need for her love was such that for my first two decades, acquiescence to her wishes, or the appearance of such, was the only tactic I'd evolved to gain her approval.

Another curious feature of the maternal drama staged at the beach was that Mother herself ate lustily and heedlessly, as I had up to that day, and never took up the cult of gauntness then sweeping fashion. She was my height, five feet nine, but far more large-boned, and she seemed to be proud of her 140 pounds. Although she was painfully insecure about some aspects of her body, particularly her large breasts, I doubt if she had ever in her life dieted. Since our arrival in the United States in 1941, our tastes had been loyal to our adopted country's robust fare: hamburgers or steak cooked very rare, butterscotch sundaes, vanilla ice cream heaped on warm apple pie. And our strikingly similar physiques—lean-limbed but large-breasted and indeed full-cheeked—reflected our lusty appetites. Why, then, had she suddenly declared that I must be utterly different from her? Was the decree related to the manner in which she propelled me ahead of her whenever we entered a social gathering, with the whispered command, "Go and charm"? Was she seeking heightened status in her world of high style by turning me—a central ornament of her life—into the faddishly gaunt woman she did not have the self-discipline to become? In sum, was she asking me to be thin for her?

One of the tricky aspects of early memories is that we assign them to whatever slot in our lives the psyche deems most orderly. The remark on the beach may well have been made in many an earlier summer and simply not sunk in until that year. For I was about to go to college, the very first occasion any young woman had, in my generation, to assume control over her intake of food. Indeed, once at Bryn Mawr I began to grab, helter-skelter, at any get-thin fad that came my way. All through October it was an embarrassingly gaseous Near Eastern diet recommended by a classmate—four daily doses of buttermilk mixed with soda water and a teaspoonful of honey. Disappointed in the slowness of the process—I was losing only three or four pounds a month—in December I contracted severe diarrhea from a regimen of prunes and tea. These privations were accompanied by a new fixation for feeling "empty," a state I associated with mental clarity and spiritual worth. Soon, hunger—controllable, light-headed hunger, just short of the passing-out kind—came to be the sweetest sensation I knew. Oh, I'd give Mother the starved daughter she craved to show off to her pals; I would be appropriately ascetic, cavernous, grave, the opposite of the noisy, distressingly big-bodied maternal figure I thought of with a curious ambivalence of repulsion and love, and felt impelled to purge out of me. I studied myself in the mirror daily to check on the flatness of my stomach, the gauntness of my cheeks. "You're lengthening out!" Mother exulted during weekend visits. "What elegance! Time to start wearing pants!"

But then, at Christmas break, my please-mommy diet crashed, for I fell in love. He was an aspiring opera singer, and, I soon found out, intolerably possessive. There would be a ring, an engagement announcement in *The New York Times,* slipping grades. By the end of my sophomore year we were cohabiting in his tiny studio flat, and I'd transferred to Barnard to be a "married student." The rough-edged, hard-drinking theatrical family my fiancé had swept me into was so vastly different from the milieu of my suave parents, and so disapproved of by them, that throughout the romance I had no need to assert an identity independent of Mother's. I resumed the hearty appetite of my youth, barely ever stepped on a scale, and probably regained every ounce I'd lost my first three months of college. The end of the affair coincided, quite precisely, with the resumption of my tortured attitude toward food.

———

On a midwinter day of my junior year in college, I stand in my parents' dining room, facing the man-child I've been living with for two years. In the past month I've refused to go to his apartment. It's nearly dawn, and I've drunk a good deal to gain the courage for this moment—I can't go through with it, I tell him in our barely developed 1950 psychobabble, I need to grow more, I must have my freedom. As I blurt this out I slowly twist and turn the pearl-and-diamond engagement ring I've worn for over a year. As he walks out of the house, slamming the door behind him—so wounded, so tall and stooped—I rush into the kitchen. I place my ring on a sideboard, head for a huge apple pie my mother's housekeeper has left on the stove for the weekend, and start glutting. Its crust is so crisp and golden, the apples so unctuous, and then that delectably cinnamony, gummy inner surface. . . . I don't even bother to put anything on a plate. Alone there in the kitchen in the early dawn, I tear and claw at my sweet, my whole hand into it; greedy for more, I stuff and stuff, the mess falling onto my clothes, my shoes, the floor, until only a few spoonfuls of it are left . . . and suddenly I feel foul, swollen, disgusting. I rush upstairs to my bathroom and get on the scale— 130! I take three laxative pills, soak in a scalding bath for half an hour to sweat out the poison, and as I emerge, crazed to perspire more of the evening's muck, I pass out from the heat and gash my forehead on the tub.

In the following weeks I moved out of my parents' house again and took a dingy room a few blocks from Barnard. But beyond my need to remain independent from my seductive parents, the true reason, as I look back on it, was that I wanted to regain control over my food. For the terror and guilt of my first real binge had determined me to become a programmed, scientific dieter. I'd read of a diuretic, high-protein regimen on which I would never feel weak, and I headed for it with a vengeance: a half grapefruit in the morning, two plain hard-boiled eggs at lunch, a quarter pound of ground lean sirloin for dinner, no substitutes allowed, keep it up for three days. "Do you always lunch on a Jean Arp?" my classmate, the future writer Anne Bernays, inquired one noon at the Barnard cafeteria, staring at my all-white lunch plate. But no jibes could affect me because . . . Zing! the weight would come sliding off like a snake's skin, two, three pounds a day. Most of it would creep back within the week, but for the forty-eight hours that followed each fast, my "wide," "plump" cheeks were as gaunt as they'd ever been; I felt wonderfully light-headed, deserving, pure.

As a senior I cut my hair very short, like Jean Seberg in *Saint Joan,* and chewed ghastly tasting caramels called Ayds to minimize my appetite. I supplemented my diets with visits to the only health club I then knew of in New York, where I put myself into an agonizing machine—rubber rollers slid up and down my body, leaving black-and-blue marks that lasted for months. For those meals I had no control over, I developed certain habits that have stuck with me for decades: Scrape the fruit out of the pie without touching the dough, limit the intake of a baked potato to its skin, consume quantities of salad for better evacuation, and above all, weave lies concerning lunch to avoid the possibility of having to eat before dinnertime—food at midday led to feelings of impurity and slow-wittedness and made me feel undeserving of any nourishment until the following day. Through these punishments I finally hit on an ideal weight that I would try to approximate for much of my life— 114 pounds.

"Such slim hips now, a true gamine!" my mother exclaimed, perplexed by the high-bohemian image yet thrilled with my stylish tomboy figure. But by this time my compulsion to thinness had little to do with seeking her approval. It had become independent, fully winged, my own wacky kind of lust, a private aphrodisiac, a sensuality of purgation, negation, and most important, of control. I graduated at 116 and dived into my first job (working the overnight shift at United Press), then moved on to a couple of dissolute and fruitfully starved years in Paris; later to a sanatorium in Switzerland, where I recuperated from an extreme case of mononucleosis partly brought on, I suspect, by malnutrition.

Marriage at the age of twenty-six, once returned to the United States, to a reclusive, fiercely independent man who gave me the best of both lives—he was adored by my mother but drew me into a world radically different from hers. Miraculously easy pregnancies from which I emerged at about 120 pounds, with little to shed to return to my Utopian weight. Two wondrously healthy children, a career. Perhaps I began to look more gaunt as I aged. Or perhaps (so I think in the more self-demeaning moments) a woman's success leads her loved ones to worry more. Whatever the rationale, at some time in my forties or fifties I discovered the great *manipulative* potential of remaining very thin.

Over Sunday lunch in Connecticut, my mother scrutinized me with a tragic air as I turned down her roast beef, her leg of lamb, to eat a single piece of toast, a cup of the salt-free broth I carried everywhere with me, in packet form, to infuse into hot water. "You look like Auschwitz!" she chided me. And then she leaned toward me, robust 140 pounds and torpedo glance undiminished since my youth, and pleaded with me, in Russian, to gain "one little pound." *"Fountik!"* she begged, *"Fountik"* (a diminutive of *fount,* or pound)! My husband, my children joined in: "You'll have no reserves if you really get sick." I remained unmoved. An anorexic's thinness is her most treasured fetish, a vocation of sorts, the core of her selfness, her only way of drawing attention and pity, her principal power over others. To put it brutally, at those times in her life when she is particularly filled with self-hatred, her emaciation is the only identity she's really got.

It is May 1991, the week of my mother's death from congestive heart failure, the roughest year of my life. I am now sixty years old. The week after my mother dies, my husband undergoes surgery in a vain attempt to restore sight in his right eye. In November my beloved stepfather has two critical heart attacks, followed by multiple bypass surgery. The following month I am hospitalized with double pneumonia, put on oxygen and intravenous antibiotics. There is also a serious case of anemia—my hemoglobin count is down to twenty-two, the level at which transfusions are recommended. For once I am too ill to check up on one of my life's most foolish concerns— how I look, how much I weigh.

The morning I come home from the hospital I'm barely strong enough to make it to my bedroom; my husband and a friend have to assist me as I climb the stairs one at a time, breathless at each step. I'm so weary, so weak that it is two whole days before I walk the twenty feet to the little dressing room where I keep the scale.

As I finally step on it I am swept by surprise and near panic—107! Ah, how interesting, how exciting, I say to myself, I'm finally at the danger line, I can finally start eating. How pleasurably I begin to gorge! Oatmeal and toast for breakfast; a muffin in midmorning; rare hamburger for lunch; ice cream around the clock; liver and onions for dinner; suddenly I feel it is my duty—to my husband, to my children—to finish at least half of my whole potato instead of just the skin, to heap a scoop of ice cream onto a piece of hot chocolate cake. For the first time since that moment on the beach, I am feeling entitled not to punish my body.

I don't know how to account for the transformation of metabolism that coincided with my most severe illness, and with the loss of my tyrannical, beloved mother. All I know is that ever since that year of sorrow and danger I can eat to my heart's content and stay close enough to that pitiful, fetishistic weight—114—that has haunted my life. In my new love affair with food, I now feel free to seek out a vast menu of fare that was taboo for forty years: creamy lobster bisques; lasagnas; blueberry pie à la mode; even, on occasion, the butterscotch sundaes of my youth. I admit to many abiding fixations: I'm still mysteriously compelled to step on the scale once a week and look for that obsessive magic number. I still panic pathetically if I go above 115, and cut down on the ice cream. I continue to associate a minimalist toast-and-cheese lunch with mental clarity—with writing well. One particularly bright doctor called me "a borderline loony," but my marginal zaniness concerning weight has been a curious source of self-knowledge. Most important, it has enabled me better to understand (and hopefully, eventually to help) women who are truly in danger of starving themselves. The notion of "Thinness is holy," the association of nutritional and spiritual purity, is as ancient as civilization. And although the obsession is hardly commendable, I, for one, seem to do better learning to live with its distress.

1999

Post-Scriptum

Beloved parents,

Whenever you stopped looking at yourselves in your respective mirrors, you occasionally worried about my scant diet, and now that you've both left this planet, I want to reassure you that I'm doing well, truly well, still at 114 pounds and holding, without those alarming swoops down to 108. Do you remember the doctor who called me a "borderline loony"? If I've improved since you've departed, it's in part because I've had to bone up about anorexia, and write about it, and now grasp its root causes. The average anorexic girl, so I've learned, is the offspring of upper-middle-class parents who tend to be success-driven, opinionated, narcissistic individuals, and who raise their child to strive for perfection: Does that sound familiar? As she balances the act of achieving independence from her mom and dad while struggling to retain their attention and approval, such a girl's best weapon may well be to go for broke on fasts.

There are often more evident sources for the ailment, such as a disgusting early sexual encounter. Having until recently repressed the memory, I've never told you that when I was eleven, my own uncle, Mother's adolescent half brother, whom you'd ill-advisedly assigned to babysit for me, grabbed me and began to grope at me most foully— I managed to escape, but the episode filled me for years with self-revulsion. And what about those adolescent syndromes—growing breasts and hips—when they're associated with the body of an angry, ambivalently loved parent: Maman chérie, how many times did I hear you say that you hated nursing me for nine months, and resented the distended breasts caused by that ordeal!

Finally, there is also that sense of unworthiness that plagues many bluestocking daughters of ambitious families. I know that issues of religion bored you to death, parents dear, but after all, I was a religion major in college, and I want to bring you up-to-date and introduce you to the subject of one of my recent books, Simone Weil, patron saint of twentieth-century anorexics. This brilliant French philosopher, one of the most influential religious thinkers of our times (and the daughter, yes, of prosperous, invasive, hyperambitious parents), started dieting at the age of six, during the First World War, in solidarity with hungry soldiers at the front; she died during the Second World War at age thirtyfour, decimated by a lifetime of malnourishment, and also by her sorrow over the Free French Forces' refusal to parachute her into France and allow her to risk her life for her country. Weil's impulse to mortify her body in order to liberate her soul, the notion that "To be thin is to be holy," had incited many earlier generations of heroic female mystics— Catherine of Siena is an example—to stop eating. One might note that they were all superbly theatrical women: Successful mystics, like successful anorexics, are endowed above all with a strong sense of spectacle.

"Enough of that bluestocking crap," I hear you saying up there, dearly departed. So I'll put it more rawly: Anorexics are also girls who suspect that no one really cares for them, and however nicely you manifested your love for me, hugs and kisses et cetera, I sensed that you were far more absorbed by each other, and with that network of friends who were enabling you to climb—faster, ever faster!—the ladder of success. And so like many other daughters in that spot, I used fasts and radical dieting as a tool to manipulate you, to cry out "Look at me! Pity me! Do something about me!" What I'm really saying is that a principal reason I'm so well today, eating fried eggs for breakfast, rich lobster bisque and ham sandwiches at lunch, second helpings of mashed potatoes at dinner, is that as of nine years ago both of you have been gone, and there is no one to blackmail anymore.

Well, it's more than you who are gone, dear Mother and Alex. I now realize that the love of my life, my late husband, was the only one who ever succeeded in feeding me properly, the only one who kept me skating and never let me fall through ice. He left me four years ago, and now I'm alone, utterly alone. Your grandchildren are too busy taking care of their own kids to notice their mom's skinny-as-ever frame; the gentleman callers who've come around seem far more obsessed with shedding their weight than with helping me to maintain mine; and there is no one left on earth to play the role of that doting tutor who alone can cure an anorexic. The nutritional problems confronted by older women who live alone—even by those who've never suffered an eating disorder—have become prominent topics in health care. In the case of women who live in isolated rural surroundings, as I do, the problems loom even larger. There are no friends, no restaurants within walking distance. Far more important, one's whole sense of identity has been transformed by widowhood: There being no man to take care of, no man for whom to effect the alchemy of food and love that goes into the making of a meal, the solitary woman will often forgo any regular eating schedule. I have a divorcée friend who grabs a sandwich at any time between 6:00 and 10:00 p.m. and chews at it while brushing her dogs. I have another friend who exclusively fixes herself onion sandwiches at those same hours. My own solution, for the first months, was hot dogs.

But at some mysterious moment, some six months or so after my husband left me—this might be an integral part of the process of grief, of the work of mourning—the memory of him began to take over. It became a commanding, nurturing presence, as he had been in real life, and it began actively prodding me to stay well and survive. I live alone in the large eighteenth-century house that he and I shared for nearly a half century; his warmth and his nurturing aura increasingly suffuse our rooms and are the essence of my days. His voice often resounds in my ear, "You must put on weight, my darling," "You're nothing but little chicken bones, sweetheart"; I abide by his wishes, as if I believed in a child's true heaven in which we would be reunited and I might bask in his praise. For the miracle of this treasured man, dear parents, is that he is the first one who made me feel worthy, and if it wasn't for the memory of his heedless, selfless affection, I would decimate myself by remaining computer-bound until midnight and grabbing a yogurt at bedtime.

But no, his voice, his tutelage, is ever present; at 7:30 p.m. I hear his voice saying, "It's time for dinner, lovey." So I go down to the kitchen and make myself fish or chicken, rice, a vegetable, maintaining a "sane, nutritious diet," as he bade me to when he was still at my side. A lifetime habit of denying food is hard to alter; like all recovering anorexics, I'm grimly aware of the duty of eating, and the obligation to stay well; moreover, my intake might be more minimal than many others'—I may consume but half the pie crust instead of avoiding it altogether, leave a tad of the potato behind. The filigreed 114 pounds I inherited from your glittering world, dear fashionista parents, is still "a private aphrodisiac, my own wacky kind of lust." But worry not if you ever did, amusing glamorous ones; I'm kept from wasting away by a benevolent ghost. As I pile on a second helping of risotto, consume crème brûlée at every restaurant that serves it, I sense my life's companion is cheering me on to preserve my health, to stay alive to the longest possible age and fulfill our shared ambition—to see what our grandchildren will do with their own lives. The cherished spirits of those who truly loved us, I'm led to think, might do more to preserve us than any human on this planet ever can.

Continued hugs and kisses,
    Your ever devoted, once starving daughter

                                                    2008

HUNGRY MEN

John Nolan

Michael Krasnow was in his teens when his life began to change from something routine into something unrecognizable. In 1985, shortly after his sixteenth birthday, Michael weighed 115 pounds. Up to this point, he had what seemed to be a stable, even happy childhood, filled with Little League and hobbies such as collecting comic books. He had loving parents. He sometimes felt distant from his brother, Neil, who was three and a half years older, but they harbored no ill will toward each other. He also had a dreadful shyness with girls that prevented him from asking them to dance—but this is a problem that millions of other young men have encountered without lasting consequences.

In his teens, though, Michael began to struggle with strong fears and compulsions. It coincided with a period when his father was diagnosed with ALS, a neurodegenerative disease, and began a gradual decline. Whenever Michael went to a bar mitzvah or another party, he began to tell himself to suck in his gut. He worried that others were thinking he was fat and judging him. He began to recopy his math homework up to six times to avoid even a single erasure mark. When he was fifteen, he also began to brush his teeth obsessively—at first for two hours a day, and eventually increasing to twelve hours a day. At the height of this obsession, he would carry his toothbrush around with him as he navigated his chores at home or did his homework. During one of these periods of marathon brushing, it occurred to him that he might not have to brush so much if only he didn't eat.

Shortly thereafter, Michael began to severely limit his food intake. He would try to survive on only seven hundred calories every day. As he did so, he entered a sort of imagined competition with both himself and others. In his terse one-hundred-page autobiography, *My Life as a Male Anorexic,* he identifies the "unusual habits" that he took up, which took on the quality of self-imposed rules: 1) A refusal to allow anyone to see him eat; 2) A refusal to be seen without a jacket or bathrobe ("to cover up my stomach"); 3) A refusal to drink water ("I have not had any water since February 1985," he wrote a decade later. "I know water has no calories, but I would still feel fat if I drank it"); and 4) A refusal to swallow his own saliva ("I always have a paper cup or a paper towel in my jacket pocket. I spit into these twenty-four hours per day").

Michael's memoir takes its reader on a tour through the depths of isolation and indifference. "I don't care if I live or die," he writes. "I have no feelings at all." Yet more surprisingly, there are also poignant attempts to reach out and connect. "Just let me say that if you think you have anorexia nervosa— or know someone who has it—and would like to get in touch with me for any reason, you're more than welcome to write," he says in a later chapter. "My address is 1776 Polk Street, #159, Hollywood, FL 33020." This war between hope and hopelessness continues through to the book's final pages, where Michael seems to be puzzling out why he bothered to write his story. By this time, he is twenty-eight years old and weighs seventy-two pounds.

"The purpose of my writing this book was to make people more aware of male anorexia," he writes in his epilogue. "I was not trying to discourage anyone or to give the impression there was no hope. . . . If I thought there was no hope, then there would be no reason to write this story." An editor's note informs us that three days after these words were written, on October 9, 1997, Michael died alone in his apartment. He had deliberately starved himself to death.

———

Michael's story is particularly compelling to me because I recognize part of myself in it. Though I was never nearly as ill as Krasnow, I, too, suffered from anorexia, and I lost enough weight to comprehend the addictive pull of self-starvation. For all the questions that female anorexia poses, the condition in men can be even more perplexing. Studies have suggested that men represent somewhere from 5–15 percent of those diagnosed with anorexia. Less than one-half of one percent of American men are expected to develop the illness in their lifetime.

In the years since my own experience, I have read the small handful of books that purport to tackle the subject of male anorexia, and I have talked to researchers and social scientists who are trying to understand the disorder. I have read scientific papers on the pathology and psychobiology of anorexia, and I've studied interviews with other male anorexics. The answers I have found are incomplete—but they have helped me begin to make sense of something that, for a long time, seemed an outlying and incongruous episode in my personal history.

To try to explain the experience of anorexia after having

emerged from it is like trying to describe a vivid dream upon waking: The disease has its own powerful, internal logic that can become fragmented at a distance. Even so, I know that if I had read Michael Krasnow's story twenty years ago, I would have felt competitive with his punishing self-discipline. I have decided to tell my story in the hope that other men might see they're not alone.

In writing this essay, I have chosen to use a pen name. I have done it with some reluctance. Though I feel shame about having had the disorder, I also believe that is not an adequate reason by itself to conceal my identity. But I have come to think it is important to try to separate my personal life—and particularly the details of my family history—from my work as a writer and as a journalist. For this reason, and perhaps for reasons less clear to me, I only feel comfortable speaking behind a veil of anonymity.

Chubby

My descent began in a way that many women say it began for them—a simple, offhand comment. I was twelve years old in 1987 when a friend of mine told me casually, "You look chubby." The criticism came during a lonely period. I had recently transferred to a new middle school in a new state, and I had turned to food for comfort. I remember spending a lot of my time in the evenings after school parked in front of a television, eating Doritos and Cokes and pecan pie, watching sitcoms such as *Full House* and *Night Court.* A relatively thin boy up until then, I began to put on weight. I remember liking the comfort of the rich food and the mediocre television. The characters on the shows seemed friendlier and more familiar than many of the new kids at school.

My friend's throwaway comment was soon paired in my mind with a discovery I made several days later. I was looking through an old picture album and stumbled upon a photograph that was taken when I was ten years old. I had qualified for the finals of the American Athletic Union's Cross Country National Championships, and my father took the picture right before the race in San Antonio, Texas. I was wearing a Windbreaker with the AAU insignia. I was smiling. I was very thin.

I carried the picture with me and began to look at it frequently, sometimes studying it for more than five minutes at a time. I liked the idea of myself in it, and I liked what the picture represented: someone who was disciplined, healthy, and happy. Meanwhile, my friend's voice echoed in my head, reminding me of a very different immediate reality: *You look chubby.* I began to think about how nice it would be if I could restore that ten-year-old's image in my own body.

———

In 1990 the social scientists Ann Kearney-Cooke and Paula Steichen-Ash attempted to create a profile of a male who is susceptible to eating disorders. They had observed dozens of clinical cases, and they began to see several similarities. They offered the following portrait:

This man appears to lack a sense of autonomy, identity, and control over his life. He seems to exist as an extension of others and to do things because he must please others in order to survive emotionally. We speculate that he came from an environment which is unable to validate his strivings for independence, a situation which leaves him at risk for symptom formation later in life. He has a history of experiences around his body (such as being teased about his body shape) which leaves him vulnerable about his body image.

As recently as a few decades ago, experts believed that the reason anorexia overwhelmingly affected women was because it was linked to social conditioning. Conventional wisdom held that the masculine physical ideal in America was very different from the feminine physical ideal. The male ideal was robust and muscular—an image forged during America's frontier days and later reinforced by such icons as Charles Atlas. Men were thought to develop anorexia so rarely because there were few social incentives for men to be very thin.

Two decades ago, social scientists and clinicians, including Kearney-Cooke and Steichen-Ash, began to look past some of these assumptions. They found that the underlying pathology of male anorexics was in many ways very similar to that of female anorexics—and that once a person became anorexic, social incentives were largely irrelevant to how the disease was experienced. Both men and women with anorexia were wrestling with larger demons than body image alone. Primary among both the men's and the women's anxieties was an overriding need to feel in control.

Michael Krasnow's twelve-hour tooth-brushing sessions also suggest that there is reason to consider eating disorders not as independent diseases but rather as "part of the obsessive-compulsive spectrum," says Laura Bellodi, a professor at the University of Milan School of Medicine. Psychologist N. M. Srinivasagam has suggested that in order for anorexia to develop, there needs to be not only a genetic vulnerability to obsessive-compulsive behaviors but also another particular predisposition: the desires for perfection, order, symmetry, and exactness. These traits have been shown to persist in male and female anorexics even after they have recovered from the disease.

Looking back, it is easy for me to recognize my own intense need for control and order, and to see how that need expressed itself in my relationship to food. As the Kearney-Cooke portrait of a male at risk for eating disorders would indicate, I had a history of experiences that made my relationship with body image particularly fraught—experiences that also go a long way toward helping explain why I tried to exert control over my body as a way of feeling in control of other aspects of my life.

———

I was four years old when my only brother went away to college in the late 1970s. He left for college at six feet one and two hundred pounds. When he stepped off the train after his first semester, he was a full one hundred pounds heavier. My family found out later that a woman he had been dating was killed in a car accident that semester—a relationship and a death that he kept from us. Unaware of the likely emotional basis for his eating, my parents focused their concern on his physical health and appearance.

When my brother was home, my parents sometimes sat down with him to talk about how he needed to lose weight. I dreaded these conversations more than anything; I was very sensitive to my brother's feelings, and I tended to cover my ears and rush out of the room if the topic came up. When I stayed, I remember how my brother's eyes would shift over the floor—or, worse, how he would shoot glances upward briefly at me, though I was still a child at the time, in the hope of finding sympathy.

So it was partly because of my brother that food had such an emotional aspect for me, and that a simple comment suggesting I was chubby could elicit fear to a degree that the friend who said it could never have anticipated.

The comment from my friend also stung because from a young age, I had a fierce desire to excel. Even my elementary school years were spent in a heady extracurricular dash in which I sought to distinguish myself. I was president of the student body, and I helped institute a student-run garbage collection program. I was founder and editor in chief of the elementary school newspaper. I once carried the trophies from my state and regional AAU cross-country races into school in the hope that the principal would put them in the school trophy case with a little note about my accomplishments. (My request was properly but tactfully denied.)

After my transfer to the new middle school in a different state, I didn't feel I had a place, and I struggled to make friends. I was not entirely comfortable with the idea that I was getting older. The picture of myself at ten years old reminded me of a time in which I felt I had achieved some distinction. I had longed for those moments all my life—and continue to do so today.

With many confusing notions of who I was and who I wanted to be, I began to spend many nights standing in front of a mirror and holding the roll of fat on my stomach that I could gather between my thumb and forefinger. My goal became to eliminate that roll altogether. I felt if I could do it, I would be less vulnerable in the ways that my brother was vulnerable. I wanted to be unassailable, and to live in a way that left no space for criticism. I had already begun what was recognizable as a diet. I cut out many junk foods, including my favorite, pecan pie. I also began to run every day, as I had when I was training two years earlier for the Junior Olympics.

This period of self-discipline seemed to produce several positive effects. Within a couple of months, I had lost five or ten pounds. I was cast in *The Sound of Music* at the local high school in my new district; I was to play Kurt. I was very happy to be part of the play, and I felt as if my life were becoming more interesting— even, in its own small way, distinguished.

During the rehearsals, I particularly admired the young woman who was playing Maria. She was exceedingly thin and athletic. At rehearsals, she wore jeans with holes in the knees and *Flashdance*-style sweatshirts that hung off her shoulders, and I felt I had never encountered a more perfect person. She was in twelfth grade and five years my senior; the romantic hopes I harbored were comic in their impossibility.

Regardless, my thoughts began to coalesce around the idea that if I became thinner—more like her—she would no doubt see more of herself in me. I continued to lose weight. During the two-month rehearsal process, I probably never exchanged more than a few words with her outside those that we said onstage. But when the play ended, I felt bereft. I realized I wouldn't see her anymore. She said she was heading off to college in another state.

Shortly after the play ended, my parents told me that I would need to travel with them that summer on my father's monthlong business trip to Japan and Australia. Though my mother and father had always been consistently loving toward me, I found the idea of the trip daunting. Just when I was beginning to carve an independent place for myself, starting to craft a life that was appealing to me, it struck me as a huge imposition.

It was during this summer journey, when I began to feel I had less control over my daily life, that a typical diet turned into something far more important to me.

Temperance

Arnold E. Andersen of the University of Iowa College of Medicine has been studying male anorexics for years, both clinically and scientifically. Andersen is considered by many to be the foremost expert on male eating disorders in the country, and his clinic helps men who have often not responded positively to treatment elsewhere. He began to recognize several years ago that all cases of anorexia, regardless of the sex of the patient, seemed to unfold in well-defined steps. "There is this myth out there that only white young women develop anorexia," he has written. "Yet the group of people with eating disorders clearly includes men, older women, and minorities."

Andersen decided several years ago that he had seen enough eating disorder cases to develop a kind of "unified theory" of anorexia—a model of the development of the disease that applies equally to men and women. At the first stage in almost every anorexic's development, Andersen says, there is simple, willful dieting behavior. Roughly 25 percent of young men and 75 percent of young women diet regularly. A much smaller percentage move into the second stage, where normal dieting behavior shifts to something quite different. There is not only the desire to be thin anymore, but also the development of a morbid fear of food and fatness.

My own latent tendency to fear food and fatness came not

only from observing my brother's struggle but also from religious belief. My mother raised me in the Seventh-day Adventist Church, which places a particular emphasis on the body as the temple of the Holy Spirit. The Church's prophet, Ellen White, wrote in her book *Counsels on Health* that "those who are keeping His commandments must be brought into sacred relationship to Himself, and that by temperance in eating and drinking they must keep mind and body in the most favorable condition for service." The religion encouraged us not to wear jewelry or flashy clothes. Excess of any kind—and particularly bodily excess—was equated with sin.

As the summer of 1987 began, for the first time I started to feel a deep fear of food and mealtimes. The fears intensified as my family arrived in Melbourne for my father's first business meeting. At the time, my parents were facing one of the few crises of what has been a long and loving marriage. On our first Saturday in Melbourne, I remember, my mother wanted to go to a Seventh-day Adventist service, and my father said he did not want to.

There had been some debate between them about religion in the months preceding—my mother was becoming more drawn to the church as my father was becoming less so. Sleeping on a cot in the same hotel room with my parents, I was awakened on successive nights by what I could tell was a heated, whispered argument. I kept my eyes closed and faked sleep, but I heard most of it. There were threats and counterthreats, and I worried that my parents' marriage might end there in a hotel room, oceans away from home.

I wanted to put my hands over my ears. I wanted to leave the room. I didn't want to let them know I was awake. I wondered whether the dispute was my fault. Maybe I had done some-

thing wrong? Maybe things would be better if I were more religious, even if my father were less so? I felt out of control. I
thought of how my life had changed since the play. I thought
of the actress who played Maria, whom I wouldn't see anymore. I thought of my brother.

In the following days, I began to become even more fearful
than before of gaining weight. In the mornings, after my
shower, I would look into the mirror and roll the skin on my
stomach between my fingers. By this point, I had already lost a
lot of weight and weighed less than I should on a five-feet-four
frame. Nonetheless, I still heard that small voice in my head
again: *You look chubby.* As I became more fearful of gaining
weight, I also became good at deception. At dinners with my
parents, I would flatten my food out on the plate to try to make
it appear I had eaten more than I had. If we ate at a fast-food
restaurant, I would put the boxes of food in my lap so they
could not see how little I was eating. If my parents got up from
the table, I would find a way to dispose of much of the food
into bags that could then be thrown away upon exiting.

When possible, I also tried to find excuses why I could not
join my parents for mealtimes. I began to make private bar-
gains with myself: *Skip breakfast, and I will allow you lunch.*
When lunchtime arrived, I told myself: *Think of how proud
you'll be if you can make it to dinner.* And when dinner came, I
would tell myself: *Think how virtuous you'll feel tomorrow if you
eat very little for dinner today, especially considering that you
skipped breakfast and lunch.*

The cycle would then begin again the next day, meal by
meal. This punishing discipline was accompanied by a growing
pride in my own virtue. I began sizing up unsuspecting (and
innocent) strangers and trying to estimate how much food they

ate. I would pass a random stranger on the street and instantly imagine all the food he consumed in the last twenty-four hours lying in a pile—hamburgers, french fries, pies, muffins, sodas, oils, fats, sugars. Then I would think about what I ate in the same period—a yogurt, say, and a side of broccoli—and imagine it lying in a separate pile next to the stranger's pile. I imagined us both standing there, comparing our respective piles of food. I thought my competitor would wither under the shock of recognition.

Besides feeling superior, I was also fearful of my closest rivals. As I walked the streets of Melbourne, sometimes alone and sometimes with my parents, I would stare at the thinnest people and wonder if I were thinner. The strangers who were near my weight were frightening to me. I sized them up as a scout would scrutinize a top prospect.

By the time my family left Australia, the tension between my parents had eased. Yet I had set myself on a course that was self-perpetuating and no longer rational. I was heading toward what Andersen identifies as the last two stages of anorexia, when the individual is no longer capable of stopping his dieting behavior. It has become "autonomous," Andersen says: a phenomenon unto itself.

The Brink

As my weight began to dip lower—and as we moved on to Japan—my emotions began to fluctuate dramatically, ascending to astonishing peaks and crashing into deep troughs. The moments of elation were so intense that I could almost temporarily forget the depression that would follow. One evening, my parents and I attended a classical music concert, and I felt as if the music were part of me, as if it were coursing through me. I could hear the whisper of my blood in my ear and see the beat of my heart against my ribs. I was the air and the music. As I grew even thinner, I also began to experience a kind of endorphin haze that I have otherwise experienced only when running long distances—it is a chemical sensation that mitigates pain and feels as if it is hard-earned.

Research has indicated that intense emotional swings are consistent with the effects of starving. The most famous study of starvation is the 1,385-page opus by Ancel Keys and his colleagues, *The Biology of Human Starvation,* published in 1950. In the book, the scientists describe an experiment involving thirty-two healthy young men, ages twenty to thirty-three, who were conscientious objectors during the Second World War. The men were fed a dramatically reduced diet over a period of twenty-four weeks, and the researchers carefully documented their emotional and physical condition. The psychological state of the men was extremely volatile. There were frequent reports of self-punishing despair, yet a significant percentage of the men also mentioned feelings of euphoria as their hunger grew deeper. "One subject experienced a number of periods in which his spirits were definitely high," read the report. "These elated periods alternated with times in which he suffered a 'deep dark depression.' "

During my family's summer trip, as I contended with new emotional swings, I began to devise new strategies to motivate myself to continue to lose weight. I have large hands with long fingers, and I had now grown so tiny that I could almost encircle my waist by placing my thumbs behind my back and trying to point my index fingers together. I convinced myself that I would be happy when I could reach that extra inch or two and be able to circle my waist entirely with my hands. *You'll be skinny then,* I told myself. *You're still chubby now.*

By the time we arrived in Japan, my parents were increasingly concerned about my dramatic weight loss, and they tried to intervene to make me eat more. I fought their efforts fiercely. My mother would take me places to eat and order nothing for herself. She would sit and watch me and not let me leave until I had finished my portion. It was profoundly uncomfortable and terrifying to be out of control in this way. Still, with no recourse to run from the room, I would chew slowly and finish an agreed-upon portion of what was on the plate. To my mother's lasting credit, she found a way to negotiate with me where she did not force me to increase my intake too much at once, which would have made me feel powerless and frightened. If we were able to negotiate, I felt I still had some measure of control.

———

To emerge from anorexia into a condition that resembles a normal life is not like walking out of one room into another. It is much more like trying to emerge out of the center of a maze, where one encounters numerous false starts, and feels at moments a strong, unexplainable desire to return to the familiar places one is leaving behind. Slowly, I began to find my way out of my mental trap. There are points along the way that stick in my memory.

When we returned from Japan, I still continued to monitor very closely what I ate and to exercise intensely, often going for runs of eight miles or more. Being at home also allowed me to skip meals more easily. One hot August day when I was jogging in my neighborhood, I became so disoriented that for several moments I could no longer remember what country I was in or how to get back—even though I was only three blocks from my house. When I regained my bearings, I was still frightened. I realized how much my hunger had for a long time been interfering with my ability to think clearly.

Two months after this incident, I competed in a cross-country race. Soon after, I was given a copy of a picture taken near the finish line. I was wearing a candy-stripe jersey, and my face had a look of abject determination. My skin clung so tightly to my whole frame that I couldn't recognize myself. For the first time, it struck me that I looked like a shrink-wrapped skeleton. It was neither healthy nor attractive. I began to see what I had become—a young man lost. Just as the picture of the ten-year-old racer had haunted me with dreams of a return to an imagined past and perfection, this new picture now offered a mirror to how distorted my self-image had become.

Anorexia had taken me to the brink of what Arnold Andersen classifies as the final stage, where the illness becomes one's identity and therefore life threatening. "The individual fears the state of nothingness associated with giving up the illness more than the consequences of the continued illness," Andersen writes.

I think my good fortune is that, by the time I began to get better—slowly, to be sure, and not without setbacks—I still had some sense of myself separate from the disease.

To Be a Man

It may ultimately be more helpful to ask what men who suffer from anorexia can tell us about the illness as a whole than it is to ask why they develop a disorder that usually strikes women.

Anorexia was not always assumed to be a female disease. The first known description of something resembling anorexia nervosa in medical literature describes both a young woman and a young man. The British physician Richard Morton's 1694 book, *Phthisiological: Or a Treaty of Consumptions,* includes the stories of a sixteen-year-old boy and an eighteen-year-old girl whose cases baffled him. Both of them suffered from what he called a "nervous atrophy," a "wasting of the body without any remarkable fever, cough, or shortness of breath." Dr. Morton saw it as a disease brought on by the "cares and passions" of the mind.

The list of men who have exhibited anorexic traits has included such writers as Lord Byron and Franz Kafka. The 511 postcards or letters that Kafka wrote to his fiancée, Felice Bauer, demonstrate fastidiousness that borders on compulsion, and some clinicians have given the author a posthumous diagnosis of anorexia. Kafka details the hours he spends swimming, rowing, and doing calisthenics. He frequently comments on how little he eats. "I am the thinnest person I know," he says. He warns Felice in advance of their living together that he considers everything secondary to his art and that he has to sleep alone. In a January 1913 letter, he writes that "perhaps the best mode of life for me would be to sit in the innermost room of a . . . locked cellar."

Like Michael Krasnow, Kafka expressed an overwhelming need to feel in control and a difficulty feeling comfortable in his personal relationships. Both also exhibited a deep ambivalence about traditional ideas of what it means to be a man. A 1990 study of males with eating disorders at Columbia University found that the men often spoke about how they believed a strong man should be: independent, aggressive, courageous.

The men said that they had trouble feeling they could be those things in their own lives. With their eating disorders, the men in the Columbia study seemed to be seeking a place for themselves outside the conventional image of masculinity, a space similar to Kafka's idea of an "innermost room."

———

Linda Smolak, a professor of psychology at Kenyon College, told me that while young women today suffer extreme pressure to be thin, young men are encountering pressures in opposing directions. "When you combine boys who would like to be thinner with boys who would like to be more muscular, you get body dissatisfaction rates that aren't so different from girls," she says. "Anywhere from one-third to one-half of boys aren't comfortable with their bodies." Indeed, some men can develop an inverse type of anorexia that pushes them to *gain* weight. A recent study of 108 bodybuilders identified a condition known as "reverse anorexia" or "bigorexia." Several of these bodybuilders believed themselves to appear small and weak even though they were muscular and strong. The bigorexics wore heavy clothes when they went to the beach for fear of being seen as too puny—just as anorexics often wear large clothes for fear of being seen as too fat.

Both the bigorexic study and the stories of male anorexics indicate that men, like women, suffer from punishing social pressures. Both sexes develop conscious or unconscious feelings about our bodies through identification with other people, just as I came to covet thinness out of my admiration for (and desire to emulate) the young woman who played Maria in *The Sound of Music*. Research has suggested that there are some precipitating factors that are particular to men, such as the desire to improve athletic performance—especially in sports with weight classes, such as wrestling. Horse jockeys, who are under intense professional pressure to be thin, have also been shown to suffer from anorexia in higher numbers than the general population. Some researchers have suggested that gay men may be more prone to the disorder since a slim physique is often considered more desirable in gay male relationships than in straight ones.

Yet the deeper prevailing issue in anorexia in men tends to be the same as in women: the desire for control and a deep fear of what its loss would mean. This desire to be in control has persisted in me throughout my adult life. It has led me to do many of the things I have been most proud of, including gaining entrance to good schools and running marathons. Yet it has also made it difficult for me to have sustaining relationships or to put myself in positions where I feel vulnerable.

While I have remained thin, though, I have never had such intense fears of weight as I did during the spring, summer, and fall of 1987. I realized how much I had changed when, as a high school junior, I visited a ballerina friend who had entered Washington Children's Hospital for treatment for her own anorexia. While visiting her, I met several other girls in the eating disorders wing. One of the young women was my age: sixteen years old. She had blond hair and weighed only seventy pounds; her body seemed to collapse in on itself like an unattached marionette. After we talked awhile, she had me sit down on her bed, and she reached over to her dresser with her frail arm and hand. The skin on her wrists was translucent and clung tightly around her bone. She extended to me a smiling photograph of herself taken two years before.

She looked remarkably attractive and healthy in the photograph, and she carried perhaps thirty more pounds. The young woman seemed to recognize that she was less healthy now, but she said she was also deeply fearful of how much food they were giving her on the hospital ward. I looked at her and thought back to the photograph that had helped to set my own course in motion. I recognized how I was once caught—as she still was—in a prison of the mind. Yet I still didn't know what to say to her, how to begin.

"You were beautiful," I said.

BLACK-AND-WHITE THINKING

Latria Graham

———

A random evening from last winter: It's dinnertime, but I don't want to go to the cafeteria, where the eating patterns of the whole campus are on display. Instead, I head to the local college hangout, Lone Pine Tavern. I enter the semidarkness and sit with my back to the other people. I resolve to pick just one item from the menu, and something to drink. I'll have a turkey panini; that will be safe if I ask them to hold the cheese. And the mayo—mustn't forget the mayo. Fifteen minutes later, I am floating back to my room with two chicken wraps, a turkey panini, and a large order of cheese fries with extra mayo packets. It doesn't take long before I am surrounded by empty wrappers that reflect my bloated face in their shiny insides. I've overstepped myself again, and there's only one way to make amends.

"How did it start?" Everyone who knows asks me, and I never know how to answer. When did I start tracking my relationship to food? When I was in the hospital last year, my father told my therapist that I was just different from other babies: If you had to feed a typical baby every four hours, you would have to feed me every three. Do I begin there, or with my awareness, from early childhood, that food defined who you were—if you were country, like my dad and his family, or worldly and sophisticated like my mom? On visits to my paternal grandmother's house, while the rest of the family dove into the mountains of food she'd prepared—oxtails, chicken brains, chitlins, "junkpots" (a congealed mass of pig's feet, tails, ears, and random cuts of beef)—I watched my mother hold back and politely say she wasn't hungry. After a while, she would fix her plate with only the more conventional cuts of meat and vegetables. The message to me was: "We don't eat that stuff." And if I wanted a piece of my grandmother's amazing butter cake with the chocolate frosting, she would say, in front of everyone, "Haven't you had enough?"

My first real memory of doing something wrong is from when I was seven years old: I ate some Girl Scout cookies I wasn't supposed to. Until that point, I was a big seller of Girl Scout cookies—one of the highest sellers in the state, in fact. (I felt like a drug pusher, foisting cases of cookies on my diabetic music teacher, Dr. Mackey.) But when it came to eating cookies, initially I had self-control. I asked my mom when I wanted some and ate enough to satisfy me. Then something switched. One night, I climbed out of my top bunk, crept past my parents' room, into the living room and around the armchair I thought of as the "Daddy chair," to the boxes of Girl Scout cookies stacked near the fish tank. I wanted Thin Mints. They were my favorite, and I knew what they looked like before I got to the crate: the green box with a troop of girls rock climbing on the front and a blurb about diversity on the back. I knew what to expect when I opened the box: There would be two sleeves of chocolate-covered cookies, but this time they would all belong to me. I sat on the tan tweed couch (the same couch that I threw up on when I was four after swallowing bleach), tore open the box, ripped out a sleeve of cookies, and sat munching and watching Mutt and Jeff, our two severely over-weight goldfish, swimming around the night-light in their tank. I didn't finish all the cookies at once, so I took them back to my room and hid them in the corner of my toy box, under my dancing ballerina doll. Later my parents would search my room for *something* (I don't remember what) and find empty flattened Girl Scout cookie boxes. When the Thin Mints ran out, I moved on to the Tagalongs . . . the Trefoils . . . the Do-si-dos, and when I got desperate, the Samoas. After I was done, I stuck the boxes under the edge of my mattress, certain no one would think to look there.

I was a clever girl, so you'd think I would learn that sneaking food was bad. Instead, I just got smarter about hiding the evi-dence. I learned by trial and error. Eating an entire box of Andes mints from my grandmother's refrigerator and putting the empty box in the trash: bad. Eating the contraband candy bar and flushing the wrapper: much better. So the closet eating started early, but it took a while to develop into an eating dis-order. It wasn't a sudden thing, like diving into a pool—*splash!* Instead, I just sort of slipped in.

At age nine, I was put on a diet. Or perhaps I put myself on a diet. I've always tried to emulate my mother in just about every way possible. I followed her around the house, learning whatever it was she happened to be doing at the moment. My contributions never measured up to hers: When she cut out a dress, her lines were perfect; my dress would be misshapen, and would hardly look like a dress at all. To an extent, my mom fol-lowed me around, too: She always dropped me off at school, was active in the Parent Teacher Association, made all the costumes for the school play, made cookies for every bake sale, taught my Sunday school class, and went on every field trip (which I loved because I got anything I wanted, even if I wasn't cool). On top of that, she managed to be social. She was—and still is—my ultimate definition of what a woman should be: tall, thin, chic, sophisticated. (Before she got married, she attended the Fashion Institute of Technology to become a designer, and modeled on the side.) She always knows what to say and never seems overwhelmed.

When she went on a diet, I decided I was going to go on one, too. It seemed like a good idea at the time—to me and to my parents. I've always been a bit chubby—more chubby-athletic than chubby-fat, but chubby nonetheless. At nine I'd already had my period for over a year, and I was bumping into things with my large hips. I didn't take these changes well. I threw a fit when I had to go with my mom to Belk's to get a training bra, and I was even madder when I couldn't get the thing over my head. "You have to undo the clasps," my mother said, but how was I supposed to know? My reasoning skills couldn't keep up with my body.

But I wanted to tame my body if I could. My mom ate salads, so I ate salads. My mom ate grapefruit, so I did, too. (I hated both.) My mom did her floor exercises, so I was red-faced and panting on the floor next to her. Most of this was well and good: I was faster when I played basketball and softball, and trading in my Hawaiian Punch for real fruit juice wasn't a bad thing. It's just that I take things to the extreme.

I'm a black-and-white thinker, and I always have been. When I want something, I have to have it. I wanted to go to boarding school; my parents said no, but in the end I won. I wanted to go to an Ivy League college, and I did—even though

I pushed myself so hard it almost killed me. Eating was the same. It became a war, in which one side had to lose: my body or my mind. For a while my mind got the better of me. I learned how to curb my hunger and turn my feelings on and off at will. But eventually my body rose up and took back what it thought it deserved.

I started skipping meals. That seemed the most direct way to make myself smaller. I didn't really like breakfast, anyway, so I stopped eating it. I had excuses not to eat lunch: My junior-high band met during part of lunch, and because the rest of the period was so "hurried" I decided it would be better not to eat at all. After getting out of my mom's car in the morning, I would go into school and dump my lunch in the nearest trash can; if I carried it with me till lunchtime, I might be tempted to eat it if I got really hungry. I became more productive with my lunch periods and tried not to think about food by occupying myself with bigger things. I used the time that I wasn't in band to create Jere Baxter Junior High's first classroom newsletter: *Mrs. Cron's Chronicles,* named after my teacher. It included all the accomplishments and awards of my peers as well as announcements for the week. When I was done with the newsletter, I spent the rest of my time playing the computer game Oregon Trail. Eventually Mrs. Cron started playing detective: When *was* I eating? I answered her truthfully—I only ate dinner—and she called my mom.

But Mrs. Cron's power over me was to be short-lived: We were moving to South Carolina. My grandfather died, my mother grew tired of my father's infidelity, and they both knew it was time for a big change. We were moving back to my parents' native state so they could give it one more shot. I saw the move as an opportunity to reinvent myself, so I changed my name. Until then I had always gone by my middle name, Nicole, but now I asked to be called by my first name, Latria, which I thought was more distinctive.

Moving meant more big family get-togethers, all of which involved food: Anyone's birthday, anyone's funeral, any special service at our Baptist church (Easter, Women's Day, Men's Day, Church Anniversary, Homecoming, Revival, and every night of Bible School, which we attended for a week each summer)—every occasion required a family feast.

There were several things I didn't like about these get-togethers. There were the boring conversations about things that didn't matter to me. I would imitate my mom, nodding politely and pretending to care. Worse was the atmosphere of judgment. When I walked through the door, one of my aunts would say, "Oh, Nicole, you look like you've lost weight," or, if she couldn't find anything nice to say about my appearance, "Oh, Nicole, I see you're the same these days." (They never agreed to call me Latria.) It affected how I ate; I didn't want to look like Miss Piggy, because it would just give them more to talk about after I left.

I tried to stick to my meal-skipping regimen, and, after doing a school project on animal rights, I decided to become vegan. But it was hard sticking to my plan with people watching me all the time, and after starving myself for a few days, eventually I would break down and eat. I'm not talking about running to the corner store for a bag of potato chips. I'm talking about the time I bought a tub of Oreo ice cream and devoured it on my way to pick up my little brother from a friend's house. I finished the ice cream and felt horrible—I'd eaten something I shouldn't have *and* I was uncomfortably full. For a while I didn't know what to do. Then I remembered something my PE coach told me in elementary school. I told him I was sick and didn't feel like running. He presented two scenarios: I could continue to sit there, sick and miserable; or, if I was really sick, I could throw up, feel better, and join the other kids. I asked him how I would go about it, and he showed me by pretending to stick his index and middle fingers down his throat. It looked painful, and I decided that I wasn't *that* sick.

But a couple of years later I was that sick, and a bit desperate, so I decided to try it. The first time I coughed and gagged and went red in the face and saw spots, only to get up a few remnants of Oreos. But I got *something*. There was hope. I could possibly undo all the damage that I had done. The thought of throwing up regularly scared me and also didn't make sense—why spend money buying food if I was going to just throw it up? But eventually purging became a system of checks and balances: When I ate something that didn't "belong," I could try to throw it up. Some things came up better than others, so I learned as I went. And I got what I wanted: I started losing weight, though not enough to satisfy me.

When I moved to Spartanburg, there were these *jeans:* designer jeans that all the other middle school girls were wearing with their matching lavender cardigans and hair ribbons. I wanted those jeans instead of the matronly dresses that hung in my closet. I wanted to be like everyone else. More specifically, I wanted to be like Hannah D. She was everything I was not: She was of medium height (not tall and gawky, like me) and medium build (not emaciated but not fat, like me), and she had long straight brown hair. She was popular, all the boys liked her, and she didn't have to get braces to have pretty white straight teeth. White. Oh, yeah . . . and she was white. There weren't many minorities where I grew up, so pretty much anyone I admired was going to be white.

You can be sure Hannah D. had those jeans. My mother and I went to J. B. White so I could try on a pair. They didn't fit well: My hips were by no means "junior-size" so it didn't make sense for me to try to fit in junior jeans. But that logic didn't matter: I was *going* to get those jeans. My mother told me I could get them if they fit; she said if I lost "just a little bit more," they would fit better. I forgot about the jeans, but I focused on the words "just a little bit more." It became my mantra.

By high school, little had changed, except that my parents were divorced. It started with a Maytag receipt—innocuous in itself, but it was for a washer-dryer in a house that wasn't ours—and before it was all over there were custody battles, police, hands slammed in car doors, broken pictures. We kept it in the family—for parties or church services, my dad would show up so that no one would guess they were divorced. But I knew: The Daddy chair was gone, and so was he.

At school I was still awkward, but now I had a group of friends who were just as awkward. We were all band geeks together. Music emerged as one of my favorite hobbies. Now I spent my Sunday evenings in the den playing my clarinet instead of up in my room, eating my dinner under the bed while reading a book. At school, I got involved. I was in every organization that didn't have conflicting schedules.

Having new close friends posed a problem for my eating behaviors. There were whispered concerns when I disappeared to the bathroom after lunch, or when I would avoid lunch altogether. I had to keep track of which lie I told to whom, because I realized that I could get in serious trouble if I were found out. I went through periods of "normal" eating, particularly during marching season, when I couldn't afford to pass out, or when I felt like I was really being watched. But the rest of the time, I'd be tired or angry or overwhelmed or unhappy about some-thing, and instead of talking about it I'd play a game with myself: I couldn't eat until, say, I finished the homework. But by the time I finished my work, I was absolutely starving, and I ate anything and everything that I could get my hands on. There was never a shortage of food in the house. Sometimes I ate lots and lots of bread (even though I hate bread), and some-times it was just whatever was there. Jars of peanut butter. A vat of pasta sauce.

You might ask where my parents were during all of this. They were there, just dealing with their own things. My mom was back in the working world: She had started a children's clothing business and went back and forth to Atlanta for meet-ings. My dad moved back to Nashville, but kept in touch. My little brother was too young to understand, or at least that's what I thought. Later, he would develop eating issues of his own. When he was about fifteen, he suddenly lost a lot of weight—so much that even my mother, who had encouraged us to lose weight all our lives, told him he was too thin.

It wasn't that I was abandoned by my parents; it was more that I isolated myself. I would get up, go to school, attend one of my many meetings, go to dinner with my band friends, have band practice, then go home for potential dinner number two, which I would take to my room so that I could do my home-work. I was gone almost every weekend during the fall, even sometimes on Thanksgiving for a parade or football game. When I wasn't at rehearsal I was in Youth Advisory Board meetings or doing community service with the Anchor Club. I kept myself busy, and my parents accepted that, since they knew that getting into a good college meant doing lots of extracurriculars.

But the pressure was getting to me. The cycle of bingeing

and purging was now regular. I had routines around it. I kept plastic bags in my room because I was too scared of getting caught throwing up in the bathroom. But it no longer gave me the original feeling of relief and release: I needed something more.

I don't know where I got the idea of self-injuring. My mom thinks I got it from white kids at school, but she also thinks I got everything bad from white kids at school: my eating disorder, the interest in veganism, my attraction to white boys. But who else was I supposed to get anything from, when they were the only people I was around?

Wherever I got it from, I used it as a way of relieving stress, and as punishment for one of many possible reasons I might be mad at myself. For example, if someone said something mean or critical to me and I didn't respond, instead of being mad at them, I would get mad at myself for being so passive. I would go to my underwear drawer, pull out the razors (I remember the brand—ironically, it was called Helping Hand), and punish myself for my sins. At first, it gave me a feeling of freedom. Over time, it became a self-made prison. I stopped wearing short-sleeved shirts because people would ask too many questions.

Yes, people were starting to worry. During my sophomore year, I read my academic team coach some of my poems; later in the day I found myself summoned to the guidance counselor's office.

Maybe my coach had seen the scars. I'd graduated from small slits from the serrated kitchen knife to long fluid lines that crept toward my wrists. This wasn't the first time I'd thought about death. In the past I'd wanted to do it naturally, by dying in my sleep. When I was nine or ten, I started making what I later called "medical cocktails," where I would mix together all of the pills in the medicine cabinet (over-the-counter and prescribed) and dump them in a mug of cough syrup. After taking the vile concoction, I would lie in bed, praying that this time I'd gotten it right. I would roll around, sweating from whatever my body was doing, and then I would get sleepy, and my head would feel too heavy for my neck. My mother would come in. I remember the sliver of light as she opened the door; it hurt my eyes. "Are you okay?" she would ask, and I would tell her I wasn't feeling so great, but I would be all right. The door would close again, and my head would continue to swim until I remembered nothing at all. Eventually my parents began to wonder where all of their medications were going, but they never figured it out.

The guidance counselor was pretty much useless. An older black woman, she tried very hard to be sweet and relate to me. We made polite talk about her new granddaughter. I told her I was fine. She said, since I liked poetry, why didn't I write about something nice—maybe her baby granddaughter?

But no one could check in on me because I was about to switch domains again: I was going to boarding school. My parents didn't want me to go, but I needed a change. They'd recently gotten back together, which meant they were fighting all the time, and besides, I was too driven to stay in my small town. So when my friend Thomas came into our German class with an application to the South Carolina Governor's School for the Arts and Humanities (SCGSAH), I knew I had to figure out a way to get there. I presented the case to my parents: I could get into a better college, you wouldn't have to take me anywhere, it might even be *cheaper* in the long run than supplementing my current public school education. They said no.

So I forged my mother's signature for her permission to audition and got a money order for the application fee. I lied and told my mother that I had a competition at the SCGSAH on Saturday morning. It was plausible: I'd had a competition there the year before. I told my mother she could stay in the car, and I would be back in a few minutes. She left the radio on and flipped through her copy of *Vogue* as I grabbed my instruments and music from the trunk. Forty-five minutes later, when I emerged from the audition room, my mother was sitting in the lobby.

> — *Did you just audition for this school?*
> — *No.*
> — *Are you lying to me? You shouldn't lie to your mother.*
> — *Yes.*
> — *So you did audition for the school. Look at me.*
> — *Yes.*
> — *Well, since we're here we might as well have a look*
>   *at the place.*

We took a tour and talked to students. I got in. I convinced my parents to let me go. I got what I wanted.

Or at least, I got what I thought I wanted. It was change: I was leaving the people who knew me and going somewhere to excel at . . . something. It didn't matter what. I spent the summer reinventing myself again and picking things out for my new life. I visited the Martha Stewart section of our Kmart for ideas to decorate my "home": really two hundred fifty square feet that I'd have to share with another girl. But my new home was going to say something about me, and thus I took it very seriously. The only thing I took more seriously was my appearance. I didn't want to be awkward anymore. I wanted to be chic. I wanted to flatten out some of the curves: The breasts were nice, but the hips didn't have to be so extreme. My shoulders could come in some, and I could have a longer neck. I read every magazine article on style and confidence I could get my hands on: "How to Get the Body You Want." "How to Have Shiny Hair Every Day." "27 Pants You'll Look Great In." "How to Make the Most of Your Shape." "How to Create Your Signature Look." I asked my mother for her opinion on everything. I became obsessed with clothes. My closet began to look like my mother's, except I was bigger than she was—way bigger— so the clothes were bigger, too. I'd been shopping at plus-size stores since the seventh or eighth grade, which had been part of the awkwardness. The prints were matronly, and things didn't fit right, or were just too racy. At age thirteen, my breasts popping out of a shirt didn't seem too sexy. But now I was sixteen, so low-cut tops were no longer off-limits. Stilettos became a fixation; they lengthened my legs so they didn't look like tree trunks. It was also part of a height complex: I stopped growing in the sixth grade, having reached only five feet eight. My mother is closer to five eleven.

Once I got to school, the work went well, at least in the beginning. I was used to not having to work too hard. In the past, I'd won competitions and placed in regional and state bands without really trying. I would pull out my instrument a couple of hours before the competition, run through the piece at home, practice a little more in the car en route, then go in and play. But this school was different: I realized I wasn't very good.

I had my first round of "juries." At the end of each semester, students filled out forms listing all the pieces of music they had learned during the term. On the day of the jury, each student waited at the appointed time until called into the room to perform. Sometimes you knew who would be there; sometimes you didn't. The professors looked at your list of music and asked you to play scales and a practice piece. Then they asked you to play whatever they wanted—it could be the hardest piece on the list, or just a piece they happened to like. It's arbitrary. Then came the critiques: The judges courteously wrote down all the things you did wrong, and after you played, they spoke sternly: "Do you think you're going to get into a *conservatory* playing like that? Are you going to get a *job* playing like that? Do you *think* you could even audition for a *gig* like that? Where's your head?" These are people with degrees from the most prestigious music schools in America—Juilliard, the New England Conservatory, the Curtis Institute of Music—so you take what they say seriously. After I got a C (a C!) as my final jury grade, I realized that this was going to be a bit harder than I originally thought.

The other kids at the school were just like me: ambitious kids looking for a chance to excel, or in some cases, just an excuse to leave home. (A lot of the guys were gay—and South Carolina is the buckle on the Bible Belt.) For me, SCGSAH was just a way to hasten my future success in whatever area. I liked music, but in my heart I wasn't dead set on being an artist forever. I needed backup plans, but I started doing too much and going too fast: taking the recommended music course load, but also four academic classes each term. The recommended amount was two.

During this time, my bulimia was at its most volatile. I was still skipping breakfast. Lunch period was short on the days that I had Wind Ensemble, so sometimes I wouldn't eat. I took German and Italian during my dinner period, so I could either take my food with me or just not eat. While working on subjunctive cases, I would smell the other students' food and get distracted. I was always hungry, and I thought about food all the time. My parents didn't want me to skip meals, so they would take me grocery shopping every week, which left a lot of food in my room. And the cafeteria was buffet style, which was dangerous. If I had the time I would eat, throw up, finish eating, sneak off to the science wing and throw up, then go to the library before my friends caught up with me and I had to sit through lunch again. Because we lived in a dorm, we could also order out. On Fridays, friends and I would get together and order Chinese food. Sometimes in my room by myself, I'd order meals from Steak-Out, and then throw up in a trash bag.

One day my roommate saw my arm and told the school nurse. I was summoned from European History to Nurse Gail's office. She asked to see my arms. I resisted. She asked again. I asked her why. She said it was important. I asked her if I was in trouble. We went back and forth for about fifteen minutes until I finally yielded. Her horror was warranted: My entire left arm was a series of strawberry gashes—some fresh from earlier that day. She called my dean, who called my parents, and we had a serious chat about my, um . . . The adults had a hard time naming what it was I was doing. My mother had sensed for over a year that I was doing something to my arms, but I think it was too much for her to fully process.

I went home for the weekend, and my mom tried to talk to me about it. She got religious—she went as far as anointing my room with holy oil—but I would have none of it. God had failed me, so I chose not to believe in him. In the end, I was given an ultimatum: I had to see someone to talk about my problems, or I had to leave boarding school. I chose the former, and ended up with a therapist who looked like Donna Karan, but dressed like a lumberjack. I hated her. I didn't trust her. She was trying to take me off my path to greatness. If I stopped cutting, I knew I would fall apart. If I could make it through the year, then I might be able to entertain the thought of stopping, but not now. (In the end, I wouldn't stop for another six years.) So I learned to fake it and play the therapist's game. She asked me how my day was, and I told her, using adjectives that had no positive or negative connotations. She tried to tease out my words, but I shut her down.

One of my roommates must have squealed about my food issues, because somewhere along the line, Donna Karan accused me of having an eating disorder. My parents and I vehemently denied it. I was fine. I mean, I was a little plump but that could be fixed with some exercise. I had my head in the toilet three to four times a day. I was spending fifty to seventy dollars a week on food in addition to eating in the cafeteria. I couldn't play my clarinet half the time because my fingers were swollen from edema, but I was *absolutely fine.*

The administration insisted on a physical examination, so I went to our family doctor, Dr. T. He did the necessary tests and asked me if I'd been throwing up. I told him I did occasionally, when I ate too much. After he wrote the word *obese* on my chart (and apologized profusely for it), he told me that I just needed some simple weight management skills (eat slowly; smaller portions; less fat; fewer calories; more water) and told my mother that I was going through a phase. Sure—a ten-year phase.

In the spring of my senior year, a friend, M., noticed that I was taking a lot of laxatives. She approached me about it, and I told her the truth. It was the first time I told anyone the entire truth. I didn't talk to my friends at home much; I was too busy. And my friends at school were harder to navigate. We all pretended not to be competitive, but we were. M. and I weren't competitive, because we wanted different things. M. was the first person I could talk to about my semiadult fears: I didn't know where I was going to college (I had applied to forty of them), and I thought my habits were so out of hand that they were going to eventually kill me. She helped me deal the best she could.

My parents wanted me to go to college in the South, but I said it was time for a change. Again, I imagined reinventing myself, leaving behind my body issues and the lingering image of my childhood gawkiness. I wanted to be the cool college girl who occasionally floated back to her hometown to have everyone admire how pretty she'd gotten, comment on her article about the double colonization of the mind, and ask her where she planned to go to medical school and if she was going to marry the nice young man she brought home on her last trip. During the summer before college, I worked with my dad—he now had a farm growing fruits and vegetables, which he sold in town. At the beginning of September, my parents packed our Ford F-150 and a U-Haul with my things and began the trek to New Hampshire.

I had chosen Dartmouth because of the name and its Ivy League status. I didn't think about how competitive it would be. When I got there, I realized I was again with the same intense students from high school. I wanted to impress people, so I pushed myself. I knew I was a great cook, so I started hosting dinner parties. I held a Sunday dinner every week of my freshman year. I shopped and cooked all day—for ten, twenty, sometimes even thirty people—but at the end of the night, when it was 1:00 a.m. and I was still in the kitchen cleaning up, I'd realize how used I felt. I was getting what I wanted—popularity and notoriety—but how was I paying for it? I bent over backward to please people who didn't give a damn about me. In addition to the dinner parties, I read other people's papers, volunteered for events, worked at the hospital, maintained a social life, and tried to go to class—the latter with mixed results. I began to wonder if I'd picked the wrong school. I'd changed everything and still there was no magic: I wasn't the beautiful, charmed college girl I'd dreamed of.

I didn't like Dartmouth, so I decided that I would get through it as fast as possible. If I was on every term, including summer quarter, for three years, I would get done early. I tried it. Not the best idea. The summer in Hanover was hot because most of the buildings weren't air-conditioned, but I had too much pride to wear short sleeves: I was self-conscious about the wide, raised keloid scars on my arms. Even now, when I'm more comfortable about them, someone will ask about the scars, and I'll just try to figure out what lie to tell them so they will leave me alone. But that summer I wasn't ready to shatter the illusion that I was perfect and completely together.

As it turned out, one of my professors would do that for me. I decided to take a Shakespeare course for my English minor, and after a couple of botched papers and many missed classes, the professor gave me an ultimatum: Talk to him about whatever was bothering me, or talk to someone in Student Health Services. I chose the latter because I could lie to the doctors there. But the night before my appointment, in my journal, I wondered if deceiving people into thinking I was fine had gotten me anywhere, and realized that it hadn't.

The therapist from Student Health Services was much better than Donna Karan. To begin with, he didn't butcher my first name; he called me Miss Graham until I could tell him how to properly pronounce it. Score one for the therapist. That first session was a turning point for me. I started to be honest about what was going on, and what had been going on for years. But even a good therapist couldn't stop the downward spiral I was in. I was cutting myself several times a day, and bingeing and purging even more. I started thinking again about suicide. One weekend I went to a gas station to buy a tank of gasoline, but thought better of it and bought cigarettes instead. The next weekend I told a friend about my idea of setting myself on fire, and he turned me in to the dean, who sent me home on medical leave.

During the next nine months, I would go to two treatment centers—the first one wildly inappropriate, where I was with people who sniffed keyholes because they thought the smell of dinner was wafting through, and where the doctors drugged me into oblivion. The next place, the Renfrew Center, which was depicted in the HBO documentary *Thin,* was better. Renfrew is only for eating disorders, so at least the patients and I had something in common. But there I focused on another level of difference. I was a double minority: the only plus-size patient, and the only person of color.

I was set apart from the moment I got there, when they gave me one of only three plus-size beds. And as time went on, although I liked and got along with the other patients, sometimes it was painful to listen to them. Women who were going blind from malnutrition talked in groups about how they felt fat, and I had to sit there, thinking that I weighed five times what they did.

But the harder part was the separation I felt because of my skin color. When I was younger I didn't think about race, but that changed completely after I got to Dartmouth. It's a very race-conscious place: There's a general sense that the white students look down on the minorities as affirmative-action admits, and as a result, the minority students tend to self-segregate intensely. There's the Native American House, the Asian Studies Center, the Latin American, Latino and Caribbean Studies House, and the Shabazz Center for Intellectual Inquiry—essentially, the African American House, though people might be offended if you called it that. I probably knew every African American student on campus. As a freshman, when I was the only black person in my English seminar, I thought nothing of it; this year, when I realized I was the only black person in my Medieval Literature class, I almost had a panic attack. That's how much Dartmouth has changed me.

Fortunately, at Renfrew I had a great therapist, who was also a minority and a plus-size woman. We talked about my family and my inability to assert myself and disentangle myself from my mother. We talked about the pressures that the white- and male-dominated atmosphere at a place like Dartmouth put on me, how there were limited roles for me to play: I could be the motherly black woman who feeds everyone, or I could raise my voice and be defined as a bitch. When I imagined myself in the future—as a corporate lawyer, which at the time was my dream—I pictured someone who manipulated people in a smooth, ladylike way, like my mother does, someone who always gets what she wants. But I've never been able to do this like she does. And as I kept talking to my therapist, I began to realize that this was not what I truly wanted to do.

Over time, I've come to realize that my mother and I are different. She is good at some things: She is artistic and stylish. And I am good at others: I like to read and write and think about things like race theory. I can admire her, and she can admire me.

I wish that I could give you some sort of miracle for the ending of this story, but there isn't one. No one rode in on a white horse and saved me. I didn't have a life-changing epiphany. God didn't perform a miracle and cure me so that I never think about food again. (You may think I'm joking, but in my quest to find stories of other black women with eating disorders—or any mental illness at all—I've read lots of recovery literature, and have come across quite a few deus ex machina conclusions.)

But God performed a different type of miracle: He made it possible for me to get the help that I needed, and now, one year out of treatment, I've begun to believe in him again. When something goes wrong that I don't understand, I realize I can get through it. I still have bad days, but I maintain hope. I have an amazing group of friends, and I'm starting to accept who I am. I'm not perfect, and I don't expect to become perfect, but I do think I can be happy. Because of the issues that I have had, I used to think I would never get married because no one could love me; I was broken. I don't know why exactly, but I don't feel that way anymore. As I've stopped exerting all my energy trying to imitate other people or fix things that are wrong with me, I've realized that I like things about myself. I also don't push myself the way I did in high school, striving toward some dream of success that I can't even define. I accept that I'm still finding who I am, and I'm allowing myself to enjoy things along the way.

Tomorrow, for example, I'm going to audition for a play. In short sleeves.

EDUCATION OF THE POET

Louise Glück

———

The fundamental experience of the writer is helplessness. This does not mean to distinguish writing from being alive: It means to correct the fantasy that creative work is an ongoing record of the triumph of volition, that the writer is someone who has the good luck to be able to do what he or she wishes to do: to confidently and regularly imprint his being on a sheet of paper. But writing is not decanting of personality. And most writers spend much of their time in various kinds of torment: wanting to write, being unable to write; wanting to write differently, being unable to write differently. In a whole lifetime, years are spent waiting to be claimed by an idea. The only real exercise of will is negative: We have toward what we write the power of veto.

It is a life dignified, I think, by yearning, not made serene by sensations of achievement. In the actual work, a discipline, a service. Or, to utilize the metaphor of childbirth which seems never to die: The writer is the one who attends, who facilitates: the doctor, the midwife, not the mother.

I use the word *writer* deliberately. *Poet* must be used cautiously; it names an aspiration, not an occupation. In other words: not a noun for a passport.

It is very strange to want so much what cannot be achieved in life. The high jumper knows, at the instant after performance, how high he has been; his achievement can be measured both immediately and with precision. But for those of us attempting dialogue with the great dead, it isn't a matter of waiting: The judgment we wait for is made by the unborn; we can never, in our lifetimes, know it.

The profundity of our ignorance concerning the merit of what we do creates despair; it also fuels hope. Meanwhile, contemporary opinion rushes to present itself as the intelligent alternative to ignorance: Our task is to somehow insulate ourselves from opinion in its terminal forms, verdict and directive, while still retaining alert receptiveness to useful criticism.

If it is improper to speak as a poet, it is equally difficult to speak on the subject of education. The point, I think, would be to speak of what has left indelible impressions. But I discover such impressions slowly, often long after the fact. And I like to think they are still being made, and the old ones still being revised.

The axiom is that the mark of poetic intelligence or vocation is passion for language, which is thought to mean delirious response to language's smallest communicative unit: to the word. The poet is supposed to be the person who can't get enough of words like *incarnadine*. This was not my experience. From the time, at four or five or six, I first started reading poems, first thought of the poets I read as my companions, my predecessors—from the beginning, I preferred the simplest vocabulary. What fascinated me were the possibilities of context. What I responded to, on the page, was the way a poem could liberate, by means of a word's setting, through subtleties of timing, of pacing, that word's full and surprising range of meaning. It seemed to me that simple language best suited this enterprise; such language, in being generic, is likely to contain the greatest and most dramatic variety of meaning within individual words. I liked scale, but I liked it invisible. I loved those poems that seemed so small on the page but that swelled in the mind; I didn't like the windy, dwindling kind. Not surprisingly, the sort of sentence I was drawn to, which reflected these tastes and native habit of mind, was paradox, which has the added advantage of nicely rescuing the dogmatic nature from a too-moralizing rhetoric.

I was born into the worst possible family given this bias. I was born into an environment in which the right of any family member to complete the sentence of another was assumed. Like most of the people in that family, I had a strong desire to speak, but that desire was regularly frustrated: My sentences were, in being cut off, radically changed—transformed, not paraphrased. The sweetness of paradox is that its outcome cannot be anticipated: This ought to ensure the attention of the audience. But in my family, all discussion was carried on in that single cooperative voice.

I had, early on, a very strong sense that there was no point to speech if speech did not precisely articulate perception. To my mother, speech was the socially acceptable form of murmur: Its function was to fill a room with ongoing, consoling human sound. And to my father, it was performance and disguise. My response was silence. Sulky silence, since I never stopped wanting deferential attention. I was bent on personal distinction, which was linked, in my mind, to the making of sentences.

In other ways, my family was remarkable. Both my parents admired intellectual accomplishment; my mother, in particular, revered creative gifts. At a time when women were not, commonly, especially well educated, my mother fought to go to college; she went to Wellesley. My father was the first and only son among five daughters, the first child born in this country. His parents had come from Hungary; my grandfather was a better dreamer than administrator of the family land: When the crops failed and the cattle died, he came to America, opened a grocery store. By family legend, a just man, less forceful than his wife and daughters. Before he died, his little store was the last piece of real estate on a block being bought up by one of the Rockefellers. This was generally deemed remarkably good fortune, in that my grandfather could ask, now, any price at all—an attitude for which my grandfather had complete contempt. He would ask, he said, the fair price: By definition, the same for Mr. Rockefeller as for anyone else.

I didn't know my father's parents; I knew his sisters. Fierce women, in the main dogmatic, who put themselves through college and had, in the remote past, dramatic and colorful love lives. My father refused to compete, which, in his family, meant he refused to go to school. In a family strong on political conscience but generally deficient in imagination, my father wanted to be a writer. But he lacked certain qualities: lacked the adamant need which makes it possible to endure every form of failure: the humiliation of being overlooked, the humiliation of being found moderately interesting, the unanswerable fear of doing work that, in the end, really isn't more than moderately interesting, the discrepancy, which even the great writers live with (unless, possibly, they attain great age) between the dream and the evidence. Had my father's need been more acute, he probably would have found a means to overcome his emotional timidity; in the absence of acute need, he lacked motive to fight that battle. Instead, he went into business with his brother-in-law, made a notable success, and lived, by most criteria, a full and fortunate life.

Growing up, I pitied him his decision. I think now that, in regard to my father, I'm blind, because I see in him my own weaknesses. But what my father needed to survive was not writing, it was belief in his potential—that he chose not to test that potential may have been good judgment, not, wholly, want of courage.

My mother was a sort of maid-of-all-work moral leader, the maker of policy. She considered my father the inspired thinker. She was dogged; he had that quality of mind my mother lacked, which she equated with imaginative capacity: He had lightness, wit. My mother was the judge. It was she who read my poems and stories and, later, the essays I wrote for school; it was her approval I lived on. It wasn't easy to get, since what my sister and I did was invariably weighed against what, in my mother's view, we had the ability to do. I used to regularly make the mistake of asking her what she thought. This was intended as a cue for praise, but my mother responded to the letter, not the spirit: Always, and in detail, she told me exactly what she thought.

Despite these critiques, my sister and I were encouraged in every gift. If we hummed, we got music lessons. If we skipped, dance. And so on. My mother read to us, then taught us to read very early. Before I was three, I was well-grounded in the Greek myths, and the figures of those stories, together with certain images from the illustrations, became fundamental referents. My father told stories. Sometimes these were wholly invented, like the adventures of a pair of bugs, and sometimes they were revised history, his particular favorite being the tale of Saint Joan, with the final burning deleted.

My sister and I were being raised, if not to save France, to recognize and honor and aspire to glorious achievement. We were never given to believe that such achievement was impossible, either to our sex or in our historical period. I'm puzzled, not emotionally but logically, by the contemporary determination of women to write as women. Puzzled because this seems an ambition limited by the existing conception of what, exactly, differentiates the sexes. If there are such differences, it seems to me reasonable to suppose that literature reveals them, and that it will do so more interestingly, more subtly, in the absence of intention. In a similar way, all art is historical: In both its confrontations and evasions, it speaks of its period. The dream of art is not to assert what is already known but to illuminate what has been hidden, and the path to the hidden world is not inscribed by will.

I read early, and wanted, from a very early age, to speak in return. When, as a child, I read Shakespeare's songs, or later, Blake and Yeats and Keats and Eliot, I did not feel exiled, marginal. I felt, rather, that this was the tradition of my language: *my* tradition, as English was my language. My inheritance. My wealth. Even before they've been lived through, a child can sense the great human subjects: time which breeds loss, desire, the world's beauty.

Meanwhile, writing answered all sorts of needs. I wanted to make something. I wanted to finish my own sentences. And I was sufficiently addicted to my mother's approval to want to shine at something she held in high esteem. When I wrote, our wishes coincided. And this was essential: Hungry as I was for praise, I was also proud and could not bear to ask for it, to seem to need it.

Because I remember, verbatim, most of what I've written in

the course of my life, I remember certain of my early poems; where written records exist, they confirm these memories. Here's one of the earliest, written around the time I was five:

> If kitty cats liked roastbeef bones
> And doggies sipped up milk;
> If elephants walked around the town
> All dressed in purest silk;
> If robins went out coasting,
> They slid down, crying whee,
> If all this happened to be true
> Then where would people be?

Plainly, I loved the sentence as a unit: the beginning of a preoccupation with syntax. Those who love syntax less find in it the stultifying air of the academy: It is, after all, a language of rules, of order. Its opposite is music, that quality of language which is felt to persist in the absence of rule. One possible idea behind such preferences is the fantasy of the poet as renegade, as the lawless outsider. It seems to me that the idea of lawlessness is a romance, and romance is what I most struggle to be free of.

I experimented with other mediums. For a while, I thought of painting, for which I had a small gift. Small but, like my other aptitudes, relentlessly developed. At some point in my late teens I realized I was at the end of what I could imagine on canvas. I think that, had my gift been larger or more compelling, I would still have found the visual arts a less congenial language. Writing suits the conservative temperament. What is edited can be preserved. Whereas the painter who recognizes that, in the interest of the whole, a part must be sacrificed, loses that part forever: It ceases to exist, except insofar as memory, or photographs, reproduce it. I couldn't bear the endless forfeits this involved; or perhaps I lack sufficient confidence in my immediate judgments.

In other ways as well, my preferences have not much changed. I experience, as a reader, two primary modes of poetic speech. One, to the reader, feels like confidence; one seems intercepted meditation. My preference, from the beginning, has been the poetry that requests or craves a listener. This is Blake's little black boy, Keats's living hand, Eliot's Prufrock, as opposed, say, to Stevens's astonishments. I don't intend, in this, to set up any sort of hierarchy, simply to say that I read to feel addressed: the complement, I suppose, of speaking in order to be heeded. There are exceptions, but the general preference remains intact.

The preference for intimacy, of course, makes of the single reader an elite. A practical advantage to this innate preference is that one cares less about the size of an audience. Or maybe the point here is that the writer's audience is chronological. The actor and dancer perform in the present; if their work exists in the future, it exists as memory, as legend. Whereas the canvas, the bronze, and, more durably because they exist in multiple, the poem, the sonata, exist not as memory but as fact; the artists who work in these forms, scorned or overlooked in their own time, can still find an audience.

Among other profound divisions in literary taste, there's much talk currently about closure, about open-ended form, the idea being that such form is distinctly feminine. More interesting to me is a larger difference of which this is an example: the difference between symmetry and asymmetry, harmony and assonance.

I remember an argument I had with someone's mother when I was eight or nine; it was her day for carpool duty and our assignment in school had involved composition. I'd written a poem, and was asked to recite it, which I readily did. My special triumph with this poem had involved a metrical reversal in the last line (not that I called it that), an omission of the final rhyme: To my ear it was exhilarating, a kind of explosion of form. The form, of course, was doggerel. In any case, our driver congratulated me: A very good poem, she said, right till the last line, which she then proceeded to rearrange aloud into the order I had explicitly intended to violate. You see, she told me, all that was missing was that last rhyme. I was furious, and especially furious in that I knew my objections would read as a defensive response to obvious failure.

It seems sometimes very strange to me, that image of a child so wholly bent on vocation. So ambitious. The nature of that ambition, of literary ambition, seems to me a subject too large for this occasion. Like most people hungry for praise and ashamed of that, of any hunger, I alternated between contempt for the world that judged me and lacerating self-hatred. To my mind, to be wrong in the smallest particular was to be wrong utterly. On the surface, I was poised, cool, indifferent, given to laconic exhibitions of disdain. A description, I suppose, of any adolescent.

The discrepancy between what I would show the world and the chaos I felt grew steadily more intense. I wrote and painted, but these activities were hardly the famous release of such pressure they are contended to be. I cared too much about the quality of what I made; the context in which I judged what I made was not the schoolroom, but the history of art. In midadolescence, I developed a symptom perfectly congenial to the demands of my spirit. I had great resources of will and no self. Then, as now, my thought tended to define itself in opposition; what remains characteristic now was in those days the single characteristic. I couldn't say what I was, what I wanted, in any day to day, practical way. What I could say was *no:* the way I saw to separate myself, to establish a self with clear boundaries, was to oppose myself to the declared desire of others, utilizing their wills to give shape to my own. The conflict played itself out most fiercely with my mother. Insofar as I could tell, my mother only wavered when I began to refuse food, when I claimed, through implicit threat, ownership of my body, which was her great accomplishment.

The tragedy of anorexia seems to me that its intent is not self-destructive, though its outcome so often is. Its intent is to construct, in the only way possible when means are so limited, a plausible self. But the sustained act, the repudiation, designed to distinguish the self from the other also separates self and body. Out of terror at its incompleteness and ravenous need, anorexia constructs a physical sign calculated to manifest disdain for need, for hunger, designed to appear entirely free of all forms of dependency, to appear complete, self-contained. But the sign it trusts is a physical sign, impossible to sustain by mere act of will, and the poignance of the metaphor rests in this: that anorexia proves not the soul's superiority to but its dependence on flesh.

By the time I was sixteen, a number of things were clear to me. It was clear that what I had thought of as an act of will, an act I was perfectly capable of controlling, of terminating, was not that; I realized that I had no control over this behavior at all. And I realized, logically, that to be eighty-five, then eighty, then seventy-five pounds was to be thin; I understood that at some point I was going to die. What I knew more vividly, more viscerally, was that I didn't want to die. Even then, dying seemed a pathetic metaphor for establishing a separation between myself and my mother. I knew, at the time, very little about psychoanalysis; certainly, in those days, it was less common than now, in this era of proliferating therapies. Less common even in the affluent suburbs.

My parents, during these months, were wise enough to recognize that any suggestion they made I'd be committed to rejecting; therefore, they made no suggestions. And finally, one day, I told my mother I thought perhaps I should see a psychoanalyst. This was nearly thirty years ago—I have no idea where the idea, the word, came from. Nor was there, in those days, any literature about anorexia—at least, I knew of none. If there had been, I'd have been stymied; to have a disease so common, so typical, would have obliged me to devise some entirely different gestures to prove my uniqueness.

I was immensely fortunate in the analyst my parents found. I began seeing him in the fall of my senior year of high school; a few months later, I was taken out of school. For the next seven years, analysis was what I did with my time and with my mind; it would be impossible for me to speak of education without speaking of this process.

I was afraid of psychoanalysis in conventional ways. I thought what kept me alive, in that it gave me hope, was my ambition, my sense of vocation; I was afraid to tamper with the mechanism. But a certain rudimentary pragmatism told me that I had not yet accomplished a body of work likely to endure; therefore, I couldn't afford to die. In any case, I felt I had no choice, which was a piece of luck. Because at seventeen I was not wild, not volcanic; I was rigid and self-protective; the form my self-protectiveness took was exclusion: That which I feared, I ignored; what I ignored, most of my central feelings, was not present in my poems. The poems I was writing were narrow, mannered, static; they were also otherworldly, mystical. These qualities were entirely defining. What was worse: By the time I began analysis, I'd stopped writing. So there was nothing, really, to protect.

But periodically, in the course of those seven years, I'd turn to my doctor with the old accusation: He'd make me so well, so whole, I'd never write again. Finally, he silenced me; the world, he told me, will give you sorrow enough. I think he waited to say that because, at the outset, the fact that the world existed at all was beyond me, as it is beyond all egotists.

Analysis taught me to think. Taught me to use my tendency to object to articulated ideas on my own ideas, taught me to use doubt, to examine my own speech for its evasions and excisions. It gave me an intellectual task capable of transforming paralysis—which is the extreme form of self-doubt—into insight. I was learning to use native detachment to make contact with myself, which is the point, I suppose, of dream analysis: What's utilized are objective images. I cultivated a capacity to study images and patterns of speech, to see, as objectively as possible, what ideas they embodied. Insofar as I was, obviously, the source of those dreams, those images, I could infer these ideas were mine, the embodied conflicts, mine. The longer I withheld conclusion, the more I saw. I was learning, I believe, how to write, as well: not to have a self which, in writing, is projected into images. And not, simply, to permit the production of images, a production unencumbered by mind; but to use the mind to explore the resonances of such images, to separate the shallow from the deep, and to choose the deep.

It is fortunate that that discipline gave me a place to use my mind, because my emotional condition, my extreme rigidity of behavior and frantic dependence on ritual, made other forms of education impossible. In fact, for many years every form of social interaction seemed impossible, so acute was my shame. But there was, after the first year, one other form open to me, or one need more powerful than shame. At eighteen, instead of going to college as I had always assumed I would, I enrolled in Leonie Adams's poetry workshop at the School of General Studies at Columbia.

I've written elsewhere about the years that followed, about the two spent studying with Dr. Adams, and the many years with Stanley Kunitz. Here's a poem, written long afterward, which simply records a few of the dreams in which Kunitz figures:

Four Dreams Concerning the Master

1. The Supplicant

S. is standing in a small room, reading to himself.
It is a privilege to see S.
alone, in this serene environment.
Only his hand moves, thoughtfully turning the pages.
Then, from under the closed door, a single hazelnut
rolls into the room, coming to rest, at length,
at S.'s foot. With a sigh, S. closes the heavy volume
and stares down wearily at the round nut. "Well," he says,
"what do you want now, Stevens?"

2. Conversation with M.

"Have you ever noticed," he remarked,
"that when women sleep
they're really looking at you?"

3. Noah's Dream

Where were you in the dream?
   The North Pole.
Were you alone?
   No. My friend was with me.
Which friend was that?
   My old friend. My friend the poet.
What were you doing?
   We were crossing a river. But the clumps of ice
   were far apart, we had to jump.
Were you afraid?
   Just cold. Our eyes filled up with snow.
And did you get across?
   It took a long time. Then we got across.
What did you do then, on the other side?
   We walked a long time.
And was the walk the end?
   No. The end was the morning.

4. Conversation with X.

"You," he said, "you're just like Eliot.
You think you know everything in the world
but you don't believe anything."

Much is said of what a teacher in a creative enterprise cannot
do. Whatever they can't do, what they can do, the whole expe-

rience of apprenticeship, seems to me beyond value. I was working, of course, with extraordinary minds. And I was being exposed to images of dedication, not of the kind I knew, which I was not wholly prepared to comprehend. The poetic vocation is felt to be dramatic, glamorous; this is in part because consecration, which is dynamic, is so often mistaken for dedication. My notions of persistence were necessarily limited by youth. I was being shown, though, what it looked like, a steady upward labor; I was in the presence of that stamina I would find necessary. And I was privileged in feeling the steady application of scrutiny—from outside, from the world, from another human being. One of the rare, irreplaceable gifts of such apprenticeships is this scrutiny; seldom, afterward, is any poem taken with such high seriousness. Those of us trained in this environment have felt, I think, deeply motivated to provide for one another a comparable readership, and that need, founded so long ago, helps fend off the animosities, the jealousies, to which most of us are prone.

I was writing, in those years, with the inspiration of those teachers, those readers, the poems that were collected in my first book.

And if I had, as yet, no idea what kind of patience would be called for in my life, I had, by that time, already ample experience of what is called "writer's block." Though I hated the condition, a sense that the world had gone gray and flat and dull, I came to mistrust the premise behind the term. To be more precise: I can make sense of that premise in only two ways. It makes sense to presume fluency when the basis of the work is some intuition about language profound enough to be explored over a lifetime. Or when the work is anecdotal in nature. Even for the writer whose creative work arises out of the act of bearing witness—even for such a writer, a subject, a focus, must present itself, or be found. The artist who bears witness begins with a judgment, though it is moral, not aesthetic. But the artist whose gift is the sketch, the anecdote: That artist makes, as far as I can tell, no such judgment; nothing impedes the setting down of detail, because there is no investment in the idea of importance. When the aim of the work is spiritual insight, it seems absurd to expect fluency. A metaphor for such work is the oracle, which needed to be fed questions. In practical terms, this means that the writer who means to outlive the useful rages and despairs of youth must somehow learn to endure the desert.

I have wished, since I was in my early teens, to be a poet; over a period of more than thirty years, I have had to get through extended silences. By silences I mean periods, sometimes two years in duration, during which I have written nothing. Not written badly, written nothing. Nor do such periods feel like fruitful dormancy.

It seems to me that the desire to make art produces an ongoing experience of longing, a restlessness sometimes, but not inevitably, played out romantically, or sexually. Always there seems something ahead, the next poem or story, visible, at least, apprehensible, but unreachable. To perceive it at all is to be haunted by it; some sound, some tone, becomes a torment—the poem embodying that sound seems to exist somewhere already finished. It's like a lighthouse, except that, as one swims toward it, it backs away.

That's my sense of the poem's beginning. What follows is a period of more concentrated work, so called because as long as one is working the thing itself is wrong or unfinished: a failure. Still, this engagement is absorbing as nothing else I have ever in my life known. And then the poem is finished, and at that moment, instantly detached: It becomes what it was first perceived to be, a thing always in existence. No record exists of the poet's agency. And the poet, from that point, isn't a poet anymore, simply someone who wishes to be one.

In practical terms, this has meant having a good deal of unused time; I came to teaching reluctantly, twenty-five years ago.

My experience as a student taught me a profound gratitude, a sense of indebtedness. In the days when teaching jobs began to be possible to me, when, to support myself, I worked as a secretary in various offices, I feared teaching. I feared that, in the presence of a poem that seemed nearly remarkable, my competitiveness would seek to suppress the remarkable, not draw it out. What I saw when, during one of my most difficult silences, I finally began to teach was that at such moments authorship matters not at all; I realized that I felt compelled to serve others' poems in the same way, with the same ferocity, as I felt compelled to serve my own. It mattered to get the poem right, to get it memorable, toward which end nothing was held back. In this act, all the forces in my nature I least approve, the competitiveness, the envy, were temporarily checked. Whatever benefits accrued to individual poems through this activity, the benefits to me proved enormous. I found an activity in which to feel myself benign, helpful—that, obviously. But I had also discovered that I need not myself be writing to feel my mind work. Teaching became, for me, the prescription for lassitude. It doesn't always work, of course, but it has worked often enough, and steadily enough. On that first occasion, it worked miraculously quickly.

I'd moved to Vermont, taken a three-month job at Goddard.

I'd written one book, and then nothing in the two years following its publication. I began teaching in September; in September, I began writing again, writing poems entirely different from those in *Firstborn*.

This difference was intended, at least hoped for. What you learn organizing a book, making a pile of poems an arc, a shaped utterance, is both exhilarating and depressing: As you discern the book's themes, its fundamental preoccupations, you see as well the poems' habitual gestures, those habits of syntax and vocabulary, the rhythmic signatures which, ideally, give the volume at hand its character but which it would be dangerous to repeat.

Each book I've written has culminated in a conscious diagnostic act, a swearing off. After *Firstborn*, the task was to make Latinate suspended sentences, and to figure out a way to end a poem without sealing it shut. Since the last poems of *The House on Marshland* were written concurrently with the earliest poems in *Descending Figure*, the latter seems more difficult to speak of independently. I wanted to learn a longer breath. And to write without the nouns central to that second book; I had done about as much as I could with moon and pond. What I wanted, after *Descending Figure*, was a poem less perfect, less stately; I wanted a present tense that referred to something more fluent than the archetypal present. And then, obviously, the task was to write something less overtly heroic, something devoid of mythic reference.

This is far too compressed a synopsis to be accurate, but it will give a sense, I hope, of some compulsion to change, a compulsion not, perhaps, actually chosen. I see in this gesture the child I was, unwilling to speak if to speak meant to repeat myself.

BIG LITTLE

Priscilla Becker

———

It began immediately after a comment made to me by a boy in the hall my freshman year of high school. The boy was Scott Calipari, my boyfriend. He was looking at my pelvis, squinting as though bringing something far-off into focus. He seemed to be registering an unbelievable truth: "Your thighs," he said, "they're kind of"—and here he paused—"big."

I had eaten until then without concern. I was thin and active. I ran track and cross-country. I danced ballet. I was fourteen and probably on my way to developing the body I was supposed to have. Meaning, I have fat genes—Hungarian, German. Great-grandmothers, dead before my birth, are described by my father as "big *mahoskas*"—fat, Slavicly fat. I could feel my body lurching toward its true form, poised to realize its heredity.

But what I was about to do would interfere with that, and prevent me from developing according to my natural physiology. Eating was never again to be a natural thing.

That night at dinner I didn't eat. The next morning I opened the cupboard door. It had dark oiled wood, the kind with black eyes, and a hinge clasp that had to be depressed for

it to open, which would occur with a distinctive click. I learned
to depress it very slowly so that the click was suppressed. I fit
my hand silently into a bag of dry-roasted peanuts and split
one open inside my cupped hands. The peanuts were reserved
for my father; he ate them while watching sports late at night.
There was food in the house designated for my mother and my
father, but no special foods for my sister or me.

This was to become my morning routine. I would try to find
a shell that contained just one peanut. Many, however, contained two. It is difficult to keep from lying about what I would
do in the event of a two-peanut shell. The truth is, I don't
know what I did with the extra peanut. I only know I didn't
eat it. I probably wouldn't have thrown it out, either, because
that would be wasteful, and waste offended either me or my
parents, though at that point it wasn't clear which. We saved
everything. Rather, I should say, there were two opposite and
potentially canceling forces at work in the household: my
mother accumulating and my father eliminating. In our case,
the former has always won out.

I thought about composing a paragraph about my elaborate
removal of the extra peanut, my systematic ritual. But that
is because I know the stories, and I am assuming you do, too:
the story of the cookie dissected into thirty-two equal seg-
ments, the story of the hour-long apple-eating excruciation;
and I am competitive and don't want you to think I was a bad
anorexic—sloppy, slack, fat.

In any case, this was to be my breakfast throughout high
school, which actually adds up to many, many peanuts, the
exact number of which I am restraining myself from calculat-
ing, as it has been part of my recovery not to weigh and reckon.
But I did wonder (and still do sometimes) about my father

puzzling over the little pile of unshelled peanuts accumulating in his bag.

My sister's body, of which I was jealous, was shaped like a boy's—hipless and naturally strong. Mine is not. I curve at the hips, and extra, incomprehensible flesh accumulates there. Thankfully, I am small-breasted. Also, I am delicately framed, which makes thinness look thinner and weight more noticeable. While some girls eagerly checked mirrors for signs of development, looking toward the onset of puberty with excitement and curiosity, I was horrified and deeply embarrassed. My tiny breasts looked ridiculous to me, but had they been bigger, it would have been much worse. I had not been warned of my first period, and when it came I thought I had injured myself by overmasturbating.

I prepared lunch at home and brought it with me to school: a bundle of carrot and celery sticks. If you were to make a circle with your index finger at the first knuckle of your thumb, that would be about the width of the bundle. The sticks were cut very thin and were three inches long. I carried them in a plastic sandwich bag. Dinner was a slice, a perfect square, of cheddar cheese. It had to be translucent: I would hold it up to the fluorescent kitchen light with one hand and, with the other, wave to myself from behind the flimsy screen of cheese.

No, that's a lie. Actually, I had already lost, with alarming speed, my sense of humor. If I laughed, it would veer off into private uncontrollable laughter, the kind I've always thought the hallmark of insanity. It was better not to laugh, just as it was better not to eat—with both I felt that if I ever started I wouldn't stop.

The family dinner was insisted upon, mostly by my mother, as some sort of symbol of normality. We rarely spoke. Currents of anger spiked around the table in complex cross-pollinations. Early in my refusals of food there were terrible fights. My mother thought my starvation an exercise of my will, an arbitrary challenge, and that I could just as well have held my breath or repeated her phrases or stuck my fingers in my ears when she spoke. And so she attempted to force me to eat. I tried the usual tactics, lying that I'd already eaten, which further angered her, or I'd say that I felt sick, an indefensible position because we were Christian Scientists.

My father and sister were mostly silent, although their faces were disgusted. My sister stopped talking to me entirely in high school, and her lip curled back as if she were tasting sour milk when I passed by. When she *had* to speak to me—it seemed to physically pain her—she'd release a few syllables from between clenched teeth and stare at a fixed point in the distance, as people do when they are addressing large groups or no one in particular.

Eventually, I removed myself from the fray by staying later and later at track practice or pretending to do homework or to practice the violin. Diligence, even the ruse of it, trumped the ruse of the family dinner.

I am writing about the early 1980s. I had never even heard the two words together: *eating disorder.* It was before such a condition was talked about, or at least no one I knew had ever had one. However, I knew very well the connection between what one ate and the size of one's body. My mother was completely taken over by physical concerns. She was generally on some sort of diet, although I hesitate to call her eating choices that, because they seemed to offer transformation beyond the body. Food had an extraordinary power in our household. As a child I was generally recruited to follow these plans with her.

There were weeks of fasting on hot lemonade, long stretches of extensive juicing during which my mother's skin turned orange. We exhausted many models of juicers and extractors, even the Champion, which was the most expensive and technically advanced, yielding the driest pulp, and to which a plastic bag had to be affixed like a diaper. We watched while orange and green waste coiled out the back like the bowel movements we hoped to enact.

We "sprouted" for a while, seeds insinuating their hairy tendrils from beneath moist towels, ate only raw food while horrible fermented almonds overtook the refrigerator, drank fizzy acidophilus from a champagne-shaped bottle (it tasted like sour socks), and lay on a "slant board" to restore our energies. There was the *Fit for Life* phase, as well as monofasts of "perfect" foods—once bananas, then avocados, then pineapple.

We activated our thyroids in shoulder stands before most westerners had even heard of yoga, jumped rope in the garage, and rebounded—which is not exactly exercise, but a lymphatic-system stimulator. We drank fish oil from a spoon, hydrogen peroxide from the bottle, apple-cider vinegar containing the "mother" (the mucilaginous substance produced by mold fungus during fermentation) lurking at the bottom of the glass like a living ghost, liquid chlorophyll, spirulina, and barley grass. All the while the water distiller, its presence on the counter like a small silver nuclear reactor, sucked the minerals out of our water only so that we could replace them, including arsenic, in a liquid extracted from a virgin sunken shale deposit below the sea in Tempe, Arizona.

Bran was to be found lacing every dish, powdered bonemeal clogged our morning juice like paste, carob bean pretended to be chocolate, and hills of vitamins waited for us at every meal.

We snacked on Scandinavian crisp bread, which boasted 85 percent bran. Buckwheat and beer pancakes were a favorite for a while.

Anything ancient or tribal was taken to be superior, and so the Dead Sea was popular, as was the Essene Gospel of Peace. My mother was sometimes heard to exclaim, "Jesus cleaned himself out with a gourd!" Every ancient grain was experimented with for a time and left behind: teff, amaranth, kamut. We chanted at Hare Krishna meetings in the Village and attended powwows on the eastern tip of Long Island.

We *fletcherized*, as per Horace Fletcher, "the Great Masticator," a Victorian-era health advocate, by chewing each morsel thirty-two times before swallowing, thus breaking down with our teeth the cell walls of all vegetables, and we took pains to ingest liquids and solids separately, as combining them would weaken the digestive fire. But when we weren't eating, we flooded our systems with liquid in order to keep things moving along. We composted, ate the seeds and skins of all fruits and vegetables, as well as the white membrane surrounding citrus (vitamin P), and we ate unpasteurized cheese and milk before it became illegal in New York State (enzymes).

I always felt we were doing much more than eating certain things and not eating certain others.

Only one thing in our household was imbued with greater importance than ingestion, and that was elimination. It seemed that no sooner were we eating the food than we were trying to get rid of it: aloe vera, pectin, wheat germ, senna, fenugreek, psyllium, cascara sagrada, flaxseed, Amrutadi, stewed prunes, beet juice, charcoal, licorice, enemas, high colonics. These were just a few of the household remedies. There was a shelf about three feet long at the bottom of the stairway down to the cellar, filled with discarded powders with such names as Colon Blowout, Intesti-Cleanse, Bowel Broom—each one defective ("This one has added sugar, this one is rancid, this one contains aspartame, this one made me gag, this one constipated, actually constipated me, this one was infested with tiny grain bugs") in some particular way, but all joined in one common offense: They did not work; they were no good.

I suspected that *no good* for my mother meant much more than that they had failed to produce a bowel movement. I think she meant something much more devastating and less physical, something about my father or God.

I cannot remember a time when I wasn't constipated. I wondered what was happening to the food. I thought it must be poisoning my system, or worse, gathering as fat. Perhaps it was waiting deep inside some cavity and one day all the unexcreted peanuts and slivers of cheese would burst out on my thighs.

So I began taking laxatives, herbal ones such as Swiss Kriss or Tam. I took them every day. Because they did not contain harsh chemicals, I let myself believe they were not harmful to ingest. I had such morbid and special knowledge of nutrition that I was continually at cross-purposes with myself. I would apply a double standard to my behavior, adhere to that part of a rule that served my concerns. I looked ahead to a time (presumably now) when all the damage I was inflicting upon myself would be corrected, as though I'd be to one side of my life, the opposite one, standing in a frozen beam of health.

I remember the day I was caught short by this behavior. By this time I had been through four years of college, but had yet to earn my degree. My boyfriend and I were visiting New York and staying at a friend's apartment on King Street. The friend was very health conscious (years later, he would burn a hole in his stomach by eating raw jalapeños), as I claimed to be. By this time I had been swallowing laxatives every day for eight or nine years. There was a place mat on the kitchen table with a chart listing just about every possible physical and mental complaint, and the vitamin deficiencies and bad nutritional practices that could cause them. As my eye looked down the chart, I saw the word *laxative, laxative, laxative, laxative.*

In that moment I knew that I was really starving, that the few nutrients I was ingesting weren't in my system long enough to do me any good. Yet as quickly as the recognition had descended, it was gone. Of course I couldn't stop taking the laxatives, because by this time I had no peristalsis of my own.

But in high school, when I was just embarking on my life of nutritional poverty, my body was still resilient. True, I was constipated, but this might have been normal enough, given my small allotment of food. I thought then it would all be temporary; I thought I was on a diet.

I would cut school by locking myself in my closet. I spent much of my time staring deeply into walls. I suppose it felt most like having been sucked away from everyone I loved, and from all desire—which is where I thought my trouble lay— with desire. I had never shared the sense of emptiness I often heard people describe, the hollow feeling, boredom. My trouble seemed the opposite: I felt too much. I was always bursting with some uncomfortable emotion or expression, feeling foolish and inappropriate.

So instead of figuring out how to get what I wanted, I slowly figured out how *not* to want. I was shocked to discover that desire is, like most things, responsive to practice. I studied joylessness. I removed expression from my face and inflection from my voice. For the first twenty years of my condition I was constantly hungry and wanted nothing more than to eat. But even hunger finally ceded. I overcame my sex drive (temporarily) in like manner; I felt peaceful, less human.

Every social situation was a test of endurance that I couldn't wait to end. I failed even to imagine enjoyment. I wanted only to be alone, hidden; once alone, I longed for love and people, for activity and interest. For each public thing I wanted to do, I had an accompanying proviso: I could do it, but just not now. I would stare at the hipless images in fashion magazines: These were the girls who desired nothing and so were desired. It never occurred to me that I might have a desire that could be met.

I had many male friends of the sort that wait around for you to love them. It was the only kind of friendship I could have—based, as it was, on their doomed admiration of me, and requiring almost nothing in return. They must have imagined a future payoff. But I slept with other men—just about anyone else, though it helped if they were ugly or abusive or actively hated. And I also pursued sex. It had no meaning for me, only purpose: to momentarily quell my nervousness—and to feed me. I lived on it.

I kept extensive lists, documenting every calorie ingested in each twenty-four-hour period, and balancing this figure with the amount—duration and intensity and, because I was a runner, this meant mileage and pace—I had exercised. On the reverse side of my calorie and exercise chart was my list of things to do for the day. Most of these tasks I would not complete, but I loved little more than crossing things out of my life.

As a child I'd read biographies of the great composers again and again. I remember that, more than stories, I had a deep affection for words. But in high school I lost the ability to finish reading a sentence without its trailing off into white gauze. I suspected I was stupid. I could read the words on the page, but they didn't correspond to anything—just symbols without meaning.

In tenth grade, as a book report, I made up a book, reported on it, complete with bibliography, and got a perfect score on the paper, which impressed my friends. One of them, unaware of how it makes me wince, still tells this story as proof, I think to her, of my ingenuity. So much of my condition, with the help of my silent complicity, seemed ready to be interpreted as will and wit; idiosyncrasy and special talent; superiority. And, in fact, this was the secret consolation: an internal elitism. My behavior seemed to prove a strange endurance because it did without a basic component of life: food. And, just as I think some nonanorexics fear, I *did* think everyone was fat and undisciplined. Anorexics generally don't like to admit this, and doubtless I shouldn't speak for them, but denial, after all, is our medium.

I would gaze at the books on the shelves in my house and my friends' houses, touch the covers and rub the pages between my fingers. I would smell the paper. But books may as well have been buried in the earth. I knew it was a world that could save me, but I did not know the way back.

While I felt a kind of dark pride when my body fit within my miserable limits, if anyone called attention to it, whether in alarm or praise, I would be filled with instant embarrassment. I dearly hated to be noticed. At the same time, I had intense yet stagnant ambitions for myself; talents that, although untried and undeveloped, I violently hoped would emerge one day, intact and whole, like an ejected egg—as though all that was required was the perfect form.

My hopes at that time were more like dreams, or really fantasies, in which I was a famous musician. I had no plan to bring this about, although by high school I was a fairly accomplished violinist. That is to say, I went as far as talent could provide. I had weekly private lessons and was expected to practice every day. I was always first chair in orchestra and would score As in the yearly New York State competitions. I won a scholarship to study violin after high school at the Crane School of Music. The music school had a good reputation and the college itself, part of the SUNY system, was cheap. I chose it for this reason. I knew I was not setting off into promise. I couldn't tell my parents this, so I did the next best thing: I decided to not waste their money.

Musicianship was a requirement for membership in our family. Of the two musical choices presented for girls (violin and piano) I preferred piano, but my sister, who was just enough older than I to choose first, had already claimed that. So I had the violin. But what I really wanted to play was electric guitar, though I had never even seen a girl holding one. Besides, guitar playing would have implied an interest in pop music, which was beneath contempt in our family, and which was also, as I left more and more behind, the only thing I was able to keep loving. I loved it in secret, keeping myself alive for it as others might go on for the sake of the children. *What if I died*, I wondered, *having not yet heard my favorite song?*

Of course by the time I was able to turn my attention to my real interests (which did not occur with any reliability until my early thirties), I found them decayed and immature. It was something like how I imagine the Sphinx must feel, arching up and gazing out of its stone form: I was an anachronism. This, at least, is one of the theories I sometimes use to explain to myself why I still look so young.

I hobbled through high school, by the tenth grade quitting most activities I once had loved or excelled in. I watched effetely from the sides of my life as my parents grew disappointed in me, then furious. I covered my tracks in a shroud of apathy equal to the intensity of my regrets. I quit track—unconscionable to my father—and would rejoin and quit several times during the rest of high school. I began to do badly in school. Meaning, I continued to get mostly As, but no longer because of my performance—rather, because I was an excellent fake, a seasoned impersonator of myself, and because brilliance was what by this time everyone and all my teachers had come to expect and thought they were still seeing in me.

I could immediately sense the most minimal passing requirement and, at the last split second, would most often fulfill it. I would rather have continued in my former excellence and obedience; I would have given anything for it; I still would. I was not, as I would be called from then on, rebellious. The way I lived seemed so strange to me, far from anything that had been presented as acceptable life or even as life. I imagined myself telling someone, and the only reaction I could conjure was deep perplexity and revulsion. I threw a hardback book at Mr. Lamoureaux, my French teacher, who threw it back at me but had excuses: A former fat man on an extreme diet, he was going through a divorce (still an uncommon thing in that place and time). I got cited for insubordination in gym, now the most troubling subject of all because it involved exposing my body—something I could not do. And in my senior year I managed actually to fail gym; I hadn't shown up for even one class. Instead of going to class I would hide in the woods just off the premises, crouching in the bushes, waiting for time to pass. Failing gym threatened my graduation and, rather than submit to summer school and shorts and public perspiration, I refused to acknowledge the grade. I simply did not allow them to fail me.

This sort of defensive offense was to become a characteristic of mine—that and the reliance on my former nature. These tactics worked for a long while: With the first, people simply did not know how to respond, and with the second, a lot could be squeezed from my past. Later, however, there would be nothing to fall back on, no remembered or defendable former life. I would rely on what had crept up in its stead: lying, secrecy, and omission.

I am assuming that I had begun much differently, but this is not necessarily true. One supposes all children are open, so I adopt this for myself as well. Actually I am mostly missing from my parents' specific memory. So, although I have asked what I was like, no real sense of me assembles. My father claimed I was putting him on the spot and so failed to produce an anecdote. My mother has the two stories, set pieces, that to her illustrate my precociousness. In the first one, I am an infant, breast-feeding, constantly distracted by some bright object on the floor and yanking my mother's nipple along with me as I jerk my head to explore. In the second one, I am also an infant, singing to myself and walking hand over hand around the perimeter of my crib. As the story goes, my parents would find me this way in the mornings, the tiny disembodied hands grabbing and releasing.

My sense of myself can best be explained by a phenomenon that I have come to call Big Little: a waking dream, not quite a feeling, but an intimation of one, a sensation. It is difficult to tell if it comes from inside or out. It slips over the body, yet has form—a column—that expands and contracts, flickering, as though trying to be brought into focus. When I would try to hold it, though, as I often did (or else close my eyes and wait for it to pass), it would escape. Big Little *is* my body: *Is it big? Is it little? Does it have feeling? Will it stay?* It is as though I am approaching myself from a distance, almost touching down, before being quickly sucked away. I rarely experience Big Little now, although for years it was a very common feeling. I suppose it has been mostly replaced by the sense of an actual body.

I had sleeping dreams also—nightmares for me—one that I had eaten at McDonald's, and another that I had moved into a fat person's body. I would awaken in terror, filled with an overpowering shame and dread. My waking thoughts were much the same: I wanted to become ever lighter, smaller, for my step to be soundless, my presence completely unknown. It occurs to me now that I have not been wholly unsuccessful. Many people I have lived with have been startled by my sudden presence, materializing without warning out of the silence. Not one former roommate has ever neglected to mention how he didn't know I was home, didn't hear me come in, never heard a sound from my room, would never have known I was there. This is, as those obliged to share their living space well know, arguably the most valuable attribute and the highest praise for a roommate to possess and elicit. And once I lived five years in an apartment in which everyone who entered left saying the same thing: "There is no evidence you live here." I liked to say I had to be ready to go, to pick up and leave at a moment's notice. But I have never been particularly adventuresome, romantic, or nomadic. Rather, I have always had the sense that someone or something is going to *make* me go, that I will not have the chance to collect my things—which brings to mind another of my nightmares: I return to my apartment to find my key no longer fits the lock.

The ability to leave, an antinesting instinct, is generally regarded as a male characteristic. It has been ascribed to me, bafflingly, when the truth is pretty much the opposite: I *stay*— well beyond good sense, personal safety, propriety, and I have spent a good portion of my writing life identifying with statues, sculptures, blighted and frozen things. But I've noticed that most often people take *appearance* as reality and the subject of one's art as pretense.

To be fair, I probably confuse people by other of my "male" characteristics: I wear no makeup and have been "cross-dressing" for most of my adult life, although this is less noticeable when one is female. I have managed, by practice of my condition, to completely suppress my reproductive system (I began, and stopped, menstruating at age fifteen and seemed not to go through puberty until I was thirty-six, having a similar reaction to the return of my period as the first time around—I thought I was dying). Until recently, I have had primarily male friends. As employment, I have mostly worked in privately owned record shops and, as anyone who has spent much time in them knows, they are almost exclusively the province of males.

I have felt separate from girls and women by nature, and I

have also knowingly separated myself from them. It is at once painful and satisfying. I hated emotions, and anything at all I came to associate with women: vulnerability, tenderness, manicures, compliance, shopping, Diet Coke, mollifying, heels, apologizing, deferment, flirting, dresses, asking permission, chit-chat, jealousy, nurturing, pleasing, breasts, neediness, laughter. I don't think I hated women so much as I hated the assumptions about them. But these I could not change, so I removed myself from women. It wasn't hard to do; they had never been kind to me.

I had always wanted to be a boy. Or perhaps I should say I have never wanted to be a girl. Boys seemed to have a natural resistance to doubt that I detested and envied. Perhaps this is what their straight bodies suggested to me—arrows, direction. I felt that gluttony or bulimia would have suited me better, that it was the very "choice" of my condition—always trying to be something I was not—and not the condition itself that suited my personality.

Recently, a male friend made a casual comment to me on the phone. "Well, that shouldn't be hard for you, you're practically a man anyway," he said. Many friends have said similar things, probably because of the masculine characteristics I've mentioned, especially the quintessential one: sleeping around. Their confusion reminds me of one I once had with a boy-friend who I thought might be gay; he was boyish, social, passive. It was a new model of maleness for me, one which, wanting to call it something, I sometimes settled for homosexuality. While no one has ever taken me for gay, I'm sure because of my appearance, I think what my friends might see in me is the female corollary to this: the absence of the convention-ally womanly—that combined with girlishness. It perplexes some—because the underfed form speaks, although softly, a confused and confusing opposition of signals: *I have no needs; take care of me.*

My immature figure is also why, I have come to think, a certain type of male finds me irresistible: generally in his late twenties to early thirties (although it has happened with men younger or much older than this), probably gay, and making a last desperate swipe at heterosexuality. For them I think I offer hope. I do not overpower with breasts and hips. I do not coax pronouncements of fidelity or commitment. I do not express an interest in marriage. I do not look like a promising candidate for childbirth. I appeal to the aesthetic senses of these men. I satisfy the condition, however slightly, of *femaleness.* And so their illusions can be pursued with minimal discomfort. I have sensed their desperation, their disappointment that I wouldn't just love them and so save them from the pain of their sexual futures. But I think, at least hope, that I have provided for them some other form of help, like a gender halfway house.

In college my tastes broadened: I began to substitute drinking for eating. A calorie was a calorie to me, and with drinking at least I had the hope of unconsciousness. And for a little while I could forget I was hungry. But I've never found drinking gratifying. It doesn't obliterate as promised. Neither do any of the drugs I have tried—I think a fair cross section. There is always a reservation, however slight; a region unaffected by my considerable attempts, like a maddeningly alert night watchman.

I binged my first year in college and returned home looking like everybody else who had been freed from their parents and done more of what they'd wanted. Only I hadn't: My extra weight was a product of the same old rules, except that I was losing my powers.

That summer my father took me aside and informed me that if I didn't do something about my weight now, it might be a problem for me later in life. My mother was away that summer, and I can't remember if my sister was home, probably because she had long ago given up acknowledging me. I had a job that summer picking up trash on the beach; at night I would ride my bike three miles, run six miles, and walk one mile, returning home well after my father had eaten. He seemed content that I was tackling my problem. I returned to college having lost more weight than I had gained, refocused in my purpose. My father never mentioned it again.

But what had begun for me that day at the start of high school, with a comment that I am certain Scott Calipari never thought of again, was an approach to life that I am tempted to say I would never shake. Twenty-two years have passed since that comment in the hall at school, and I still cannot imagine my life entirely free of rules about food. Not long ago, talking to a friend who has known me for fifteen of those twenty-two years, I remarked at how far I had come. And she conceded my view—up to a point. After all, many things are different, better. Whereas once I wore baggy clothes from neck to toe, never allowing an unnecessary inch of flesh to show, and never ate in restaurants but would order various flavored waters while my friends dined self-consciously away, I now have come to some sort of resigned and inevitable terms with my body and generally wear clothes appropriate for my size. And I eat in restaurants almost every time I go to one.

Guilt does not describe my feelings about eating, although there is always a moment, a change, during a meal. Perhaps it happens when I have finished half my food or—depending on what it is and also how it appears on the plate: one-third, five bites, two-thirds. Usually I cannot eat beyond two-thirds of the food on my plate; at that point I fear it might seem that I am eating too much, or that my interest in food might be apparent. Certainly it is not a sense of satisfaction that I am responding to. This is the point at which all enjoyment is over. Sometimes I will eat on, shamefully; sometimes I will stop, disgusted and sad. Not guilty, but ugly and conspicuous—as though I'm sitting under a hot white lamp.

What my friend had said, however, sounded about right, although I remember being startled by it at the time. I was on the way to proclaiming near recovery when she said casually, "It doesn't sound like you've been cured of anorexia, just that you've raised the bar a little." What she meant was that I now permit more calories and a broader range of foods, and I don't exactly count calories anymore—I don't have to; I calculate them instantly, reflexively, so quickly that the math is subsumed. I know the science behind all food, even in the case of foods I've never seen before; I can accurately hypothesize the ingredients, their proportions, and the caloric content. So now, when selecting what I am going to eat, I weigh my considerations in a flash and make my choice accordingly. You cannot see me do it, although I imagine that in that flash, my brow nettles and my eyes cloud. There are now also smaller considerations of desire and mood, hunger, and a larger one of nutrition, because of the damage rendered to my body from decades of abuse. But there was a time—most of my life—in which only the math had authority.

So if I was premature in the assessment of my progress, perhaps it is closer to the truth to say that my behaviors are less extreme and my appearance less severe. I have settled into a kind of *working* anorexia: not careening toward death, but— two words frequently used to describe me—disciplined, self-contained. It is, I suppose, anorexia's middle age, in which I give up my ideals and try to be more reasonable.

THE GHOST OF GORDOLFO GELATINO

Rudy Ruiz

———

"What's it gonna be, kid? C'mon! We ain't got all day," croaked the withered cafeteria worker, hulking behind the buffet counter in her mustard-colored polyester uniform. Her smoker's gargle bubbled in unison with the stews, gravies, and soups simmering between us.

I'd just begun to survey my options, determined not to choose hastily and end up with something less than the most savory and satisfying set of flavor combinations. After all, eating out with my *abuelito* and *abuelita* on Sundays was one of the scarce bright spots within the otherwise bleak rituals of my childhood in south Texas. Like civilized denizens of another era, my family would gather in their best outfits around the Formica tables of Luby's Cafeteria on Boca Chica Boulevard. I listened attentively as the grown-ups around me held discussions in Spanish on such serious subjects as the value of the peso, beef prices, and political corruption in Mexico.

Several times during the meal, the heads of other families would pause at our table to give their regards to my grandfather. I loved my *abuelito*. He was my hero. He was a tall and

149

ample patriarch, with pristine white locks combed back in neat grooves atop an angular Italian face. I adored the tales of his success, and I marveled at his spartan restraint. My grandfather owned over fifteen thousand acres of ranch land flanking the Gulf of Mexico, three thousand head of cattle, and blocks of downtown property in Matamoros—the city across the border from where we lived in Brownsville. But despite his wealth, he was devoted to austerity. As my *abuelita* frequently reminded me, my *abuelito* grew up as one of fourteen children during the Mexican Revolution. He learned how to mend his own clothes and to eat frugally so there would be more for his siblings. He left home when he was fourteen, and later raised nine children during the Great Depression. Even years later, during those lunches at Luby's, he ate little. He always ordered the Luann platter—the child's plate—which consisted of a half serving of baked fish, a lump of soggy spinach, and a dollop of mashed potatoes. He drank ice water. He was an icon to me—one whose powers of will and restraint I could only hope to someday inherit.

As I stood paralyzed before the splendid smorgasbord behind the counter, gazing across the growing space between me and my *abuelito,* the cafeteria lady brandished her tongs.

"Kid! Make a choice!" she barked. "What's it gonna be?"

But how to choose? My eyes nervously scanned the options. There was the fried fish in its neat little rectangle: crunchy on the outside, mushy on the inside. There was chicken-fried steak; tough but tangy. There was also fried chicken, fried shrimp, fried okra, french fries, fried rice. Mashed potatoes, gravy, broccoli smothered in cheese sauce, rolls, desserts lined up in endless rows. And, as the "healthy" option, a giant presentation of lime Jell-O salad. To immigrants like my parents, eager to be as Betty Crocker–American as possible, Jell-O was a salad, despite the marshmallows suspended in it.

The next man in line pressed against me in impatience. "Rodolfo!" my mom called, waving frantically. My baby brother shrieked in the next room.

"Kid, someone's gonna die of starvation if you don't do something here!" The cafeteria lady's lips curled into a sick smile, and her smoke twined its way through the steam above the counter. Tears pricked my eyes and my tummy jiggled as I fought back rising sobs.

My mother's heels clicked rapidly across the floor, and my cheeks flushed as red as the ketchup that squirted from dispensers on every table in the dining area. In pity, the restless mob behind me fell silent at last as my mom pulled me away, leaving my tray behind.

At the table, I sulked. My parents, preoccupied with feeding my disabled younger brother, Raul, and the baby, Gerardo, ignored me. While nobody was looking, my *abuelito* quietly slid his Luann platter my way.

I don't know why this memory stays with me out of so many uneventful Sundays at Luby's. Looking back, however, it seems to foreshadow what would happen to me in high school—when, not knowing what to eat, or how to eat healthily, I opted for nothing at all. I began to emulate my grandfather's discipline that I so admired. But, in my fervor to exercise restraint, it turned out I lacked it: I went too far and lost control.

In my nuclear family, I did not have examples of how to eat healthily. We ate the same hearty food as earlier generations—except they had worked in the fields all day and hadn't supplemented their three home-cooked meals with corn syrup–sweetened soft drinks and snacks of potato chips and Oreos. My parents fed us in accordance with tradition, but they were not familiar with the modern-day science of nutrition. In middle and high school, I used to anguish about my rolls of fat and ask my mom if what we ate was healthy.

"Mom, is bacon good for you?"

"Yes, Rodolfo. Bacon is meat."

"Mom, is Coke fattening?" (Our family hardly drank anything else.)

"No. Coke has zero grams of fat. Look at the label."

When I was twelve years old, my pediatrician told my mother (after my annual checkup) that I had a "propensity toward fatness." I felt humiliated and defeated. Did my doctor mean I had no control over my physical destiny—that I had no choice but to be fat? My mother, who struggled with her own weight, thought the pediatrician was overreacting to what she considered healthy plumpness for a growing boy. We looked at the diet she recommended, and it seemed like a way of eating from another planet, or perhaps for another species. People actually ate celery sticks? I thought that was rabbit food.

But my mother also felt guilty, worrying that she might have caused my "propensity." After that doctor's appointment, she admitted to me that she force-fed me as a baby. She blamed it on her obsessiveness (she was diagnosed with OCD) as well as on her unhappiness at the time. Lonely and trapped in a doomed marriage, she would hold me hostage in the high chair, trying to make me eat even when I rejected it. Sometimes, she said, she fed me until I threw up. As a new mom, her only way of feeling okay about herself was if I was plump and "healthy"—our culture's paragon of the perfect baby.

Years later, I was still that "healthily" plump boy, causing me torment both at home and at school. I have another painful memory from that period about our Sunday ritual.

Every week, after Luby's, we made the pilgrimage back across the border to Matamoros, where my ancestors were born. It took only five minutes. Driving over the bridge that spanned the tiny, dammed-up creek otherwise known as the Rio Grande, we would arrive smack in the middle of the residential neighborhood known as Colonia Jardín. In stark contrast to the rest of the chaotic city, the Colonia was a lush and tranquil oasis, offering tree-lined streets and gardens, night watchmen on every corner, and a sense of security behind high walls crowned with broken glass. Half of the houses in the neighborhood must have belonged to one of my relatives. Beyond my grandparents' home, there were those of Tío Oscar, Tío Alfonso, Tío Lalo, Tía Lulu, Tía Lili, Tía Lilí (whose names were distinguished only by the accent falling on a different syllable). During the afternoons, between lunch at Luby's and evening Mass at the cathedral in Matamoros, we'd visit my aunts and uncles. Everywhere we went, we were offered pastries, snacks, coffees, and sodas. The adults rocked on porches or sat in formal living rooms while the children played in a sprawling game room separated by a courtyard from the main house.

One Sunday, I bounded eagerly toward the game room, seeking a break from the dueling drooling of my siblings. The Luby's lunch-line fiasco was a rare exception from my habitual overconsumption of fried food, so my jiggly tummy would have stretched the fabric of my Polo shirt as I lumbered in. Panting, flushed, I squinted through my steamy glasses. Holding court among his friends, my older cousin Juanito grinned as he lowered his pool cue onto the green felt of the table and beamed sarcastically at me. "Well, look who it is!" he said. "My little cousin, Gordolfo Gelatino!"

It took a few moments for the joke to dawn on me, while the cackles rose in front of me like an invisible wall. Juanito and his entourage laughed so hard, a couple of his lanky friends collapsed onto the leather couches to catch their breath. "Gordolfo Gelatino, get it?" they panted in cruel glee.

The gears in my head slowly clicked. Rodolfo Valentino was the Spanish version of silent-screen legend Rudolph Valentino's name. *Gordo* means "fat" in Spanish. Hence . . . Gordolfo. But perhaps the coup de grâce was the second half of my new nickname: Gelatino. Need I say more? This was bilingual punnery at its best.

Sucking in my stomach, I hung my head, turned, and left the room, retreating to the adults and their political discussion. But the name echoed in my mind. Juanito addressed me by it on every occasion thereafter. Suddenly, family gatherings were no longer especially fun. They ceased to be a haven from the mockery at school. The insults were in another language, but they weren't that different, and, because this was family, they cut more deeply.

I came to dread seeing Juanito. I started wearing loose-fitting shirts and spending time in front of the mirror, staring at my pudgy self in disgust. Turning sidewise, I assessed my protruding profile, breathing in the rolls that rendered me "Gordolfo."

Then, one scorching summer day on the two-lane ribbon of road between Matamoros and the Laguna Madre, Juanito and his dad had an accident. Their truck flipped over onto the side of the road. My Tío Alfonso died in the tangled wreckage, and, according to the story told in horror by my aunts and uncles, Juanito supposedly walked for miles before finding help, bathed in a mixture of his own and his father's blood. After that, Juanito morphed into a forlorn shell of a person. He didn't bother calling me Gordolfo Gelatino anymore. He limped slightly, rarely looking people in the eye. Guiltily, I wondered if this was his punishment.

———

But my own minuscule emotional crises, and real crises like Juanito's accident, were rare dramas in the general tedium of life on the border, which usually flowed as slowly as my passage through the lunch line at Luby's. The faces around me remained the same from kindergarten through high school. The same family members attended every event. The grass was always green; you couldn't even mark the changing of the seasons. Sometimes I wonder if my self-conscious relationship with food—how, as a child, I measured the week by those beloved Sunday lunches, and how, as a teenager, I marked hours by what I *didn't* eat—was just a way to carve a shape into the seemingly endless stream of time.

The discipline I began to exercise over food was also a way of gearing up for my escape. As early as grade school, I dreamed of attending Harvard, just like so many of the presidents whose biographies I devoured in the school library while other children ran about on the playground. Amid the provincial monotony I was born into, I yearned not only for change, but for a remarkable life.

———

Unfortunately, my grades did not always reflect my high ambitions.

On the last day of eighth grade, I stared in shock at the report card quivering in my hands. Sixty-eight? Who gets a 68 in PE? My gym teacher, Mr. Finger, was a hard, mean, less-than-brilliant man, one of those jock bullies who never stop taunting the misfits who linger on the bench and get picked last when teams are formed. But the fact was, Coach Finger had every right to fail me. I had failed PE. I hated "dressing out," fearing that all the other boys would see my flabby pale skin and mock me. I hated my legs, which were covered in pimples. I hated how my glasses fogged up as we exited the gym and trod onto the damp, mosquito-infested fields. I yearned for rain so there would be no PE class at all, but the south Texas sky was stubbornly cloudless. Instead, I sat fully clothed on the bench for days on end, watching the other kids run, play, laugh, and make friends. Coach Finger never offered me a hand. He just joined the other kids in poking fun at me.

One of my classmates, a hulk named Omar, christened me Toad, after a character in a Saturday-morning cartoon we were all familiar with. Toad was the sidekick to the show's villainous vampire. Whenever Toad screwed things up, which he invariably did, his master admonished him: "Bad Toad!" Then Toad would self-flagellate, swatting at the flies that buzzed about his slimy, fat head and subserviently repeating: "Yes, Master. Bad Toad. Bad Toad."

On that last day of middle school, as the other kids signed each other's yearbooks, I quietly climbed on my bike and rode home crying. A 68. Sure, there were nineties and eighties on my report card, too, but I knew my parents would focus on the 68, as if it were the only number on the page. I had come to St. Joseph's, the school where my father had played football in his youth, to blossom into a scholar. Yet so far, to my parents' distress, I was underachieving, lethargic, an enigma. And I was entering my freshman year. From that point on, every grade would matter for college applications.

———

"If you do not make Dean's List this quarter, I'm pulling you out of St. Joe and putting you in public school," my father threatened as he drove me to school one morning during my sophomore year in his rattling pickup truck.

"But, Dad, I'm just starting to like St. Joe. I have friends now," I pleaded.

"I don't care about your friends," my dad snarled, pulling the truck over to the side of the road. "I care about you. You're smart enough to be number one in your class. That school costs me a lot of money. You better make something of yourself. I had to mow the football field—"

—*in order to pay my way through school.* I silently finished his sentence.

He concluded, "So you better get this straight. It's now or never. No more chances."

My dad had used this scare tactic before, but this time I sensed a different tone in his voice, and I knew he meant it. He didn't care that at last I had a couple of geek friends at whose houses I played Dungeons & Dragons after school. He didn't care that I was the band's star trumpet player. All he cared about was my making Dean's List.

Like my beloved *abuelito,* who was my mother's father, my dad extolled the virtues of perseverance, willpower, and determination. He had been the first in his family to graduate from college. To him, I had it easy, and he couldn't understand why I would waste the opportunities he had worked so hard to give me.

My dad intimidated me, but by high school, I couldn't look up to him the way I did to my *abuelito*. Dad was obsessed with being professionally successful, but not nearly as devoted to being a good husband. He hid behind his work as a pharmacist, spending long hours behind his drugstore counter and leaving my mother alone with three children, one of whom was severely handicapped. He didn't give her the support she needed.

Still, although my doubts about my father were growing, I was moved by his threats about taking me out of St. Joe's. I yearned desperately to live up to his expectations. I knew that, even if it didn't always seem like he cared about me right now, he certainly cared about my future.

At school that same week, I overheard several of the class brains heatedly discussing their class rankings. Class rankings? I didn't know anyone was keeping track! But then I learned that our college guidance counselor had made our rankings available so we could start planning for college.

I met with the counselor, whose name (and figure) reminded me of an avocado, in her office. I watched intently as she leafed through her papers.

"Your rank, Mr. Ruiz, is eleven," Mrs. Avocado said.

"Eleven?" I asked.

"Yes, that should get you into the University of Texas if you get a decent SAT score." Her job done, she smiled in satisfaction.

I summoned up my courage. "But I want to go to Harvard," I said.

The Avocado nearly rolled off her seat.

"Harvard?" she said, giggling like a nervous schoolgirl. "Ha! Run along, Mr. Ruiz. I have an appointment."

"Can I look at the brochures? Can I see what it takes to get in?" I asked, scanning the catalogs on her walls.

"You can look all you want," she pursed her lips. "But we don't have that book on the shelves. You should focus on UT or SMU. St. Mary's isn't all that bad, either, you know."

That day, I sat in class and tuned out the drone of my teachers while I calculated my averages. The new grading period had begun a week earlier. Already, I had netted a sixty-eight on a pop geometry quiz and a forty-four on an English quiz about a book I hadn't liked enough to bother reading.

In the months that followed, my study habits underwent a radical transformation. I began reading every line of every assigned book or short story two or three times, anxious that I would forget something that might be on a test later. I grew so focused on perfecting my scores that not only did I obsess over making sure that my answers were correct, but I also fussed over my penmanship, fearing that the teacher might misread one of my answers and mark it wrong out of habit. In geometry class, I volunteered to tutor other kids for extra credit. I cleaned the blackboard after class in order to talk with the teacher. When the tests were handed back, I was the first to dash to the teacher's desk with a knot in my throat to fight for every measly point that I thought had been incorrectly deducted. Sometimes I argued so intensely I was sent to detention. Still, week by week, my grades rose. By midway through the grading period, my grades had moved up into the eighties in both English and geometry. I also noticed that I was losing weight; my new focus on schoolwork had cut down the time I

spent watching TV and eating junk food. According to my
D&D dork buddies, a girl or two had possibly even looked
at me.

As the end of the semester drew near, I was summoned to
the guidance counselor's offices. Mr. Dean, an older gentleman
with a bushy mustache and flouncy-bouncy salt-and-pepper
hair, sat in the office next to Mrs. Avocado's. His job was to
help the crazy kids. What did he want with me?

"Have a seat, Rudy." Mr. Dean smiled, motioning to the
ripped vinyl chair in the cramped supply closet that served as
his office.

"Is something wrong?" I pictured Mayra Vera, the girl from
our class who had locked herself in the library closet and
refused to come out for hours. She was the kind of kid that
spent time in Mr. Dean's office, not me. Maybe it was the
Dungeons & Dragons. Maybe it had scared someone into
thinking I was a Satanist. (That's what my paternal grandma
believed.)

"Nothing's wrong at all," Mr. Dean replied, amused. "Rudy,
remember when I did that inkblot assessment for you last
year?"

I nodded.

"Well, I think you're a very talented kid with a lot of potential. Talk in the teachers' lounge is you're turning things
around."

"Really?" I gaped. *People talk in there about me?*

"Anyway . . ." Mr. Dean produced a bulky envelope from
a desk drawer. "I overheard your conversation with Mrs.
Avocado." (Of course he didn't call her Mrs. Avocado; he used
her real name.) "Don't tell her I did this, but I went ahead and
ordered you something."

He handed me the heavy package. Tearing it open, I was delighted to find a shiny crimson brochure full of photos and information about Harvard.

My eyes danced with glee. "Mr. Dean, I don't know what to say."

"Don't say anything. Just study hard. I know you can do it."

At home that night, I locked myself in my room, turned down the heavy metal, and pored over the materials from the Harvard admissions office. They said most of the students accepted were in the top 10 percent of their class. There were only seventy students in my class, so this meant I had some work to do, but I had a chance.

I tried harder than ever at school. I lost more weight. When the report cards came out at the end of the year, for the first time they included our class rankings. My classmates in English and geometry huddled around as I opened the envelope. Nineties lined the page. I'd done it. I'd reached the goal. My eyes settled on the class rankings at the bottom. I was now tenth in the class. And for the grading period, I was number one.

That day, when they handed out the yearbooks, I loitered until my mom would wait for me no longer. I gathered as many signatures as I could. And I made myself a promise. That summer I was going to keep losing weight, get in shape, and get a tan. I would return for my junior year ready to take the world by storm. For the first time in my life, I felt empowered. I was controlling my own destiny, steering my course out of the shadows of both Gordolfo Gelatino and the stultifying border world.

———

I started skipping meals. Total restraint seemed easier than moderation. I started jogging, too.

I avoided the flour tortillas, and the delicious little *taquitos* that explode in your mouth because the tortillas have been fried to a crisp and then proceed to melt warmly, oozing with cheese, greasy ground beef, and rich Mexican cream. It was hard to eat just one bite, so better to avoid them altogether. At the grocery checkout aisle, I picked up a handbook for counting calories.

For the first time, I learned how rich my family's staple foods were, and since they were too delicious to eat in moderation, I avoided them altogether. I cut out the *barbacoa* tacos, the chorizo *con huevo,* the *queso fundido,* the pork rinds, the eggs cooked in leftover bacon grease. I stared at the pantry in fear, ripping through packages, reading the labels. A tiny chocolate chip cookie had how many grams of fat? How many calories? Oh, my God!

That summer, I survived on Lipton's Diet Iced Tea. I had my parents buy it for me like I was a baby and that was my formula. It came in a little blue jar. Two heaping spoonfuls of that powdery panacea and I was good to go for hours, my tummy temporarily filled with saccharin and cold water.

The rolls came off. When I looked in the mirror, I was no longer Gelatinous. At my heaviest, I must have weighed about 145 pounds, which was husky for a five-feet-four fifteen-year-old. By fall I weighed in at 120.

The feedback was positive. I suddenly had more friends. I was even spotted occasionally with the popular crowd, many of whom appreciated my new look or harbored a newfound respect for my intellect. I was on a roll. I kept skipping meals. My mom worried. A coach at my school encouraged me to get serious about jogging, allowed me onto the track team, and helped me learn techniques for long-distance running. Suddenly, unbelievably, I was almost an athlete. I didn't look like Toad anymore. Who was I becoming? I convinced myself I was evolving into my dream vision: a cool, smart, athletic, musically talented, Harvard-bound guy. No Gordolfo Gelatino in sight.

As I continued to lose weight, some people began to inquire if I was sick.

"No, of course not," I'd tell them. "I just run a lot, three miles a day. I'm in shape, that's all."

My mom and *abuelita* nagged me incessantly to eat, so I avoided them as much as possible. I stopped going to my *abuelito's* house. The food there was too fattening, and I resented the constant attempts to feed me. My mother may have had the power to fatten me up as an infant, but she wouldn't get away with it again. And as my weight plummeted, even my dad became concerned, although he'd never express it directly. Instead, he tried to sneak some extra calories into me by slipping an egg into the morning smoothie he'd started making for me since I refused to eat anything else before heading off for school. When he wasn't watching, I dumped it in the sink.

———

By the middle of junior year, my Harvard prospects were brightening. But people kept asking if I was sick. My clothes hung loosely. I weighed 104 pounds. My parents—who juggled taking care of me, my two younger siblings, financial problems, and a collapsing marriage—had little time to delve deeply into my situation. They worried, but they were ill-equipped to help. They never asked what might be at the root of my eating disorder. They never probed what I might need or what might be missing in my life. They never took me to a counselor or psychologist, despite the fact that my behavior was coupled with hypochondria and interminable hand-washing. They just begged me to eat more. And I didn't.

That spring, our school band took a trip to Dallas. Band trips were always a blast: an escape from parents, the boredom of life in a small border town, and a chance to romp around with friends. Aside from the competition, we had an itinerary full of excursions, including South Fork Ranch (where the TV show *Dallas* was set) and Six Flags.

Without my parents to pressure me, I didn't eat. It wasn't even hard for me to skip meals. I knew I didn't have to lose more weight, so that was no longer my motivation. At this point, I derived a sense of power and superiority as I watched others eat. They were mere humans who required their three meals a day for survival. I looked down on them from my ethereal pedestal. In my mind, I was above them. I saw not eating as an extension of the trait I believed was the key to my success: my will. I could will myself to lose weight. I could will myself to be top in my class. I could will myself into Harvard. My will was indomitable.

On the last evening of the trip, we went to the rodeo. I don't know when I'd last eaten a meal, and I wandered about in a daze. My vision blurred. My thinking became fuzzy and shapeless. The center of my torso became a small, cold stone grinding its way to the surface. I stared at a campfire for a long time, wondering if I would faint. I observed the other kids laughing, watching the cowboys do rope tricks and ride bucking broncos. I watched them happily eat their sloppy joes and their baby back ribs. I finally questioned what in the world was wrong with me. I knew then something had to change. Something had to stop. Or better yet: start. I needed to eat . . . if I could remember how.

———

Strangely enough, I did. I began to eat again. I realized if I kept jogging, I didn't gain much weight. It was comforting to learn I could eat and still maintain control. Steadily, I gained enough over the course of my senior year to appear healthy in my school photos. I was accepted to Harvard. I jumped up and down on the front lawn, waving the thick acceptance packet in the air. Two months later, I shed Brownsville, the border, and my dysfunctional home. And it seemed for the most part that I'd left my bout with anorexia behind, as well.

However, my weight has continued to yo-yo over the years. The pediatrician's warning that I would battle with my weight has become a self-fulfilling prophecy—although it is not fat and normal I alternate between, but normal and too thin. Every time I hit my maximum of 160 pounds or so, I begin to freak out, becoming uncomfortable in my own skin. And I start the dance again, cutting back, skipping a meal here or there, jogging. But I only drop to 145 before my self-preservation instinct kicks in, triggered by the memories of my high school days.

Just like those Sundays when I was a child, when my family would drive back and forth across the Mexico-U.S. border, today I oscillate between the realms of healthy and unhealthy eating. My feelings about my adolescent eating disorder are also divided. I regret it and yet simultaneously cherish the role it played in shaping me. It coincided with a period of academic success that helped me change my future. The combination filled me with a sense of accomplishment and gave me an enduring faith in my power to mold myself into who I want to be.

While the days of hurtful nicknames and clever cousins are over, to this day I am haunted every time I raise a fork, or choose instead to put it down. I pause and wonder: Am I in control? Or is it the ghost of Gordolfo Gelatino?

EARTHLY IMPERFECTIONS

Lisa Halliday

———

The summer I turned fourteen I began cleaning houses for money. I took out a small advertisement in the local newspaper, pinned flyers to bulletin boards and telephone poles around town, and soon accumulated about a dozen clients whose houses I cleaned at a rate of two per day. Each house took approximately three hours. The money I earned went into a savings account earmarked for the eventual purchase of a car and college tuition. Some weeks, working steadily, I made as much as $300.

To each of these appointments I rode my bicycle. It was large, a man's bicycle that once belonged to my father, and to ride it without bruising my groin I had to stand on the pedals.

In my customers' houses I picked up toys, tidied dens, made beds, dusted and polished furniture, vacuumed rugs, washed dishes, scrubbed counters, swept and mopped floors, scoured sinks and toilets, and laundered and folded clothes. I moved quickly, anxious not to arouse suspicion that I was taking advantage of being paid by the hour. For the most part, I enjoyed this work, particularly the glimpses into other people's lives, the ample time alone, even the physical demands. Moving furniture, lifting vacuum cleaners up and down flights of stairs, pushing mops across linoleum—the exertion made my muscles ache and my skin shine with sweat. Between six hours of brisk domestic labor and my unwieldy mode of transportation around town, I must have burned an extra thousand calories each day. Yet despite always having a free hour or so between my morning and afternoon jobs, despite having had no more than an apple or pear for breakfast before starting out, I never ate lunch. This was not because contending with strangers' soils ruins the appetite (though of course it does), but because it was during this summer of heightened financial conscientiousness that I developed anorexia.

My mother married for the first time when she was eighteen and became pregnant with me within a year. She separated from my father, eleven years her senior, when I was four; we moved with my younger sister into a house with another man—my future stepfather. This man, at that time, was an alarmingly temperamental person whose tolerance of my sister and me felt so brittle, so strictly conditional on our quietest, most inconspicuous behavior, that it seemed to require vigilance even in our sleep. Neither he nor my mother had gone to college, but during her first marriage my mother had taught herself to sew and gradually acquired an impressive clientele as a seamstress. Her boyfriend was a pest exterminator, and in addition to sewing my mother realized a business plan for a little pest-control company. Still young and intently focused on her own entrepreneurial pursuits, she gave no impression of living vicariously through her daughters. Certainly she was the most present and influential of our four parents (our biological father, with whom we spent every other weekend, eventually remarried as well), yet her presence and influence were remarkably unobtrusive, her parenting style sensible and responsible while in the main laissez-faire.

It was outside home where I sought attention. I was an eager, gregarious student who thrived on good grades and adults' approbation. I acted in plays, tap-danced in musicals, sang the national anthem at basketball games, and gave impassioned orations on the facts and fictions of democracy. If I heard a good joke I repeated it a half dozen times before the day was over, caring little if an interlocutor responded with a blank look or a groan. Of course there were moments of embarrassment and self-consciousness, but these were discrete and appropriate to the circumstances. As late as in preadolescence there was still nothing of the sadness and anxiety that would accompany the relentless self-evaluation of my teens.

In junior high and high school I continued to perform onstage and in the classroom, but the pleasure of performance, and indeed of my playful tendencies in general, became stultified by self-consideration and self-doubt.

I cannot think of any distinct critical event that might have been responsible for this shift. I attribute it to years of feeling on guard at home, followed by the bewildering biochemical effects of puberty. Friends were no longer merely easy afterschool companions; now they were public accessories, tenuously allied. I wasn't so fickle as to renounce anyone in favor of a more prestigious social profile, but I was terrified of being renounced myself. I wasn't so shallow that I valued looks over intelligence, but I wasn't sufficiently confident in my own cleverness not to feel vacuous when someone listened to what I had to say with his eyes on my breasts. And whereas I had been content previously to measure my academic and extracurricular abilities against a set of unambiguous standards—an A-plus was a perfect test score; a violin concerto played according to tempo and without a single wrong note was a perfect performance—with adolescence, a stern skepticism of these same standards set in. Surely an A-plus at the public high school I attended was no better than a B at the private academies to which some of my classmates had defected. An instructor having more worldliness than mine would probably rate my violin playing no more favorably than my cat, who at the sight of the instrument used to run out of the room. And now that I had a job, a real job—not babysitting or a paper route but my own, bona fide business—I worried that no matter how conscientiously I worked, my services would not be deemed worth $10 an hour. In short: It became impossible, except in fleeting and infrequent spells, to forget myself.

In the interest of achieving safe, indisputable competence and acceptability, I sought standards against which I could measure my existing faculties. Objectivity seemed to me of especial importance. Possibly what I truly craved, rather than objective standards, were standards higher than those I had encountered so far—guidelines along which I could evolve with direction but without limit.

Meanwhile, my mother, whom I never considered overweight, went on a diet. My girlfriends, also thin enough to my mind, became preoccupied with their bodies and what they were eating in a tacitly competitive way. In the houses I cleaned I saw magazines advertising weight-loss advice and cupboards and refrigerators stocked with dietetic foods.

Enter the scale: a substitute adjudicator. While it would not rate my intellect, my musical capacity, or how well I waxed a floor, it nevertheless (and despite its intrinsic relativism) became my standard for truth in an ill-advised pursuit of objectivity. Appealing to the scale for an indication of my personal value was at once an attempt to measure my success among humans and my retaliation against human subjectivity. The machine's needle, every morning settling into its silent judgment, black against white—the very mode of anorectic thinking—seemed to me proof that objectivity, and therefore truth, exists.

———

"Hunger," wrote Hemingway, "is good discipline." At the Luxembourg museum:

> [A]ll the paintings were sharpened and clearer and more beautiful if you were belly-empty, hollow-hungry. I learned to understand Cézanne much better and to see truly how he made landscapes when I was hungry. I used to wonder if he were hungry too when he painted; but I thought possibly it was only that he had forgotten to eat. It was one of those unsound but illuminating thoughts you have when you have been sleepless or hungry. Later I thought Cézanne was probably hungry in a different way.

Not long after I started cleaning houses and stopped eating properly I began to experience the altered consciousness of being hungry as something like a drug-induced high. The colors of my suburban surroundings took on an almost hallucinatory brilliance. Music acquired a crystalline quality. Words in books appeared more starkly and urgently against the page. It is commonly supposed of people who refuse to eat that they perpetuate hunger partly for its anesthetizing effect. Paradoxically, hunger can also expand one's aesthetic sensitivities.

It was during the evenings of my first summer of not eating, when I had ridden my bicycle home from the day's last house-cleaning job, that I felt most painfully hungry. To curb the discomfort, I lay virtually motionless on my bed. To distract myself from it, I read.

Reading and not eating were pursuits to which I would become addicted over the next few years. Some of what I read as a teenager were books I had been introduced to in school: *The Good Earth, The Great Gatsby, The Grapes of Wrath, The Old Man and the Sea, Of Mice and Men,* and *Moby-Dick.* Others I took home from the library by the half dozen: some pulp, but also some genuine literature I would not have had the quietude and concentration to read if not for my chronically underfed condition. By the end of the day, stomach long empty, I had minimal energy for output. Resigned to eat nothing other than a piece of fruit in the morning and, when my mother was home, as little dinner as she would let me get away with, I fed on words instead.

I had always been an ardent reader, but it was not until this period, contemporaneous with my strict experiments in avoiding food, that reading took hold as a source of calm and contentment. Reading was my retreat, my submission to remote authorities, and my escape from otherwise relentless self-regard. Reading often meant coming up against an empathetic connection, even in physical solitude. For anyone besieged by hormones and apocalyptic surges of self-consciousness, such a connection is a rare solace—felicitously, one that comforts without threatening a teenager's fledgling senses of privacy and self. The reader remains largely in control; the submission to authority can always be aborted, the book shut.

In literature, hunger is often a romantic notion. For Hemingway, the years described in *A Moveable Feast* were his hungry years—hunger being not merely the dues paid by the starving artist but also an indispensable part of his aesthetic education. Hunger also appears in fiction as a by-product of happiness. *Anna Karenina*'s Levin, elated at having his love for Kitty reciprocated, goes an entire day and night without eating, while feeling "not only fresher and better than ever, but completely independent of his body: he moved without any effort of his muscles, and felt capable of anything." Levin's happiness is not the result of going without food; on the contrary, not needing food was a symptom of his happiness. Food is the last thing on Levin's mind during the hours leading up to his and his beloved's engagement. His strength and ecstasy have another source.

As a teenager, I knew nothing firsthand of Hemingway's Paris, nor of the magnitude of happiness Tolstoy's Levin felt at being in love. What I did know was what it was like to experience a sustained abstinence from food. If neither artistically nor romantically, then at least hungrily I could imagine myself in good company. Never mind that my discipline wasn't directed toward producing serious literature and that the happiness I felt each time the scale's needle shifted leftward wasn't the real thing. Familiarity with the severe sensation of prolonged hunger seemed to me a prerequisite for an adult intellectual and artistic life: for living hard, for living romantically, and, ironically, for living well.

By the time I started high school, I had lost about twenty pounds. I am naturally a small person, only five feet two, and I'd never weighed much more than a hundred; these were twenty pounds I did not need to lose. My period became irregular. I was often cold. I didn't believe I would never eat well again; I believed that once I was happier with myself and with my prospects in life—and such a moment would reveal itself unmistakably, like a bright yellow finish line passing under my feet—whether and what I was eating would cease to be an obsession. Deferral, however—of nourishment, of indulgence, and, perhaps most important, of this amorphous future happiness—was itself a perverse pleasure I resisted giving up. It was my first taste of anticipation as more delicious than the object itself.

The harm I might have been causing my body was not a consideration. Possibly this was because my eating disorder only approached, never actually became, seriously dangerous. More likely it was because as a teenager I had little conception of death and therefore little regard for protecting my life. I felt invulnerable. In fact, I believed the enviable condition of thinness could only make me stronger. Later, when the addiction to hunger surpassed any regard for my weight, the damage I was doing might have alarmed me—but not more than the prospect of surrendering what I thought to be a superior state of mind and self-control. I maintained a fierce conviction that friends and family urged me to eat out of resentment—because they had not my well-being and self-esteem in mind, but their own. I mistrusted attempts to persuade me to eat because I suspected them actually to be attempts to divest me of my crucial, self-protective strengths: willpower, self-awareness, self-control, effectiveness, resistance to being dissuaded by others . . . even my humility. That such well-intentioned tendencies, carried out to extremes, can be self-destructive I was too blinkered to comprehend. Nor did I understand yet that when a virtue becomes self-destructive it ceases to be virtuous. I rejected any intervention that threatened to undermine my pursuit of perfection.

———

According to geometry, a perfect circle exists only in the mind. In the physical world, a circle drawn on a page or arranged out of rope can be improved upon an infinite number of times without yielding satisfaction; a microscope will always reveal a wobble or dent in its curve. To live in the physical world is to contend with imperfections.

And yet *perfection* is one of the words most commonly used by anorectics to describe their goal. Why aspire to be something categorically elusive? The answer may be more approachable via a slightly different question: Why aspire to *create* something perfect if perfection is categorically elusive? For a composer, or a cabinetmaker, the word *perfection* must have a different significance; it must remain the act of trying to make something perfect while being aware that the condition is unattainable. There is no such thing as perfection in human-made creations, only gradations of imperfection.

The viability in perfecting one's own body also relies on perfection being limited to the act merely approaching the condition. To be perfect is to be beyond improvement, finished. What would this mean for a living body? In Nathaniel Hawthorne's short story "The Birthmark," a man regards the "crimson stain" on his wife's cheek to be "the visible mark of earthly imperfection" and urges her to have it removed. Uncertainly, she agrees, and for a moment the procedure is a success: Seeing his wife without the birthmark, her husband declares her "perfect"—but then she dies, because the mark had been "the bond by which an angelic spirit kept itself in union with a mortal frame." It's a fable, of course; removing a birthmark should not kill a person, or at least not for the paranormal reason Hawthorne suggests—however, the potential lethality of trying to become physically perfect is certainly real. Among the disturbing considerations of anorexia is that one of its virtuous-sounding guises, "the pursuit of perfection," effectively entails the erasure of oneself. Many anorectic people lose so much weight that it would seem the perfect person they aspire to become is no version of the original. And for some the project of bodily perfection ends in death.

———

I continued to clean houses throughout high school. From September through June I scheduled customers' appointments around play rehearsals, violin lessons, softball games, and homework, while each summer I resumed housecleaning full-time. By my junior year I had saved enough money for a used Oldsmobile. During my senior year I was accepted by a college I'd felt certain was beyond me, news received over the phone from my mother while I stood in someone else's kitchen holding a mop.

The summer before I left for college, still reading volumi-nously about countries and cultures that were unfamiliar to me, I became impatient to move on. Not eating then served as a way for me to prepare for the future. By losing weight I felt I was cleaning myself, priming the slate for new relationships and impressions.

And yet there was an undercurrent of apprehension about leaving home. Not eating became newly remedial.

Literature had by now impressed upon me the inexorability of time. *You Can't Go Home Again,* the title of Thomas Wolfe's novel, spoke precisely to the source of my anxiety: While the households in which we grow up aren't always happy places, they are still the shelters of our youths, often difficult at age seventeen or eighteen to leave behind.

But not eating alters one's perception of time. When I was fiercely hungry, time swelled, and decelerated. While I would wait, and wait—to eat, for time to pass while I wasn't eating—I perceived each moment to be longer than the last and therefore imbued with greater intensity and potential. My breathing slowed; my heart beat less frequently. As a result I felt more in control, that I had more temporal and mental space in which to check myself and undertake self-improvements for a more successful future.

Meanwhile, anorexia, my taste in prose, and even house-cleaning began to appeal to a common aesthetic that continues a decade later to govern aspects of my life.

My literary taste tends still to be ascetic, lean: not in terms of a book's overall length, but a line-to-line spareness of text, often the cleverest conduit for an unwieldy idea. Crystallized language, nothing extraneous, an elegance of proportion and unfussy style, streamlined passages: These are the artistic qualities of literature I am most often drawn to.

Though I no longer clean houses for money, I remain fastidiously neat and predisposed to spartan, immaculate surroundings.

Anorexia I seem to have evaded. There were intervals in my late teens and early twenties when I would eat as little as a couple of oranges per day. But I was enormously lucky. I had no formal therapy or treatment for this, and yet, with time, the intransigent mind-set and lifestyle of avoiding food became an insupportable bore. In college I focused increasingly on the classes I was taking: music theory, astronomy, philosophy, African art, Renaissance art, Russian avant-gardism, French, German, and Italian. I joined the drama club and the literary magazine and fell in love with a man from New Orleans. I had sex. I edited travel guides, applied for my first passport, and flew alone to Rome. There no longer seemed to be any boundaries to life and therefore no limit to my potential evolution within it. After college my intellectual and social universe expanded further: I moved to Manhattan, worked at a literary agency, traveled to London, Finland, and France; fell in love twice more; and began seriously to write. My anorectic tendencies never wholly subsided; in fact, they still compete with other, saner and worthier petitions for success. I call myself lucky because today the latter virtually always win out, whereas for many people with eating disorders the opposite is true.

I still struggle with the limitations of control, but I no longer feel the same frustration I used to feel with the exhaustive subjectivity of human judgment and ideas.

The only certain pleasure in reading is that it enriches the consciousness. I have long given up trying to read "everything" in pursuit of some tidily quantifiable body of knowledge. *Plus on lit,* I heard once: *plus on se rend compte de n'avoir rien lu.* The more one reads, the more one realizes one has read nothing.

Perfectionism appealing exclusively to outside reinforcement will not remedy feelings of self-dislike and insecurity. Often, as a child and younger adult, I was unsatisfied by anything less than a broad consensus of unqualified praise. Not for many years did my perfectionism evolve to be more concerned with my own opinions; it took even longer before I was able to recognize and accept my own opinions' sundry and changeable nature.

Anorexics are generally believed to seek perfection because they have a "distorted self-image." But what would it mean to have an undistorted image of oneself? The tension among our multiple selves is a fundamental part of being human. We are not consistent objects; striving to be so, mechanical and inorganic, is unnatural and futile.

And: Despite humans' unique capacities for communication, despite so much effort to the contrary, we cannot fully know one another. Ostensibly we want to know one another in the names of transparency and compassion, but usually, actually, we want to know one another for the egotistical reason that it is a way of knowing ourselves. Living well is to negotiate a balance: preserving the self while still remaining receptive to external influences, however sprawling and chaotic.

The self, too, can be sprawling and chaotic, fluctuating and disarrayed. Humans' internal disorder, our flawed mortal frames, and our perseverance in trying to make sense of these perplexities give rise to culture—in which the gradations of imperfection are infinite. Perfection, the condition, is an abstraction. The pleasure in pursuing it must remain in never getting there.

LITTLE FISH IN A BIG SEA

Sarah Haight

My first job after college was an unlikely one, given my medical history. After sending out résumés to nearly every publication west of the Mississippi, I landed at a major fashion magazine, whose sleek offices overlooked Times Square. Because I worked in Features—the department responsible for the articles, not the fashion spreads—many of my immediate superiors had come by way of newspapers or "serious" magazines. Style to these women was about the way a writer wielded a verb, not simply the way she carried her Balenciaga motorcycle bag. I felt mercifully cloistered from the Fashion department, where women with angular silhouettes scrambled between racks of beautiful clothes.

I grew to love my work, but I often felt as if I were keeping a vicious secret. In the elevator one afternoon, shortly after I started, I stood next to a few junior editors from the Fashion department. They were my age, midtwenties, and their hands cupped yogurt parfaits and Diet Cokes. "I had half a bran muffin for breakfast, so I'm only going to have half of this," one said to another, a blonde who was leaning against the elevator wall. The third tore open a bag of dried fruit with her teeth, popping a wedge of pineapple in her mouth. "Just do one meal a day," she said, chewing. I listened, staring at the floor. The words were familiar, like old songs whose refrains you could belt out on cue.

The dichotomy of my current life, in which I wrote about $4,000 Valentino gowns and stood quietly to the side as models shimmied past me in the hallway, and my old one, in which I had worked so hard to shed my preoccupation with size and appearance, was inescapable. I told no one at the magazine that I had once been hospitalized for anorexia. There were moments when I felt as if I was clenching back the admission: After listening to a quiet discussion in the art department over one cover subject's "arm jiggle," say, or while watching a new assistant whittle down her lunches over the first few weeks, from turkey wraps to leafy piles.

I observed all this with a mix of feelings: relief that I was no longer so vulnerable to these pressures; moral superiority; a hint of nostalgia. I knew how it felt to lose yourself in a haze of self-induced starvation, but I also knew what it meant to return to consciousness. Though I wondered if I still had the will-power to starve myself down to scrawniness, my memory stopped me, forcing me to buy real lunches in the cafeteria instead of the pseudomeals—cups of edamame or oatmeal, razor-thin slices of strawberries and kiwi—that in the past would tip the scale backward. Some part of my brain remembered that particular hell of being eating-disordered, and so when I eventually left the magazine to attend graduate school, I was the same dress size I'd been when I got there.

Anorexia is one of the most difficult illnesses to trace the origins of: Its roots are tangled, and the delicate unbinding of each contributing factor can be done only once the patient has truly agreed to get help. In my case, the disease was the product of a complicated mélange of emotional pain, perfectionism, societal pressure, and genetic bad luck. Every anorexic has a narrative of where things started to go awry. Of course, as with so many sad stories, mine is about high school.

———

It is 1996 and my senior year, in a small town in upstate New York, where I'd moved two years earlier from a larger city with my parents and younger brother. There is a tradition at my school in which the girls wear garters to the prom, and at midnight their dates remove them, by tooth or finger or any other appendage, to the theme music of that old standby, "The Stripper." I've never seen it happen, but the stories in the cafeteria are told so gleefully that I think perhaps the feminist movement never quite reached this pocket of farm country. Garters? Theme music?

"It sounds weird, but it's really fun," a friend tells me at tennis practice one afternoon. "The guys like it, and we all go buy garters together."

I'm vaguely disapproving, but I'm also bored. This is the sort of town where the seniors smoke pot down at the train tracks, where the lacrosse team gets its own parade, where there is a literal Main Street, and no other. The previous fall I'd been elected as the representative to the Board of Education (to be fair, no one ran against me) and so, in my next speech to the all-male board, I mention that there's this little event that has been going on here for about fifteen years, and I'm thinking that it's rather outdated, not to mention potentially uncomfortable for girls who attend the prom with dates whose fingers they'd rather not have running up their thighs halfway through the evening.

"I didn't know this was happening," one board member says. He squints at me across the long wooden table. I am standing in front of the men, shifting my weight from foot to foot, suddenly feeling like a petulant child.

"You've given us something to consider for next year, certainly," another announces. They nod their heads.

All in all, it's not exactly a success. As I'm leaving, a reporter for a newspaper in Rochester approaches me. I speak with her for a few minutes and then drive home. The next day, I am quoted on the front page, calling the garter tradition "patriarchal and sexist."

The principal's phone began to ring that morning, and from what I'm told, it did not stop for a full three months. In addition to my own statement, a neighboring school's principal was quoted in the article as saying, "We'd never let something like that happen here." By afternoon, the white van of a local TV news crew idled in the front drive of the school, and several other reporters waited outside the doors to interview students about what they thought of the tradition. At the end of the week, a class meeting was held in the high school gymnasium.

"It seems we've got a situation on our hands, folks," the principal, Mr. Walker, said, running his hand through his plume of dyed black hair. The senior class lounged on the bleachers, all dangling arms and legs. Mr. Walker stuffed his hands in his pockets. "Someone has made it clear she's not comfortable with this sort of thing, and you know, my hands are tied, guys. I've got to tell you, this isn't something you can do this year."

The only thing I remember from that meeting, besides Mr. Walker's stilted words, is the heat on my face. It rose up my neck, burnishing my cheeks so quickly that I put both palms to them, as if to hide. As all one hundred and twenty of us clambered off the bleachers and back to class, the other students chattered around me like a swarm of mosquitoes buzzing around my head. On the second floor, on my way to English class, a girl who I had sat next to during sophomore World History turned from her locker. She smiled slowly, and then dumped an entire bottle of peach Snapple on my head.

I remember trying very, very hard not to cry. I stood still for a moment, as if stuck to the floor, and then, the liquid seeping through my eyelashes and down my face, I walked to the bathroom, where I plunged my head under a sink. The bell rang, and I walked to class through an empty hallway. My English teacher, a gray-haired, wide-hipped woman, met me in the doorway. The look on her face, examining my slicked-back ponytail, was one of pity. She prodded me back down the hall before any of my classmates could get a look.

Threats had been made against me, Mr. Walker said when I arrived at his office. People like their traditions here, he continued—and the way he leaned back in his chair, rolling a pen in his fingers, made me suspect he was one of them. I was to go home for a few days and complete my assignments from there while things blew over. The secretary had called my father's office to explain. I often drove my mother's car to school then, as she used it only sporadically for work, so I drove myself home that afternoon. My memory, so sharp on the details of that particular day, goes fuzzy in the aftermath. I'm not sure how I passed the time during my house arrest. I think I did my homework, read, and watched a lot of daytime television. I walked our dog.

My father, the vice president of the local college, and my mother, a teacher, said relatively little about what had happened. That their child would object to such a stupid and retrograde tradition was so assumed as not to be worth remarking upon; my protest was simply confirmation that I had absorbed their own value system.

As we were eating dinner in the dining room a few days after I was sent home, a group of girls with sherbet-colored streaks in their hair zoomed down our street in a sports car. "Lesbo!" they shrieked out their windows, the screens in our house vibrating.

My mother, sitting at one end of the table, hardly looked up. "We're very proud of you," she said, calmly spooning out more ravioli for my brother, who scraped at his plate obliviously.

In the months that followed, I chose to cope with the situation by owning the spotlight I'd been thrust into. I offered up quotes to reporters who called our house. I snapped back when the boys who sat next to me in AP U.S. History lobbed flirty, resentful remarks: "Hot skirt for a lesbo." "Nice shoes, party-crasher."

I'd be lying if I didn't admit I sometimes enjoyed the feeling of moving from invisibility to notoriety. At the same time, my confidence was predicated on a romantic fantasy of my future, and my imminent escape from this narrow-minded backwater. I had accepted a place at Barnard, and I knew that in a few short months the garter saga would be just a funny piece of cocktail party repartee. Until that time, I could bask in a kind of attention no one in this town had ever before thought to pay me, while dreaming about my future life, which I was certain would be full of vigorous political debate and good-looking boyfriends.

When the prom came, I went stag. Chaperones lined the walls of the dinner club, sipping seltzers, and fidgeting with disposable cameras. I had been elected prom queen by a majority vote consisting largely of classmates eager to toss garters at me when I went to retrieve my crown. The school didn't want a scene, however, so I sat on a lipstick-red banquette and watched as a very tan cheerleader named Penny, who had apparently received the second-highest number of votes, was crowned. I wore a Laura Ashley silk dress that looked like an elegant pillowcase, and, despite the lacy lime-green and pink garters popping out of their pockets, I danced with all the guys who asked me.

Two months later, I left for New York.

At first, the garter ceremony, and my role in it, was indeed a funny piece of college party banter. Particularly in those heady first few days of school, as everyone scrambles for a story to mark her spot in the rapidly forming social circles, the ceremony was my currency: *You did what? People do what? Where?* Without acknowledging the pain of my experience, I used it now to define myself among a new and intimidating crowd.

From the beginning, it seemed clear that my new classmates' lives were far more glamorous and full than my own. Standing at the elevator to haul my high school wardrobe (pressed dresses from J.Crew) and CD collection (no Pixies, plenty of Sarah McLachlan) up to my dorm room on the first day of school, it dawned on me that I was rather out of my league. One of my floormates had a mullet and a banker boyfriend and had spent the summer interning for Errol Morris. Another had a brother who was in Blues Traveler. In particular, I envied the beautiful, thin dancer who lived across the hall, and it was partly her influence that propelled me to begin changing the way I ate.

She was precisely the kind of college student I was not: vaguely detached, cool, tall, and thin. I, on the other hand, practically vibrated with anxiety and eagerness. One evening while walking from the bathroom she told me she had been on a diet with her mother since she was eleven.

"You don't eat anything brown," she said—a designation that encompassed most carbohydrates, including pasta and cereal. "Except baked potatoes, but without butter."

At first, as is often the case, my dieting seemed benign. I am five feet, six inches tall, and since hitting adolescence had always weighed around 125 pounds. I have a swimmer's broad shoulders and full, round cheeks. In high school, I had spent time in front of the bathroom mirror, teeth clamped on the flesh inside my mouth, examining what Michelle Pfeiffer–esque qualities might emerge if my cheekbones were just a bit more prominent. I have thin, fine feet and hands, and these were always my favorite parts of my body. When it came to the rest of me, I was lacking in ambition; I played sports, and I ate a lot. I liked bacon, and I liked apples dipped in peanut butter. I liked nearly every single food out there, except pâté. And though I admired thinness—marveled at women who had that perfectly flat, ridged belly or that slice of sunlight between their thighs—my admiration was that of a distant observer. Like Irishness and high blood pressure, an athletic build was my genetic draw. Reedy thinness was simply never an option.

The beginning of my illness, then—a ruling out of certain foods, the forgoing of dessert—was precipitated less by a desire to look a certain way than by a need to create a persona, to fit in with my edgier classmates, some of whom had been shoving food to the edges of their plates for years. I made friends relatively easily, but I was also startled by how discomfiting it was to be the proverbial small fish in a big sea. I was not a local celebrity, or reviled crusader, or even one of the smartest girls in the class. I was simply Sarah.

Nor was college itself as romantic as I had expected. When I left home, I had visions of lounging in hallways discussing the Brontë sisters while drinking cheap Pinot Noir out of mason jars. I thought I'd go to class in sweats and band T-shirts, and that on weekends my friends and I would all hunker down in the library together, sharing trips to the deli on Broadway to pick up bagels and hot chocolate. But I found the reality of campus life riddled with contradictions (also, of course, I didn't actually own any band T-shirts). Many of my classmates, it seemed, hadn't wanted to go to a women's college; this was their safety school, or their parents' idea of the right place. On weekends people scattered across the city, and by Saturday afternoon the campus was practically abandoned. Suddenly my own reasons for choosing Barnard seemed worrisomely off base. The garter business had led me to imagine college as the highest possible rung on the ladder of human happiness. But I was here, and it wasn't. Now what?

Years later, as a graduate student in clinical social work, I studied the psychologist Karen Horney, who explored, from a feminist perspective, the connection between women's self-identity and their basic needs for food, love, and sex. Horney cites the often-uneasy relationship women have with their own essential self, suggesting that narcissism, or an inflated sense of self-importance, is a reactive instinct rather than an innate one. When I read this, I felt an immediate tug of self-recognition: the outsize sense of purpose and mission atop a bottomless pit of worry. The more vehemently I protested Geneva's antiquated policies and embraced my role as feminist heroine, the further alienated I had become from my own self and needs. By the time I arrived at Barnard, my identity was so predicated on achieving things that I'd lost track of how to enjoy just being myself, or how to feel good about myself without a constant external affirmation of my own uniqueness. Horney says that those who are accustomed to feeling good about themselves through these external events end up finding the absence of them so intolerable that they find other ways—extreme, frequently addictive behaviors—to cultivate the missing attention.

During that first fall of college, I began rising earlier and earlier in the mornings, chugging across Broadway to the gym, where I ran on the track, followed by a climb on the elliptical machine. I'd return to my room in time to meet friends for breakfast, a meal that dwindled from four cups of Froot Loops, or granola with Greek yogurt followed by a buttered scone stuffed in my bag for a midmorning class bite, to a sliced Fuji apple and one dollop of cottage cheese. Lunch consisted of Diet Pepsi and a scooped-out pumpernickel bagel. In the evening I'd join my group of friends for dinner. I would slice open two steaming baked potatoes and slather them with ketchup. I piled broccoli with soy sauce on the side. I ate half of what was on my plate.

"Your wrists look smaller," my friend Lissy remarked one afternoon in November. I looked down. To me, they looked the same as they always had, but she clasped one in her hands as we sat on her bed, our Political Theory reading open on our laps. "You're losing weight," she said.

A flush of excitement washed through me. It had been difficult to tell if anyone else could see any changes in my body. I knew I was smaller; I had lost about ten pounds and had jettisoned several now-baggy pairs of jeans for a tiny pair of vintage Levi's that I bought at a boutique in Soho. The gentle seesaw of skin that hung beneath my biceps had shrunk. The satisfaction I felt was unmistakable: I was proud.

By Christmas I had lost fifteen pounds; now there was no question that people noticed. My mother's eyes narrowed when she picked me up from the train station to head home for the winter break—a new home for our family, since my father, after realizing the problems my younger brother might face at my high school, had accepted a job in Massachusetts. While home, I stuck to familiar foods: baked potatoes, piles of steamed vegetables soaked in miso paste, and the occasional cup of frozen yogurt. I told my parents I was on a cleanse, or was becoming a vegan, or had decided to cut out wheat. My explanation changed, depending on what was being offered at the dinner table.

"We're concerned," my father finally said one evening. We were sitting in the living room, the blue glow of the muted television illuminating our faces. My father, like me, worries about what people think of him. On some level, I thought he would approve of my new discipline around food and exercise. A competitive rower, he is meticulous about his routine: waking at 5:00 a.m. to work out, picking up coffee from the same 7-11. He looks ten years younger than his age. When I was a kid, my mother would sometimes catch him squinting at his own reflection in a sliding door or toaster, and she would say, "Still looking good, honey."

By February, I had lost another six pounds. I spent the half hour before class each morning slicing apples into sad little squares before biting into each one. I'd get up earlier and earlier, pulling on two pairs of nylon tights and wrapping a scarf around my neck, setting off across Broadway in the dim morning so that I could have a longer workout and still make breakfast with my floormates. Hairs like fine corn silk sprouted on my back and belly. I brushed my teeth four or five times a day, trying to scrub off the rank smell of a diet composed nearly entirely of vegetables.

My friends were worried and encouraged me to eat. My friend Kathleen treated me to silver-dollar pancakes at Tom's Diner on a day when I said that I had skipped the gym. My deception, at first, was a means to avoid disappointing them, although the result, of course, was precisely the opposite. "I'm not losing any more weight," I would stammer at dinner, sipping my Diet Coke as they rolled thick twines of spaghetti around their forks. I was ashamed, and guilty for jeopardizing their trust. Over the winter, I noticed their looks of concern giving way to head-shaking, shrugs, hushed talk that halted as soon as I reached the cafeteria table. When they told me to eat, an edge had crept into their voices. They were tiring of me.

Around Valentine's Day, they held an intervention. Kai told me that we were all going to watch a movie in her room, and when I arrived, they were sprawled across the twin beds.

"We don't know what to do," Jean said. The others nodded.

"You look really sick," Kathleen said.

I promised I would schedule an appointment at the campus health center. "You have to," Lissy said. "We'll take you."

In fact, I put off going to the health center until early April. For the previous few nights, my heart felt like it had been leaping and stuttering in my chest, and I was scared. Something else strange had happened: In spite of ramping up my exercise routine to two hours in the morning, and eliminating the pumpernickel bagel from lunch, I had stopped losing weight.

At the health center, a resident took my pulse and quickly called in the medical director, who brought with her an EKG machine.

The electrodes stuck like barnacles to my bare chest, and the director, Dr. Wheat, leaned over me, her breath cool and sweet. I remember wondering if she had just eaten ice cream. I had not had real ice cream in so long.

"Your heart rate is thirty-six," she told me.

"Is that bad?" I asked.

"It's very serious," she said quietly.

I wrapped the threadbare cotton robe around my waist and hauled myself upright on the table, answering yes and no to Dr. Wheat's questions ("Do you have a strict exercise routine? Are there foods you will not eat? Do you write down calorie intake?").

"We're going to call your parents," Dr. Wheat said. "I think you should be admitted to the hospital."

My father was having a business lunch in the city when Dr. Wheat called. When he drove up to the campus gates in his rental car, he was wearing a suit. He looked terrified.

We drove to the medical center in Westchester that evening in silence. I was exhausted, though relieved to be with him, relieved to be turning over my well-being to someone else. I spent five nights at the hospital. My heart rate was monitored twice daily. Our food was measured by two nurses in a small linoleum kitchen and served on cold orange plastic trays, a slip of paper with our names taped to each one. The USA Network played *Disclosure* on a continuous loop on the TV in the common area, and our beds were covered in plastic sheets.

In our group therapy sessions, I began unraveling the origins of my anorexia, a process that would continue for several years. So many things—my predisposition to depression, the isolation and extreme conventionality of our town, my choice of a college filled with intense and ambitious women in the most intense and ambitious city in the world—had come together to trigger the disease. In this perfect storm, I reached for the same tool that had been used by so many other women to create an illusion of control: dieting.

Years later, when I was in graduate school, I learned that women in vastly different circumstances often try to cope the same way. I did my clinical internship at a facility that operates as an alternative to incarceration for women who have been convicted of crimes such as robbery, child abuse, and drug dealing. Nearly all the women were African American or Hispanic, and although our group focused on general mental health, many of my clients had eating disorders. A lot of our time was spent discussing the impact their childhoods, riddled with sexual abuse and drugs, had on the development of these disorders. It often seemed easier for my patients to trade stories of restriction, or bingeing, than it was to describe their drug problems, their experiences in jail or halfway houses, or the pain of knowing a child had been placed in foster care. These were shameful, divisive stories; bingeing and dieting, on the other hand, are universal ones. After all, as one client pointed out one evening: Rich white women do this, too.

As I sat with my clients week after week, listening to their stories of standing on street corners, hustling cocaine to make money, and racing home to binge on Big Macs as a way to assuage the guilt, I couldn't help but think about my own experience. I had been so comparatively lucky, with my suburban childhood and family dinners, yet I had fallen into the same desperate patterns of using food as a means of control. I chose not to reveal to the group my own past food issues. I was still in training, and therefore still too much of a novice to steer the delicate conversation productively; plus, I felt slightly foolish comparing my own struggle to theirs.

During my five days in Westchester, I gained three pounds

in four days. I left on Sunday evening, napping in the backseat of my parents' car as we barreled down the West Side Highway. When I arrived back at my dorm room, there were a dozen colorful cards wedged under my door, with notes of support from my friends. Someone had cut a crown out of orange paper and taped it to the door. There was a flattened bouquet of white roses squeezed between the knob and frame.

I did not get better right away. I got a therapist, and the summer between my freshman and sophomore year, I visited her office three times a week at lunchtime. I would bring a tuna fish sandwich, or chicken salad, or grilled cheese, and she would unwrap her lunch, a hero from Subway bursting with layers of salami, and we would eat together. My parents joined me for family sessions with another therapist. She sat in a rocking chair, which my mother said reminded her of the old Lily Tomlin skit. The fear I'd had that our fragile family structure might spontaneously combust if I were to tell them what kind of loneliness and confusion I'd experienced in the past year slowly dissipated.

"So much of our work is just sitting with people and holding their pain," an advisor told me in graduate school. "Not taking it away, or trying to erase it, but acknowledging that it exists."

There were fits and starts, good days and bad ones. I ate split-pea soup and Caesar salad and Frosted Flakes. I ate pasta with olive oil. I ate brown food. I gained weight, then panicked and lost it. I gained back the weight, lost it again, and by the middle of my sophomore year, gained it back for good. I had a standing appointment with Dr. Wheat, who made me turn to face the opposite wall when she weighed me, so that I wouldn't see the number. I haven't known my weight in ten years.

Three years after arriving at the fashion magazine, I left to pursue my master's degree in social work. The move seemed odd to colleagues who knew me in an atmosphere so far removed from the dingy clinics that my program assigned its students to work in, and yet the leap made perfect sense to me. I considered my life to have been saved by therapy. One of the benefits of surviving anorexia—in addition to a revived sex drive and shinier hair—is a greater insight into the struggle others engage in against demons you might otherwise never notice. My illness left me curious about the delicate binds between the mind and body, and the ways in which people eventually heal from wounds much deeper than my own had been. It was a strange thrill to be on the other side of the couch, as it were—though my early work environments were a far cry from an analyst's tidy office. At Coney Island Hospital, where I started my internship three weeks after leaving the magazine, the patients called me Alice because of my long blond hair. "Good night, Alice," a Russian man who was schizophrenic and always in pajamas would say as I unlocked the ward door to leave for the evening.

"Good night," I would reply, moving from one end of the rabbit hole to the other.

HOW THE FAERIES CAUGHT ME

Francesca Lia Block

But the faerie won. She won. And the thing is, I can't even recall how. I just remember fragments. Sharp as shards of mirror.

I have often read about the dangers of anorexia, while at the same time I am bombarded with visuals of Hollywood twenty-somethings shrinking before my eyes into the abyss of their slip dresses. But what is it about this disease that seduces? What are its initial lures? Without understanding them, it is difficult to heal, especially with the spectacle of thinness paraded before us as both angel and demon.

Actually, a better metaphor for anorexia, for me, would be that perfect blend of angelic and demonic—the faerie. Ethereal, delicate, able to fly. Also dangerously seductive, beckoning us into worlds unknown.

It is summer, 1982. The house I rent with a group of other students is an old, wooden, northern California two-story with bare wood floors and a glassed-in sunporch. This is the room I share with my boyfriend. It smells bitter and sweet from fresh white paint and the straw mat we have laid out under our frameless futon. We are embraced by the plum tree in the yard. A tree house. Appropriate for a sylph, a nymph, not necessarily a real girl.

I walk to the Berkeley campus for summer school in the mornings, shop at the co-op, lie in the sun, and read all afternoon. In the evening I go running around the high school field. The air is softly fragrant. I prepare healthy meals for my boyfriend. On a budget, and sick of dorm food from the previous semester, we mostly eat tofu, brown rice, and vegetables for dinner. We snack on fresh fruit—fuzzy peaches, dusky plums. In the morning I eat sugar-free wheat squares (they look like tiny bales of hay and don't taste much more flavorful) with nonfat milk, and for lunch I usually have a sandwich and an apple. I am losing weight.

I gained about fifteen pounds my freshman year in the dorms. An aspiring vegetarian, I avoided the mystery meats that were served in the cafeteria and opted for mountains of white rice, peas from the salad bar, and cold tofu seasoned with yellow mustard. For breakfast I had scrambled eggs and cold cereal. For lunch I gobbled up peanut butter and jelly sandwiches. I drank beer on the weekends. I was on the pill.

One day my roommate, a tall, thin woman who was dating a boy I'd had a crush on, was watching me change my clothes.

"Does the pill make you gain weight?" she asked me, her eyes on my distended belly.

I was disgusted with myself. I'd never had to diet before, but now it felt imperative. I was afraid my boyfriend would fall in love with a certain Germanic-looking blonde poet. I was afraid I wouldn't be able to keep getting straight A's. I was afraid my father would die of the cancer that had been discovered the previous summer, before I left for college.

I went off the pill and moved into the sunporch room with my boyfriend. I was afraid that otherwise he would take a room in another communal house with the blonde poet. I lost weight.

Initially, when I started losing weight, I felt better than I ever had in my entire life. I was incredibly clearheaded. My skin was also clear, my stomach flat. All my thrift-shop clothes seemed more chic. Feeling gamine, I cut my hair short. I had a lot of energy—and not just to run and study. I experienced sex in a whole new way. My body was alive and free and full of sensation. I felt pretty for the first time since I was twelve years old.

At that time, my older brother's friend took some photographs of me. She applied my makeup and dressed me first in a silk piano shawl, then draped a leopard-print scarf over my black leotard and tights. In the photographs I have long hair that reflects the sunlight. My eyes look big and dreamy; my lips are full. I have a slender body, long legs. You can tell that the girl in the photo feels loved, cherished, appreciated, seen. A year later, in junior high, I brought one of these pictures to school for an art project. A boy who often teased me about my appearance said he didn't believe I was the cute girl in the photo. By that time my hair had been cut into an unflattering pageboy; I had acne; my nose seemed too big for my face. Though I was still slim, my body felt awkward and often swollen with menstrual blood. The preadolescent sprite had vanished into the ether.

Back at Berkeley, I have changed my diet: I now eat a tiny serving of the same cereal and nonfat milk for breakfast. At lunch I have a sharp-tasting green apple and one slice of whole wheat bread. Dinner is tofu and vegetables, a little brown rice. I go running minutes after I've eaten but it doesn't seem to bother my stomach. I walk everywhere.

I walk to the UC Berkeley Cowell Hospital, which perches castlelike on a hill above the city. It is a long walk. As usual, the streets are empty. The air smells blossomy.

The doctor who sees me for a diaphragm fitting says she thinks I am "preanorexic." Part of me is surprised—I've just lost a little weight—while another part of me is already angry that she has qualified the condition: I never do things halfway. And look at me: I'm nineteen years old, five feet five and a half, and I weigh ninety-five pounds.

I'm home for a few weeks before school starts, and my father says, "I know that doctor said you were preanorexic or whatever, but you look very pretty to me."

It's the first compliment he has given me on my physical appearance in a long time. It feels like years, since before I was an adolescent. He compliments my writing. He proudly tells me not to work too hard, to get a B once in a while. He writes me loving notes and sends me drawings of our dog, the flowers in the garden, my childhood toys, me as a girl. But there aren't any drawings of me now.

School starts. The sunporch is not supposed to be a bedroom. It is always cold. Most of our roommates were away for the summer; now there are five women and two men in the house. My boyfriend and I have to step over two of the women, in their sleeping bags on the floor of the adjacent bedroom, when we get up in the morning. The dark, overcrowded kitchen feels threatening—a dirty refrigerator stuffed with other people's food, a grease-spattered stove, a sink piled with unwashed dishes. There is only one small bathroom. Two of the women in the house are bulimic. I saw a photograph of one of them from high school and asked who that pretty woman was. My friend started to cry; I felt sick for hurting her, and was reminded of the boy from junior high's comment about my photo. Another woman in the house is losing weight, but not as fast as I am. I am secretly very competitive: *Look, I'm the thinnest one!* And I would never stick my finger down my throat to vomit food I shouldn't have eaten in the first place.

For my Shakespeare in Film class, a group of us have to shoot a scene from a play. We pick *A Midsummer Night's Dream.* I cast it, and one of my roommates films it. He is Oberon; his girlfriend, who also lives with us, is Titania. My boyfriend is Puck. I am the Faerie.

I wear a lace thrift-shop dress and combat boots and we perform in a barren-looking stone-sculpture garden; this is our punk version. As I recite my lines, I feel possessed. I feel so light I could fly away.

Afterward, we go to a café to eat. I order a turkey sandwich and devour it. I never eat birds now, but I still remember that sandwich. Mustard and mayonnaise and white meat on whole wheat bread. It is raining and the café feels steamy, cozy, and warm. My body swoons with desire for the food.

But the faerie won. She won. And the thing is, I can't even recall how. I just remember fragments. Sharp as shards of mirror.

I wake once in the night and say to my boyfriend, "I'm hungry."

He replies, "Go get something to eat," and rolls over.

I don't even know it at the time, but what I want is for him to walk me downstairs, prepare a plate of food, talk to me, and hold me while I eat. But I have gone too far. My patient love has finally had enough.

Still, he tries. When we walk on campus I am always cold. He rubs my hands in his while I wish I could vanish inside his wool peacoat.

I sit in the lecture halls. The wooden seats hurt. I have no padding to protect me.

Gray hairs appear on my head.

I have a dream about a chocolate cake climbing the stairs of my house. It wants to devour me.

My periods stop. The sexual energy I initially experienced is gone. I no longer have to worry about birth control or the needs of a lover. I am becoming a child again, except that I am almost twenty years old, with some gray hairs, and have wished since I was four that someday I would have children of my own.

I don't remember much else about this time. I struggled with school and fought with my boyfriend. Finally, I dropped out. My parents came to get me. My father was still being treated for cancer, but he managed to drive the whole way, pack me up, drive me back.

I stared out the windows at the twisting, starving trees, the silvery, sorrowful sky. I wrote strange, surreal poetry. My father stopped at a Dairy Queen, and I ate a vanilla cone. It tasted delicious. It tasted fearsome and frightening. Like mortality.

I could choose to lose myself in a forest of emaciated dryads or find comfort in sugar and fat. Both were escapes from the reality that my father's cancer was spreading throughout his body.

Back in Los Angeles, I chose my escape route: I gained weight, eating junk food and drinking alcohol again. I missed my boyfriend. I missed Berkeley. Most of all, I missed, wistfully, the faeries who had fled somewhere along the highway on the way south.

How did I recover? I'm not sure I really did, at least not until much later. I stopped the junk food and alcohol. I abstained from sex, mostly because the only man in my life was my gay best friend. I attended school again locally and once, in a lecture hall, I saw a woman gnawing voraciously on a large green apple. Her head looked too big for a body that was mostly elongated bone. I knew her in an instant. (Sometimes I see them still—in yoga classes, running—my sisters with their flat chests, twig limbs, and wispy hair. Others are hidden in big, dark clothes so that even I can't recognize them.)

After a year I forced myself to return north to complete my education. I spent most of that year alone, studying, walking, writing. I tried to eat healthfully. My boyfriend had graduated, but the Germanic blonde was in my feminist studies course. She wrote a beautiful poem about me, and I wondered if my jealous fears about her and my boyfriend had been more off-base than I'd imagined. I saw a therapist who fell asleep during my session more than once, suggested I change my makeup brand, and seemed shocked when I brought in some surrealist collages I had made. My father died a few weeks before my graduation. I moved back to LA and maintained a normal weight. But had I recovered?

Once I saw a television program on anorexia. It featured a doctor who took girls into her home for treatment. Part of the therapy involved holding these long-limbed teenagers like infants cradled in her arms. Love was literally the cure. I have received unconditional love from my mother since the day I was born. Perhaps I felt abandoned by her during the years of my father's illness, but her love never really left, and it heals me still.

I like to think I've found a balance now. I eat healthy vegetarian food, meditate, pray, do yoga, don't drink or consume sugar. I have a wonderful therapist, and I also share my anxiety with my friends, some of whom have also suffered from eating disorders. I write about what is painful to me. This process transforms the pain into something meaningful, possibly even beautiful. It physically removes it from the prison of my body so that I can look at it with perspective and share it with others.

The gray hairs disappeared for twenty years when I started eating again, and have just recently returned. My periods came back and, after two miscarriages, I gave birth to two healthy children. But if I were to tell you a story of the twenty-plus years between my college days and now, there would be more visitations by the faeries trying to claim me. And I learned that I'm not as pristine as I once thought—girls under the faerie spell do binge on rice cakes and plain nonfat yogurt and purge with aerobic dancing, running, and ballet.

I told a man I was dating that one thing I couldn't take was the idea of someone judging my body.

"I have to tell you," he said. "I'm judging your body right now."

I was horrified and almost walked out of the restaurant. He explained that he thought I was anorexic. I told him that I had been anorexic in college, and possibly two other times after that, but that I was fine now. He apologized and told me that it was partly his issue. His parents were Holocaust survivors, and his grandmother had been killed in the camps. His younger sister had gone through a period where she cut off all her hair and lost weight in imitation of, or perhaps homage to, her grand mother. My small size brought up his "Holocaust stuff." He told me that on a trip to Auschwitz, he photographed the ruins of the camps and, due to a mysterious accident of overexposure, ghostlike images of men and women appeared in the pictures.

I am Jewish, and images of emaciated Holocaust victims haunt me. If I were to give my self-loathing a face, or rather a body, it might look like those tortured, skeletal figures. Yet in the throes of anorexia, I didn't think of myself as courting death. Ironically, I felt I was escaping from death by starving my adult body back into the body of a child. Subconsciously, though, I *was* trying to die. It was one way to avoid the grief and fear I felt at losing my father to his illness and my mother to her own fear.

Escape from the confines of the body is, ultimately, escape from life. Escape from adulthood back into childhood is, if taken far enough, escape into death. Anne Frank, symbol of innocence annihilated; fashion models, the unattainable bane of my existence; prepubescent girls who do not yet carry the responsibility of mature sexuality; and of course, those harbingers of enchantment, but also of death, the faeries, have all stood on the banks of that other world, beckoning.

The other day my friend sent me a picture of us at a party. We have shiny hair, happy smiles, clear skin, cute clothes, strong, well-exercised bodies. I liked the picture, but my belly was protruding above my low-rise jeans, in spite of the many sit-ups I can perform. I felt humiliated by this pregnant-looking image of myself and mentioned it to my therapist. I have been frustrated because a lot of foods don't agree with me now and I feel bloated after I eat.

"Think about what you do in a day," she said.

I wake up at 5:00 a.m., prepare breakfast and pack lunches for my two young children, and feed my two dogs. I meditate, shower, check my e-mail, and try to write while eating my bowl of oatmeal. My kids wake at around six-thirty, and I help get them ready for school. Three days a week I take them there, then do errands or yoga and walk my dogs until I have to pick up my kids three hours later. Two days a week I work at their schools. I usually eat lunch in about ten minutes; I couldn't tell you what I have most days. In the afternoon my children and I play, do homework, visit friends. Whenever I can, I try to write. I make dinner. I try to eat as much as I can stomach—a mild grain, a vegetable, a little protein. I give baths. I read storybooks. We say prayers and fall asleep together at eight-thirty; my exhaustion feels like it has seeped into my bone marrow. On the weekend their dad takes them for one night; I do hard-core yoga, run errands, take care of my dogs, organize, clean, and write. I eat a little more than during the week because I have the time and energy to focus on myself. My favorite foods are nori plum rice wraps and tomato vegetable soup, stuffed grape leaves and lentil soup, green-tea matcha soy lattes, pumpkin raisin muffins, and vegan carrot cupcakes. Gentle food, comfort food. My kids come back Sunday night, their arms outstretched, their round faces shining. They are fresh from the bath their dad has given them. Their curls are damp and smell mildly of vanilla. They look taller every time. It shocks me how much I have missed them: bone-marrow deep. I think of myself as a child, happy in my body, graceful, innocent, beautiful, free. Deeply loved by my parents and able to feel that love before death threatened to take them away.

"You need to eat," my therapist said. Her words stated so simply and warmly are the equivalent of an embrace.

So the point is, I'm hungry. And I can't afford to be a faerie anymore. I have two young humans who need a warm, soft, well-fed mommy. Someday soon they will be adolescents, leaving the purity of their childhood bodies, needing a guide to help them in this world. Then they will be adults, facing my death with what I hope will be courage and acceptance. I can teach them how to do this only by embracing this world fully, with all its love and loss. My children, the loves of my life, the salvation of my body and spirit, are reason enough for me never to go back to the faerie world again.

THE VOICE

Trisha Gura

——————

I remember standing with my husband, Kevin, in the bathroom. Pants down, I braced against the sink, as Kevin held a syringe like a dart.

"On three," he said, counting and then plunging the needle into my left buttock.

I winced and felt the burn as hormones, extracted from the urine of pregnant mares, flooded my muscle. I was thirty, and we wanted to get pregnant. The only problem: I had never menstruated in my life.

At nineteen, when I was diagnosed with anorexia, I had whittled my five-feet-four frame down to eighty-nine pounds. My blond hair split at the ends. My skin flaked. My nails broke. Four years of treatment coaxed my weight up to 110. I left therapy in 1986 with my hair longer, my smile surer, my body curved more like that of a woman. My psychiatrist considered me "better." For the next decade, I felt better. I earned a doctorate in molecular biology and became a medical reporter for *The Chicago Tribune*. Of course I was better.

Wasn't I?

There was one obvious inconsistency: Because of my ongoing low weight, food restriction, and intense exercise (I did three triathlons), I never menstruated. Perhaps many women would envy my never having to deal with the backaches, bloating, and bitchiness—but only because they wouldn't understand the consequences.

I am like many other women with histories of eating disorders. We are diagnosed as teenagers and then get well enough to evade diagnosis, but not enough to feel eating disorder–free. Researchers term our condition *subclinical.* They believe that far more individuals fit into this category than the fifteen to twenty million Americans who have full-blown eating disorders.

Based on studies, experts estimate that at least one-third of those diagnosed with eating disorders recover just enough to become subclinical. But there are also many more who never quite meet the criteria for diagnosis. In conducting interviews for my book, *Lying in Weight: The Hidden Epidemic of Eating Disorders in Adult Women,* I discovered dozens of people like this, who did not have clinical eating disorders but who nonetheless lived in the grip of obsessive food issues and/or exercise habits.

There is a man in my office, for instance, who is so terrified of becoming fat that he restricts his diet to vegetables, dried figs, dates, and pretzels. He exercises two hours a day, even through his hernia, forgoing surgery because it would prevent him from exercising for several weeks. He is normal weight.

And then there is Dana, who cannot go a day without running. Rain, sleet, or snow; tired, sick, or injured; she laces up and sets off no matter what. She consciously limits her runs to forty-five minutes, worrying that if she didn't, she would increase the time each day.

Throughout my twenties, I also flew below the medical radar: privately obsessive but, on the surface, better enough to seem "normal." Until, that is, I wanted to get pregnant. Then my husband and I had to go through two years of fertility treatment. There were the tests: temperature taking, pelvic exams, and squirts of dye into Fallopian tubes to check for blockage. Kevin shot sperm into a cup and had it counted. There were the failed procedures: Hoping for ovulation, I unsuccessfully swallowed drugs such as Clomid (clomiphene). Next, Kevin administered to me the nightly injections of egg-prodding hormones, and I managed the daily trips to Northwestern Memorial Hospital for blood tests and ultrasounds.

My egg sacs grew: 13 millimeters, then 15, then 17. At 18 millimeters, the doctor scribbled a prescription for hCG, human chorionic gonadotropin, a hormone that triggers the release of a growing egg. After each injection, Kevin and I would have thirty-six hours of the most fraught lovemaking to try to create a new life.

At first, it didn't work. After years without menstruation, I remember getting my period in the middle of a science journalism conference in Atlanta and rushing to the bathroom to cry.

We continued, however, and eventually I conceived. I felt giddy. Electric.

And then my body began to shift.

For the first three months of pregnancy, I felt nauseous and bloated. At the same time, my job became more demanding. I had to commute an hour each way. I was given a beeper, a new beat in the suburbs, and therefore an excuse not to eat. I told myself that I had no time on the road with such tight deadlines.

I also wanted to hide my pregnancy to protect my job. I had heard the stories of reporters who went on maternity leave and returned to bottom-of-the-barrel assignments. I had landed this job less than two years ago; I worried I hadn't yet paid my dues and that the editors would not be kind to my shifting priorities. There was always the chance I might miscarry, in which case the issue would be moot. If not, I figured that I could at least work for a few more months and prove myself on several big stories before I told my editors the news. So I wore loose clothing and sneaked naps at lunchtime in the shower stall of the bathroom. Out in the field, I skipped lunches. I welcomed morning sickness because it would keep me smaller longer.

For five months, none of my coworkers guessed my secret; I gained only four pounds. Then, one summer afternoon, I was assigned to report on a solstice festival sponsored by Wiccans, a neo-pagan group that draws from the pre-Christian traditions of Britain. Arriving at the site, I chuckled at all the chanting and drum banging, watching through the detached cover of my journalistic position. But then, at sundown, as the women stood in a circle and shared coming-of-age stories, I felt myself suddenly pulled in. I realized that I had no such stories. I had no first period. The pregnancy was my first organic identification with femininity.

From that moment, I felt connected to something much larger. I wanted to take care of this baby more than anything else. I wanted to heal for her. My body even felt physically different: soft and warm, like it was submerged in honey.

I began to steal midday walks through the forest preserve near my office, on which I rubbed my belly and talked to my child. I found a therapist who drew on the methods of psycho-analyst Carl Jung to explore my dreams and find positive images of femininity. I wrote in a journal about my fears of mothering. I carried around prints of Botticelli-like figures, whose rounded bellies and pendulous breasts allowed me to embrace a gentler, more realistic view of myself.

After a sobering talk with my obstetrician, I quit my job. He was concerned because at seven months pregnant, I had gained only seven pounds. I listened to him. I gained ten pounds in a month, snacking on trail mix and sleeping most afternoons. Two weeks early, I gave birth to a healthy, six-pound, nine-ounce girl. And I felt wonderful.

Soon after my daughter was born, though, I separated from my husband and embarked on a four-year, bitter divorce. The cracks in our marriage had become evident while I was pregnant; they only widened with the stresses of sleep deprivation, lactating, and my overwhelming disgust toward my slack abdomen and misshapen body. With my womb empty, my happy acceptance of my maternal shape faded. Where had my body gone? And beyond that, I wondered, where had *I* gone? At thirty-one, without a job, and soon to be without a partner, I had lost my identity as both wife and worker. Who would I be now?

Unfortunately, the ensuing court battle over custody fueled my distress. Kevin used my eating disorder to argue that I was an unfit mother. His attorney brought in a psychiatrist, an eating disorders expert, who testified that mothers with eating disorders compete with their children and neglect feeding. He argued that I would starve our daughter so that she would not supersede me. The attorney brought in journals that I had left behind in our house in which I had described my struggles with my body while pregnant. I was forced to read my private insecurities aloud to the judge.

And so it went for four years, during which the stress

nearly overwhelmed me. Although I am certain that my eating problems did not cause my divorce, the divorce did stir up my latent anorexia. Ironically, I turned to my old habits to cope, relapsing into the very behaviors that were being used against me.

My weight plummeted, but never to the level of my worst illness. I knew better. Somehow, after the first year of postpartum chaos, I found a way out. I watched my daughter, pink and pudgy, crawling and later walking. I had bonded to her when pregnant, and I held on to that connection during the divorce. I fought back both in the kitchen and in court, regaining the lost weight and gaining full custody. I began to move on with my life. In my mind, I closed that chapter with relief. I decided that the book of anorexia, for me, was complete.

———

One winter morning in 2002, I met my friend Lauren in a café in Cambridge, Massachusetts. We had met during a yearlong science journalism fellowship at MIT and Harvard. This particular morning, we were luxuriating in the absence of deadlines and brainstorming new writing projects.

We were also getting to know each other better. Lauren, who writes a great deal about her personal tribulations, brought up the topic of her past. "You know, I had an eating disorder as a teenager," she said.

She went on to describe her recovery and subsequent relapse after her first pregnancy. Late at night, she would tell her husband she was going to the grocery store, where she would buy bags of junk food, gorge in her car, and then make herself throw up in the parking lot. Only after two years, and with the aid of therapy, was she able to stop.

"It was me or my baby," she said. "I had to choose."

My mouth dropped open. "I had an eating disorder, too," I said.

I used the word *had* instead of *have* because, in my mind, my eating disorder was in the past. But Lauren was not easily deterred.

"Did it go away for you?" she asked.

"Of course," I said.

"Are you sure?" she said. "I don't believe they do go away."

I paused, thinking.

"Well," she said, taking another sip, "you should write about it."

I went home that day, trying not to ruminate on Lauren's words. But I couldn't help it. Her question nagged me: Had my eating disorder gone away? I'd always said it did, but now I realized that I was lying to myself. I did not feel liberated at all. I still have a voice in my head. It whispers that no one will love me if I am fat. It says that what I do is never enough. It promises that if I follow its rules, skipping meals, swimming extra laps, not eating this or that, avoiding meat and chicken and fish and dairy products, I will be safe. But I don't feel safe—just closed up and isolated.

I did what Lauren suggested: I wrote about it. In interviewing women who had suffered from eating disorders, not one told me that she was completely symptom-free. There were always remnants: an overattachment to exercise or appearance, regularly skipped meals, a need to measure out portions in plastic bags to avoid a binge. And where such "slips" occurred, I saw patterns. Stress and emotional upheaval made women more vulnerable. Major life transitions were often cited as triggering a relapse: changing jobs, marrying, divorcing, getting pregnant, parenting, being widowed, coming to terms with old age. The oldest woman in my book was ninety-two.

In fact, my grandmother died from complications of undiagnosed bulimia. In her eighties, she complained of diverticulosis, an inflammation of the intestines exacerbated by stress. While that is a common ailment connected to aging, it became the catchall for her worries, including her fears of mortality. After my grandfather died, she rarely engaged in social activities. She lost interest in cooking for herself, so she would eat either frozen dinners or nothing at all. Then, when invited to family gatherings, she would stuff herself. She would go home feeling sick and then make herself throw up. "My diverticulosis," she would say. She even joked about it: "Every so often, you just have to have a good upchuck."

She died at age eighty-seven, after a party at which she ate so much that she felt ill. She went home that night and threw up so violently that she ruptured her gastrointestinal tract, aspirated her vomit, and got pneumonia. Because of many reasons—her age, her diverticulosis, my family's reluctance to discuss the possibility of an eating disorder—no doctor ever diagnosed my grandmother with bulimia. My mother and I now wish we might have known more, and done more to ameliorate my grandmother's pain and fear.

———

If an eating disorder can last that long—if it can be a chronic illness like alcoholism—then is it possible it actually begins before birth, lying latent in one's genes? Are the anxiety, hypersensitivity, and perfectionism that characterize anorexia the consequence or the cause of disease?

Right now, researchers are trying to figure this out. People like Cynthia Bulik, a psychologist at the University of North Carolina at Chapel Hill, are searching for the genes that might put an individual at risk for anorexia. Thus far, the strongest candidates to emerge are genes that encode neurotransmitters in the serotonin system, which controls and affects mood; genes for neurotransmitters that work in the dopamine system, which is related to reward; and a brain-housekeeping molecule called brain-derived neurotropic factor (BDNF), which plays a role in the growth and maintenance of nerve cells.

This last molecule is particularly interesting to researchers and could revolutionize their thinking about anorexia. BDNF is in charge of *general* nerve connections and maintenance—not just the complex circuitry related to appetite or satiation. If BDNF turns out to play a pivotal role in causing anorexia, the finding suggests that anorexia represents a misguided attempt to cope with anxiety, rather than simply a pursuit of extreme thinness.

I personally understand this concept. In times of great stress, I deny myself food in an attempt to distract myself and numb out difficult emotions. Other anorexic women I've interviewed have told me the same thing. According to Walter Kaye, a psychiatrist at the University of California, San Diego, the way we process our emotions and experiences is actually different from people without eating disorders.

Kaye is using a brain-imaging technique called fMRI scanning to shed light on those differences. In a recent experiment, he asked women who had recovered from anorexia, as well as women without histories of eating disorders, to play a decision-making game while sitting in the brain scanner. The women had to guess if a hidden number was greater or less than five;

they won $2 for every correct guess and lost $1 for every incorrect guess.

With the women who had no history of eating disorders, Kaye's team could clearly see the difference between a win and a loss on the fMRI scans. The wins lit up the women's brains in a structure called the anterioventral striatum, which contributes to reward processing. By contrast, women who had recovered from anorexia did not register any activation in the anterioventral striatum. In simple terms, they showed little drive for pleasure, even after recovery.

Instead, in the recovered anorexics, wins caused overactivity in another brain region, called the caudate-dorsal striatum. This circuit works to anticipate long-term consequences; it helps a person attach a reward sensation to a particular stimulus so that he or she can make a future decision when offered the stimulus again.

According to Kaye, the finding shows that "anorexics cannot live in the here and now." Instead of feeling the pure momentary joy of a win or disappointment of a loss, individuals with anorexia live in the future, worrying about consequences and planning for all contingencies in order to avoid making mistakes.

Kaye's team also did another experiment in which they gave the same two groups of women either water or sugar water and compared their brain responses. The control women had no trouble judging the pleasant taste of sugar as opposed to the neutral one of water. The sweetness lit up the insula, a brain structure important for recognizing taste.

By contrast, the women who had recovered from anorexia showed no activity in the insula when they tasted the sugar water. Either such women failed to recognize the pleasantness

of sugar, or they had trouble responding to that pleasure. Both
suggest that, even after recovery, anorexics don't process food
rewards in the normal way.

These experiments suggest a frightening question: Without
the normal motivations to eat, how can those of us with a pro-
clivity to anorexia want to eat, especially in a culture that
rewards thinness? For me, life has turned into an attempt to
find such incentives. They are slowly emerging, as I face the
consequences of self-starvation on my long-term health and
strive to be a healthy role model for my daughter, now on the
verge of puberty.

———

It's 3:00 a.m. Every twenty minutes, the nurse tiptoes into
my room. She screws the syringe into a plastic tube inserted in
my vein and draws out exactly half a teaspoon of blood.

I am participating in a clinical trial at Massachusetts General
Hospital that is looking for connections between cortisol production and osteoporosis. Cortisol is a stress hormone, secreted
as part of the body's "fight or flight" response. Doctors believe
that heightened levels of cortisol may explain both some of the
gratifying feeling associated with the early stages of anorexia
such as increased energy, and some of the destructive long-term
consequences.

In five hours, I will learn the results of a bone scan, which
will reveal whether I have osteoporosis; because I do not men-
struate regularly, I am at serious risk of bone loss. In twelve to
eighteen months I will also find out if, like most women who
have recovered from anorexia, I produce too much cortisol.

I have volunteered for this trial because I need a motivation
to gain weight. Working on my book, I came to realize how

much I still cling to my unhealthy behaviors. Now I want something to help me let go.

At 8:00 a.m., the doctor tells me the news: I don't have osteoporosis. But I do have its precursor, osteopenia. The bones in my hips, wrists, and spine are all thinning too fast. There are no drugs for me to take. The only things that will help are calcium, vitamin D, and walks outside for twenty minutes a day—the ultraviolet light will help my body absorb nutrients and preserve my thinning bones. I can also attempt to restore my periods by gaining weight. I will learn the overall cortisol results of the study when they are published in a year or so.

I listen with a mixture of worry and relief. It's not too late to change.

———

After the trial, I begin therapy at the Cambridge Eating Disorders Center in Massachusetts. During the course of five months, I gain nearly ten pounds. Part of my treatment is a meal plan: three a day including foods I had heretofore eliminated from my diet, such as bread, pasta, and sugar. For the first time in my life, at age forty-three, I start having monthly periods. To me, this seems a miracle. And it happens just as my daughter, now twelve, is on the brink of puberty. We are sharing a unique adventure.

Throughout the writing of *Lying in Weight,* I talked to my daughter, a little bit at a time, about the struggle I have had with eating. I did this because I worried that she might go down the same road, or some other bulimic or bingeing path. I knew that she had picked up the signs of my eating problems. I remember her coaxing me to eat with her at breakfast and frowning when I refused. When the school nurse weighed her for health class, she came home morose. "I wear the same size as you," she cried, "and I'm only ten years old." And then came the startling question after a weekend with her father and paternal grandmother: "Granny says I'm fat and should be on a diet. Am I fat, Mom?"

I knew what to say in such situations. I didn't counter her claim, but asked: "Now, why do you think Granny would say something like that?" In the ensuing discussion about her grandmother's diabetes and the special diet she is on, my daughter realized that her grandmother's comment was much more about her own insecurities than about my daughter's body. I stood her in front of the mirror and told her to list ten things that she loved about herself. I talked about how she and I are different shapes and sizes, and the difference is beautiful. Beauty is about being authentic.

But all along, I knew no words were as powerful as the actions I was modeling. And this became the strongest motivation to let go of my symptoms and inflexible rules. The other day, my daughter made me macaroni and cheese, and I ate it with relish, grateful for her act of love in cooking for me. When overwhelmed by the stresses of work or single parenting, I ask my daughter to give me twenty minutes to shut myself in my bedroom and meditate. She absorbs my lessons and then turns them back on me. One day, when I was bemoaning a setback in a parenting article I had been writing, my daughter said, "Wait, Mom," and ran to the bathroom to retrieve a mirror. She held it up in front of me and said, "Say ten things that you like about yourself."

I cried joyful tears, watching my face contort in the hand mirror. My daughter had gotten it. She had learned from me how to love herself. We are learning profound lessons together.

I have taken Walter Kaye's findings to heart. I focus on living in the moment rather than anticipating what is to come. The other day, for the first time in twelve years, I made and ate tapioca pudding—simply because I hadn't allowed myself to eat it in the past. I tasted it. I mean really *tasted* it. I laugh with my daughter at the antics of our cat, Alex. I have traded aerobics and triathlons for yoga and meditation, which deal with the body and its relation to the present moment.

As I do these little things, the cruel voice in my head is fading. Finally acknowledging the consequences of my eating disorder has prompted me to try, in midlife, to let it go and find a new identity outside of anorexia. I used to think that I could recover for my daughter if for nothing else. But I now know I want more than this: I want healing, promise, and joy for myself.

FINDING HOME

Maya Browne

Living in Los Angeles, producing feature films and writing, I am part of a culture so wonderfully open, and so alien to the New York and San Francisco I grew up in, that sometimes I can scarcely believe I found my way here. In the entertainment business, it doesn't matter where you come from—Park Avenue or Harlem, Pacific Heights or Hunter's Point. You are only what you have created here, nothing more and nothing less. You are only as good or bad as your last movie, screenplay, or book (if it got optioned or you are visiting from New York, that is), and everyone has an expiration date. Last week I drove by the home of a college classmate in the hills, only to find that the house had been sold and gutted. Once a successful executive at a studio, she had simply disappeared from the LA landscape. It happens so often that people hardly notice. Though this lack of security can be unsettling, it also means there is little to lose in trying to define yourself and your life here. Also, neither of my parents has ever lived in LA. They have no influence in my current business, which leaves me completely free of their oversight for the first time in my life. And it is good to stand on my own.

My parents are two very beautiful, intelligent people who happen to be from different planets. My mother is artistic, a quintessential southern belle. She grew up in Nashville, Tennessee, and both her parents were professors. She is eccentric, generous, a bit in her own time zone, a great teacher, and was always devoted to doing everything she could to protect and nurture me, her only child. My father is a businessman from the South Side of Chicago—self-made, driven, charming, detail-oriented, sometimes ruthless, yet also a doting papa who surprised me around my sixteenth birthday by picking me up from dance rehearsal in a brand-new Saab. My parents met and married in New York City, and they moved to San Francisco when I was four.

Because they have very strong personalities, and very different perspectives on the world, they argued frequently. When I was eight and they decided to start a company together that would design and import children's shoes, the fighting got worse. I was a fairly popular kid and often went over to my friends' houses after school. But I rarely invited them to my house—partly because my parents were rarely around, and if they were, I never knew when the next fight would erupt. An only child, I was also happy to get away from the constant supervision by either my parents or our housekeeper and to hang around with other kids my age. Plus, my mother was an early adopter of the health-food movement, so there was never junk food in the house, unless my father snuck it in.

On days when I didn't have play dates, I had lessons of one sort or another. I realize now that this was an innovative alternative to sticking me with a babysitter. As my parents got busier and started to travel more, my schedule of extracurricular activities expanded. Every day, I would be picked up from school by someone who worked for my parents and driven to ballet, violin, piano, tennis, or gymnastics. By the time my lesson was finished, one or both of them could usually come get me, and we would go out to dinner. These dinners were the happiest times I spent with my parents. Usually, one or more of their employees came with us, and much of the conversation revolved around the company. I found these conversations interesting and chimed in whenever I could. Plus, with other people around, my parents were charming—even to each other.

———

My parents both grew up in racially charged environments in pre–civil rights movement America, in comparison to which the Bay Area was a utopia. Race was seldom discussed. The private elementary school I went to was full of racially mixed kids with enlightened, NPR-listening parents, so I didn't think of my identity as defined by race. As I got older, I did notice that, even though most boys flirted and would seek out my company, the only boys who actually asked me out were usually black or at least of mixed race—which was fine, except that I wondered why the other boys didn't.

My parents' increasing wealth and worldliness also divided me from my peers, both black and white. Around the time I started junior high school, they expanded their business dramatically. The housekeeper who had been coming once a week started coming almost every day. I went along with them to Europe about twice a year on buying trips, and we spent Christmas holidays in the Caribbean. All of this was great, but it made it difficult for me to relate to the few black kids I knew, who were bused in from the projects at my public junior high school and were usually scholarship kids at my private high school. On the other hand, as glam as it all looked on the outside, I still knew we didn't have the kind of money that many of my white classmates had. Our house, although very nice, wasn't nearly as grand as the Pacific Heights mansions they lived in. Our situation was difficult to explain and made people jealous. I had learned early on not to talk about my family life much, and now there were just more things I couldn't talk about.

Throughout my childhood and adolescence, I always felt most comfortable with the people I met when I was away from home. I didn't have to worry about being embarrassed by some outburst between my parents, and I didn't have to explain anything. These people tended to be a bit more sophisticated than my peers at home and to have fewer barriers to interracial dating. We understood each other, and I felt at ease.

In junior high, although on the surface I would have seemed popular and well-integrated—president of the student body and a cheerleader—I felt like an outsider. I didn't want to accept that the reason I felt this way was something as utterly out of my control as my race. I began to think that maybe, if I just put a bit more effort into being as pretty as I could be, I would finally be admired enough to feel really accepted. And so high school began. . . .

In 1986, when I was a freshman, the kids in the San Francisco public schools knew University High School as a place where every girl had "a Saab, a shrink, and an eating disorder." I heard this from my boyfriend at the time, a motorcycle-riding football star at one of those public schools.

In some ways I was well suited to the high-pressure atmosphere at University, but I also felt isolated there. I was kept busy by a full schedule of extracurriculars: studying violin at the San Francisco Conservatory of Music, voice lessons, piano lessons, dance lessons, tennis, skiing, waterskiing, and traveling out of the country at least three times a year. On top of all this, I was a straight-A student.

I loved standardized tests, auditions, and sports—any competitive arena. Excelling at these served a dual purpose: It was a way to both console myself and make sense of the isolation I felt as a black girl, no matter how pretty or affluent, existing in the predominantly white environment of my peers. It convinced me that if I was isolated, it was because I was in some way superior. I embraced my isolation as a badge of honor. This worked all right until I turned sixteen. Then the entire playing field changed: A perfect storm of hormones, boys, and my warped worldview shifted my focus from achievement in the world of academia to achievement in attracting male attention. Having a tall, popular boyfriend became more important and more gratifying to me than beating my opponent in tennis or getting a 100 on a test.

Since it was the 1980s, and every guy I knew was salivating over Cindy Crawford, Linda Evangelista, or Naomi Campbell, I decided to become a model. My parents were horrified and disapproving, but I didn't care. I got myself an agent and started getting booked for jobs without their consent, which was made easier by the fact that they were often out of town. My parents believed I was still the dependable, levelheaded little adult they had known for the first fifteen years of my life. But a major transformation was under way. By age sixteen, securely in the driver's seat of my own car and—so I thought—my own life, I began making changes. I quit all of my extracurriculars except for dance, took up running, and made friends with two exercise-obsessed fashionistas from another private school.

The daily drill went something like this: I would wake up to my Bang & Olufsen stereo and use the remote to turn on the news from bed. I would go down to the kitchen and prepare my own breakfast (one serving of Cream of Wheat made with nonfat milk, and a few pieces of fresh pineapple—its acids were rumored to boost metabolic rates). I would also make my lunch (half a chicken breast cooked with non-fat cooking spray, some steamed veggies, and half an apple). While I ate breakfast, I would ride the Exercycle I had in my room and finish watching *Good Morning America*.

After extensive grooming and wardrobe selection, I was in the car and off to school. I had a parking space about three blocks from school, so I got in a little extra exercise on the way there and back. I went to classes and raised my hand often. During free periods, I went to the library to do the next day's homework and to socialize—there was a lot of note passing in those pre–cell phone days. After school, I headed either to dance rehearsal or to the tennis club, where I would meet up with my two new friends (one an actress, one a model) to work out. On the way home, the three of us would often grab sushi or something equally "healthy."

In trying to look healthy, however, I was becoming an anorexic. The amount of calories I was burning with exercising (not to mention growing) far exceeded what I was consuming. Still, the booking agents and photographers I was working with told me I looked "amazing," and on top of that I was getting more attention from the boys at school. I spent the summer after junior year at dance camp and then studying at Alvin Ailey in New York. Everywhere I went in the city, men followed me around. It was a little frightening, and I definitely didn't have the social skills to interact with them except by pretending not to notice, or smiling and saying "Thank you" when that wasn't possible. I was expending even more energy than during the school year, dancing eight to ten hours every day and then going out clubbing at night. By the end of the summer, I wanted to transfer to The Dalton School and stay in New York. But my parents said no, so I accepted the bribe of a trip to Spain and reluctantly came home to San Francisco to start senior year.

I knew I wasn't going to be able to focus much on academics; I was too concerned with how to get back to my glamorous life in New York. So I flipped through the stack of college applications I had ordered before leaving for the summer and identified the schools with early admissions programs. My college counselor encouraged me to apply early to Harvard, because I'd be notified in December but would have until May to respond. When I visited after getting in, I told a friend who was already a freshman there that I didn't think I would like Harvard much, but surviving it would serve me well. She agreed; she felt lonely and isolated at Harvard. But she was surprised that I looked at it the same way she did—after all, she was on financial aid. Still, I saw Harvard as a way to get away from my parents and on the road to the adult life I had already tasted in New York.

Shortly after I received my acceptance, everything started to fall apart. I should have been happy, but the future I was headed toward didn't actually look like a lot of fun, and I was, suddenly, uncertain about what I had gotten myself into. I felt pressured and wanted to take a year off to figure things out, but my parents, who were then at a very difficult point in their marriage, were so thrilled about my college choice that it felt impossible to put on the brakes. So I looked for ways to relieve my stress and depression.

Thanksgiving that year came right after my second Harvard visit. I had looked forward to the trip because it meant I could spend a few days in New York before heading back home. Everything was going great: I had a meeting at Ford Models about East Coast representation, I was reasonably sure I was going to Harvard in the fall (unless I could convince my parents to let me go to Columbia or NYU instead—fat chance), and I was back in my native city and reunited with the growing group of friends that I had met on holidays in Europe and the Caribbean. In the more ethnically diverse, more international and sophisticated context of New York, a girl who looked like I did was very dateable—especially if you'd met her in, say, Barbados. I felt a part of things in New York in a way I didn't in San Francisco. I remember walking happily around the city, thinking I couldn't wait to get away from home and get on with my life.

But in the midst of this came a crisis. I spent Thanksgiving night at my aunt's brownstone on Riverside Drive. In the past I had always loved Thanksgiving meals, but this particular evening the smells permeating the house—of turkey roasting, candied yams bubbling in pools of butter and brown sugar, and pumpkin pie baking, with its golden brown buttery crust— filled me with terror. I tried not to inhale too deeply, imagining that even smells this rich would be enough to put cellulite on my thighs. Stepping from the shower, I proudly surveyed the slender dancer's body I had worked so hard to create. Just a little more to lose, I thought, scrutinizing my thighs. I believed that my appearance was my ticket to the life I wanted—on my own terms and without parental supervision—because the money I earned modeling would give me some financial independence.

As I dressed for dinner, I imagined each item that was to be served as a small pile of lard. At the dinner table, I sat down next to my cousin Christopher and began to pick at my plate. By the time he had finished seconds, I had scarcely eaten a third of my food. When he returned with his third helping, Christopher brought a piece of pumpkin pie for me. I looked at it in terror, but I couldn't resist. I took one bite, and before I knew it the entire slice had disappeared, along with the rest of the food on my plate. I excused myself and headed for the small bathroom downstairs where I would not be discovered. I locked the bathroom door behind me, then bent over the toilet bowl, stuck my index finger down my throat, and gagged repeatedly.

In exact reverse of the order I had consumed them, the turkey, stuffing, yams, pie, cranberry sauce, and string beans came up. Finally there was nothing left but bitter green bile. With a feeling of relief and accomplishment, I flushed the toilet and turned to the sink to wash my hands, splash cold water on my face, and rinse the bile from my mouth. Meeting my own gaze in the mirror, I tried to reassure myself that everything was under control. I remember thinking then that I would never need to throw up again. I could stop myself whenever I wanted to.

Unfortunately, my body was beginning to fight back against starvation, and it was just the start of the food-filled holidays. My parents were no longer able to turn a blind eye, because the binge-and-purge cycle left evidence (disappearing food, bloodshot eyes). They finally confronted me; wanting to put their minds at ease, I went to see a therapist. But I wasn't ready to change my behavior. We spent the first few sessions talking about current events and travel. In an attempt to draw me out and open the discussion about my behaviors around food, the therapist started asking me questions about which behaviors I indulged in: Do you induce gagging? Do you take laxatives? Do you ever . . . A few of the things she mentioned I wasn't even aware of. I promptly incorporated this new skill set and, shortly thereafter, stopped seeing her.

It is probably not coincidental that the real onset of my disease coincided with the unraveling of my parents' marriage. The worse things got at home, the more I turned up the pressure on myself to be, or at least look, perfect. During a school break in January of my senior year, my father and I went to Barbados. We usually went between Christmas and New Year's, but that year I had my coming-out ball. I hadn't wanted to have one—I didn't see any point in all the teas and ridiculous rehearsals—but my mother, who had been a debutante herself, insisted on it.

In Barbados, away from the pressures of boys and school, I felt relaxed. Then one day, my father invited me to lunch with himself and a "new friend." She turned out to be his mistress. At least, though, I had regained control of my eating. I wasn't purging, just restricting, so overall, I felt better.

Fortunately, Harvard turned out to be a better experience than I had anticipated, by far. I found my first real set of close friends there. We lived in dorms, so isolating the way I did at home just wasn't possible. The people I met were more like me, their economic backgrounds much more varied than those of my high school peers. They made me feel valued, understood, and accepted as a person. Also, at Harvard, I didn't have as much control over my food choices as I had in high school. My social universe revolved around eating in the dorm and at the clubs I belonged to (the Signet and the Hasty Pudding). In my view at the time, I was fat during college. But it just didn't matter as much to me anymore. I had friends and boyfriends. I was part of the social life of school in a way that I had never been before. I wasn't purging or starving, so I thought of myself as cured.

During the summer after junior year, I took my first solo trip to LA to visit my half sister. Always observant, she suggested that I go to see a film called *Eating* that was then in the theaters, a faux documentary about women in LA and their attitudes toward food. During the film, one of the characters spoke about having realized that her issues with food were only one symptom of obsessive-compulsive disorder. She had gone from food to men and shopping. I felt a shock of recognition: Hadn't I just come from a shopping spree in Paris and a week-long whirlwind romantic trip with my latest gorgeous Italian boy? Maybe I wasn't as well as I thought.

When I got home from the movie, I had a long talk with my half sister about my thoughts, and she suggested that I write about my experiences. At the time, there had never been an article about black women with anorexia or bulimia, and there was no research to support that black women were even at risk. I pitched the story to *Essence,* and they bought it, and also sponsored a study to run along with the article. Writing about my own experience was far more difficult than I'd anticipated. It went against everything I had been taught by my parents about discretion and "keeping our business private." But ultimately, it was also liberating, because it put a flaw of mine into the public eye in a way that ensured that I could never be mistaken for perfect again.

My short biography in *Essence* described me as a "recovered anorexic and bulimic." The reality was that my battle would go on for another decade.

For a few years, I successfully made my disorder into a career. As the Beauty and Fitness editor of a magazine aimed at African American women, it was my job to embody the attributes in my job title. At my interview, the editor in chief said that part of the way she would be able to justify my salary (I had negotiated a much larger amount than they had initially offered) would be to use me as a model for some stories. I went to parties and did some TV spots. Ironically, since I had always viewed it as my "job" in the world to be thin and attractive, making a career out of it took some of the pressure off. It helped me to explain to my friends why I placed so much importance on my appearance: It was a prerequisite for my blossoming editorial career. Anyway, none of them minded going to the parties and fashion shows I took them along to as part of my job.

Then, in the fall of 1996, I met a Swedish artist and fell madly in love. Peter loved me in a way I hadn't experienced ever before. He didn't care about Harvard; he didn't care about parties and fashion shows; he didn't care about who my parents were or what they did. He cared about me. And we lived together, which meant that I could not hide anything from him. Consequently, I had to choose between holding on to an old way of doing things and embracing something new: letting someone in completely; thinking about what was best for us both; wanting to have children. Ultimately, things didn't work out between us, but we have remained good friends. I felt a safety and security with Peter that I had never felt in my own family. And that shelter allowed me to grow, change, and see my own worth as an individual—not just as a commodity.

Peter thought I was beautiful and didn't understand why I put so much pressure on myself about maintaining a certain weight.

Had I moved to LA without already having had an eating disorder, I would surely have found one here. In West Hollywood, where I live, it is a rare day when I see anyone on the street who is older than forty-five or younger than about twenty, much less anyone seriously out of shape or unattractive. My neighborhood isn't reality. It's the entertainment world.

Because I work behind the camera and primarily deal with writers and investors, my livelihood is not wholly dependent on the way I look—but it does play a part, as in almost every business. I still go to the gym often, watch what I eat, and shop for nice clothes. But I experience nothing like the pressures that my friends who are actresses face. On one film I worked on, the entire production was delayed for weeks so that the lead actress could do double workouts and starve herself down to her prepregnancy weight. My own past gives me a lot of compassion for actresses, making me a better producer and, I hope, a better friend. But I find it strange that the tabloids run stories about actresses suffering from eating disorders. That's not news to anyone here.

LA is a kind of enabler to people on perpetual diets. Any restaurant will happily make changes to any item on the menu. Bread is rarely served unless specifically requested; at the very least, you'll be asked before it is brought to the table. Organic and vegan restaurants are plentiful, and no one raises an eyebrow if you only ever order fish, despite warnings about mercury.

New York is a different planet. My friends there will tell me

I am being ridiculous when I spend twenty minutes going to different coffee places looking for one that will make my latte with almond milk instead of soy. In LA, that passes for acceptable adult behavior.

Today, I am definitely on the vigilant side of weight awareness. But for the first time, about six months ago, I saw someone I thought looked too thin. She was at my gym, wearing an '80s getup of leotard and tights. Her legs were so spindly that it looked like she might just collapse. Her skin was sallow and gray, and her hair was thin and limp, although she could not have been over twenty-five. For the very first time, I saw what other people must have seen when I was an anorexic: someone who looked ill.

For the first time in my life, I am living alone. I run my own company. I eat well and take care of myself, because I like who I am and value my health. Progress, not perfection, is what I strive for.

Sometimes, at a dinner party, I will notice a woman slip into a bathroom after the meal, or push the food around her plate and then have it cleared as soon as possible. In her eyes, I see the darkness of hunger, and it sends a shiver up my spine. Once I would have felt a kind of twisted solidarity. But these days, I look away: I take a deep breath, and thank God that I am well. And then, sometimes, I even have dessert. . . .

SHAPE-SHIFTING

Amanda Fortini

———

I watched the doctor's hands as he wrote out the diet. He had large hands with thick, truncated fingers. He wore a wedding band that appeared permanently embedded in the flesh creeping up around it. These were the hands of a man who liked to eat.

I focused on his hands as a way of distracting myself from the anger tightening its grip on my chest. I was convinced that if I looked at his face, I might snatch his expensive pen from his meaty paws and throw it across the room. This was the fourth time in two months I had come to my doctor—let's call him Dr. F.—complaining of a radical change in the rhythms of my digestion, a shift accompanied by a swift, inexplicable weight loss, both of which had occurred after I'd returned from a trip to Belize. He had performed a few routine tests, found nothing. And so he was writing out for me a beef-heavy, cream-rich, high-lipid diet on his letterhead. It read:

Breakfast: Scrambled eggs, bacon
Lunch: Red meat (hamburger, steak), potatoes, cheese
Dinner: Steak, potatoes
Snack: Milk shakes (w/ full-fat ice cream)

"For the milk shakes," he said as he tore the "prescription" from his pad and pushed it across the desk with a self-satisfied flourish, "be sure to use Häagen-Dazs ice cream. We have to fatten you up."

I studied the sclerosis-inducing regimen—milk shakes? Was this the 1950s?—and tried, one more time, to explain the situation to him. The problem was not that I was depriving myself. The problem was that I was eating just as I always had, and I was still losing weight.

"You've gotten far too thin," he said, not listening. "Obviously you're not eating enough."

For him, the equation was elementary: Calories consumed equaled pounds gained. If I was losing weight, it had to be because I was starving myself. In a way, I understood the source of his bias. Here I was, a young woman in her early twenties, a former dancer, an assistant at a fashion magazine, my hip bones and collarbones shockingly (and, yes, fashionably) protuberant. The context clues pointed overwhelmingly one way: I must be anorexic.

I tried again. I described for him, in the most graphic images I could conjure, the revolt under way in my intestines. I told him about the relentless nausea and bloating, the humiliatingly frequent trips to the office restroom. I explained that, for obvious reasons, this was affecting my work life, my social life, everything.

He patted my hand and gave me an indulgent smile. "Just give the diet a try."

———

In the most superficial sense, my doctor was right: I needed to gain weight. Since returning from Belize two months earlier,

I had shed the fleshly equivalent of a small child. At five feet six and a shade over 120 pounds, I had always hovered on the thin side of normal, but after my rapid, post-Belize attenuation, the needle on the scale barely hit the hundred mark. My soft, slightly rounded physique had become all sharp angles and flat planes: prominent clavicles; concave abdomen; visible, countable ribs.

I have to admit that, in the beginning at least, as the weight began to fall away, I enjoyed my metamorphosis. All those epithets we have coined to describe annoying areas of recalcitrant flesh—bat wings, back fat, love handles, muffin tops—no longer applied to me. I remember standing beneath the harsh fluorescent lights in the dressing room at Saks and thinking, *Give me tight! Give me diaphanous! Give me sleeveless!* For the first time since I was a teenager, I could take a photograph in which I did not appear to have Nixon-like jowls. I began to look more frequently in mirrors. So thoroughly had I internalized our culture's idolization of the very thin that I was secretly pleased by a weight loss I knew to have sinister roots.

All of this must sound vain, perhaps shallow, and no small part of it was. But there was also an anthropological aspect to my curiosity; I came to regard my ever-transfiguring form with a fair amount of detachment. Watching my face and body shape-shift during such a short period of time was a bit like watching a natural disaster play itself out. I understood the phenomenon was pernicious, and that the final outcome might be catastrophic, but I could not look away. And then, my recently acquired narcissism was nourished by a bizarre sense of disassociation. When I looked at myself in the mirror, the self I saw did not align with the self I felt I was. Viewing my reflection initiated an eerie sort of time travel, transporting me at once backward and forward: to the ridiculous teenager I was long ago, the gangly ballet dancer who for two years ate only fat-free foods, and to the wizened old woman, her cheeks sunken and forehead pronounced, I might one day become. I grew to understand, in a profoundly tangible manner, the way inner identity arises from outward form. And I like to think that my literal navel-gazing was an attempt to get a fix on my drastic transformation.

———

I remember the moment I first became aware of weight as a measure of self-worth and a standard for external appraisal.

I was in ballet class, and we were moving through our daily warm-up exercises at the barre. The sequence on this particular day required that we bend forward, the fingertips of our extended arms lightly brushing the floor, before rising up onto our toes in a slow, controlled manner and arching almost imperceptibly backward.

"Hey," whispered the girl behind me, a pretty brunette about five years older than I was (or so, at age eleven, I assumed—she already wore lipstick). As we collectively bowed, I looked behind me and caught a glimpse of the back of her head, her unruly curls pulled into a severe bun. "How do you stay so thin?"

"What?" I whispered back. I had no idea what she meant. *Overweight, diet, calorie, anorexia:* these words had not yet entered my lexicon.

"I mean, what do you *do*? Do you take diet pills?"

I did not know how to answer her. "I don't do anything," I answered. Which, at the time, was true.

But as I spoke, I was bothered by a vague awareness that it

was not just the smear of fuchsia lipstick that separated me
from this girl. In some subterranean region of my mind, I
understood that I had not yet met with certain changes that
she, and many of the other girls, had experienced. In fact, I
had only the dimmest apprehension of what those changes
were. (That I was in class with these young women, cram-
ming my still-growing feet into pointe shoes to dance at the
advanced level, now seems to me one of many examples of
the ballet world's complete disregard for the realities of the
body.) I knew, in the visceral way dancers have of knowing such things, that when I lifted my arms or arched my back,
my hips and ribs and collarbones still created the jagged lines
of a professional dancer, the angular geometries that appealed
to audiences. I could still move easily and lightly, without the
huffing-puffing effort it took some of the older girls. I did
not possess a bothersome layer of midsection padding that
bunched up inelegantly when I executed an arabesque, and
that our teacher, Madame M., would poke at with her fearsome cane—or, worse, pinch with her manicured hands—as
she strolled past, commenting that the bulk "ruined the line."
No part of my taut, childish body continued to bounce after I
completed a jump. This was because I was still, essentially, a
child: I had neither breasts nor a monthly period that made a
leotard a sometimes risky venture (and would not have either
for another five years). I knew that for a young dancer such
changes were undesirable, but that they were on the horizon
just the same.

A few months after this incident, I began to manipulate my
food intake. I found in my mother's bedroom a diet book by
Victoria Principal called *The Body Principal*, in which the former *Dallas* actress shared her tips for keeping trim. A bowl of

Cheerios with skim milk was the ideal breakfast; eating cheese
was tantamount to "rubbing it on your thighs." I sat on the bed
and read the book cover to cover, absorbing every word as
gospel. Here was a concrete strategy, easily followed, for avoiding the flabby pitfalls of adolescence. Here was a method for
preserving "the dignity" of my childhood body, to borrow a
phrase from Naomi Wolf. Tuna fish, plain yogurt, and bananas
ranked high on Ms. Principal's list of acceptable foods, so they
also came to figure heavily in my own diet. ("Amanda's smelly
lunches," teased my fifth-grade friends, whose own brown bags
contained lunch-meat sandwiches and packaged fruit snacks.)
For several years, I ate Cheerios every morning. I categorically
avoided the menace of cheese. Eventually I became a "vegetarian," which, in my interpretation, meant pulling the meat
out of a sandwich and consuming only lettuce, tomatoes,
and bread. I always ate enough of my "allowable" foods, and I
didn't obsess over numbers—my mother didn't own a scale—
but my relationship to food was rigid and, as I entered my
teenage years, heading toward injurious. If an eating disorder is
loosely defined as an abnormal fixation on food, then I had the
malignant mind-set, and I was flirting with real illness.

In ballet class, my efforts to keep my body at the low end of
what it would tolerate were met with approval. We were never
provided with dietary guidelines or cross-examined about what
we ate, but the importance of remaining blade-thin was communicated to us in myriad other ways. There was the cane that
prodded bulges, the chorus of girls who snickered at the jiggling thighs of a fellow dancer as she performed *grand jetés*
to an unfortunate lyric from "Love Shack" by the B-52's: "Hop
in my Chrysler / It's as big as a whale / And it's about to set
sail!" I was frequently commended for my physique, held up

as an example before my fellow classmates, some of whom battled with their weight. In the middle of an audition for a prominent ballet school in Chicago, the head teacher pushed my leg high up over my head and announced in her thick Russian accent, "You look like a dancer. I will make you a dancer." My part of the bargain was to continue to deprive my body for the sake of my craft. The balance demanded of us was delicate: Remain strong enough to dance and yet free of even an ounce of excess flesh.

At age sixteen, weary of missed school and endless teasing ("bean stalk," "mosquito bites," and the like), I quit dancing. Within a few months, I began to develop as my nonballet peers had long before. For a time, I continued to select from my menu of fat-free foods (many of which, incidentally, were processed, and I shudder now to think of the chemicals I ingested), but gradually my palate revolted. Then, as a freshman in college, I became completely absorbed in my studies and lost interest in dieting entirely. All around me, anorexia was in full flower: the skeletal girl who ate piles of cucumber slices for every meal; her doppelgänger, who forced "just a bite" on others while refusing to take one herself; the hollow-eyed member of the Kennedy clan, all pointy elbows and knobby knees, who appeared in the dining hall for every meal but never, ever ate. To me, it seemed that these young women were not only wasting away, they were wasting a fleeting opportunity. Counting calories, worrying about weight, not to mention starving your brain of nutrients: Suddenly it all felt shameful, wrong, *boring*.

Not long ago, I read an article about anorexia in *The New York Times Magazine,* in which Daniel Le Grange, an associate professor of psychiatry at the University of Chicago, was quoted as saying, "If you are constitutionally slender and it's easy for you to diet and you like ballet, and you live in the United States, and you're 13, and your personality is perfectionist, your chance of developing this illness is very, very high." The sentence stopped me cold. I had been, I realized, a prime candidate for anorexia. For many dancers, habitual dietary restriction creates neurochemical changes that manifest as depression, anxiety, bingeing, social withdrawal, ruminating about food—all of which create fertile soil for eating disorders to grow. And yet my problems with food always remained low-grade and manageable. For whatever reason—a mother who didn't obsess about her weight, or perhaps a lucky genetic draw—I had escaped a dancer's usual fate.

But in my twenties, upon becoming ill, I once again slipped into a perverse romance with thinness. This ran deeper than a delight in my ability to wear slinky, body-skimming clothes. Suddenly, I found myself able to glide around with an unencumbered ease I had not experienced since adolescence, and I liked it. I would call the sentiment nostalgia if it hadn't felt so physiological, so chemical. Studies have shown that in the minds of those predisposed to eating disorders, starvation can create a sense of euphoria by altering the levels of certain neurotransmitters in the brain. In my experience, *any* considerable weight loss engenders a similar feeling. Although I was eating as much as I could, my body wasn't absorbing the calories, so from my brain's perspective at least, I was starving. Even as I worried I might truly be dying, I was reminded of how keenly I relished being exceedingly thin. *How fabulous to be able to eat whatever I want and not gain a pound!* How demented, given the circumstances, to have this thought at all.

———

When I think about it now, I can't really blame myself for obsessing over my slimness, even for taking some pleasure in it. Because if I was paying an inordinate amount of attention to my changed shape, this was nothing compared to the attention it was getting from others. I learned, for instance, that many men, whatever they may claim to the contrary, are drawn to frighteningly lean women. As an average, medium-size woman, I was unremarkable and innocuous. As a slip of a thing, I was a minor sensation. Men flirted with me extravagantly. A critic for a highbrow magazine slipped me his business card, whispered, "Call me," and, after an almost comically pregnant pause, leaned in to add, "socially," as though we were actors in a noir film. It was not that I had never been hit on, but never—and never since—with such audacity or frequency. And I could only point to my sudden waifishness, my newly excavated cheekbones and sinewy upper arms, as the source of all the silly come-ons and smoldering glances. Had I dyed my brown hair platinum blond or augmented my breasts, I imagine the effect would have been similar—an almost overnight alteration of the way I was perceived by the world.

Like those other fetishized symbols of a stereotypical sort of femininity, thinness, I came to realize, carries its own set of misperceptions. If, according to the antiquated logic of some men, blond women are wrongly thought to be less intelligent, or buxom women to be, well, more willing, then thin women are often viewed as weak, vulnerable, in need of protection. My figure, it seemed, conveyed all this about me without my saying a word. During those months I was ill, I came to believe there is something primal in the male gravitation toward female frailty, an attraction the media may have reinforced but did not create. A physically small woman serves, perhaps, as a visible affirmation of the differences between the sexes (however superficial those differences may in reality be). One literary type with an overblown streak of romanticism captured this notion for me when he said I reminded him of a heroine from a Joan Didion novel. As anyone who has read Didion knows, the comment was hardly the compliment he intended, but I thought I understood what he meant: all bones and big eyes. Insert macho rescue fantasy here.

If men took notice, women took it upon themselves to comment. There exists a type of woman who is drawn to another woman's weight loss like a shark is drawn to blood: *Look how tiny you've gotten! Are you eating? What are you eating? You should eat more.* At work, an editor, walking behind me down the hall, hollered, "You're such a whippet!" And one afternoon, while I stood at the photocopier wearing a pair of pin-striped black pants that had long since grown baggy, the photo editor passed by and said aloud, as if to no one in particular, as if I weren't standing right there, "Okay, now you're really going too far! Being that thin is just gross."

I learned that people feel it's appropriate to comment on weight if it falls toward the low end of the scale. The assumption seems to be that, as the saying goes, one can never be too thin, so telling someone she's too skinny is like telling her she's too smart. But that's not how it felt: It was like being constantly reminded of how sickly I looked. And of course, had I gained weight, not a soul would have asked about my dietary habits.

Perhaps I'm being too cynical. It's true that some of the remarks were made out of genuine concern for my well-being. But an equal number were motivated by the tangle of complex feelings stirred by the sight of a skinny woman: jealousy, admiration for her (supposed) discipline and willpower, pity that she feels she must conform to an impossible cultural ideal. More than once, I was asked, in a single conspiratorial breath, "Are you eating enough . . . and how did you lose the weight?" A slender woman is treated like some kind of human bulletin board; or perhaps a chat room is the era-appropriate metaphor. Her body becomes a locus for people to air their thoughts and anxieties about weight.

Granted, I worked at a fashion magazine. We were in the business of perpetuating thinness, and on birthdays we ordered cakes that went untouched. But the women I knew outside the office were just as vocal on the subject of my weight loss. And while it bothered me to field public editorializing about what seemed to me a private topic, it bothered me more that the comments, even the well-meaning ones, were almost entirely off the mark. The insinuation was always that I was eating too little or exercising too much when, in truth, I was seriously unwell.

———

Why, I've often wondered, are women so invested in the weight loss of other women? Few, suspecting a colleague's alcoholism or depression, would feel compelled to comment. Why do eating disorders provoke such strong reactions? Why does anorexia (or the possibility of it) at once intrigue and repulse? The easy explanation is that our culture worships an unrealistic ideal of thinness, which few healthy women will ever attain. Newly svelte women are closer to meeting that preposterous standard, and thus arouse the ire and insecurities of other members of their sex.

But this theory is far too simplistic. The problem is not only that our society celebrates slenderness, but that this celebration occurs in a country where food is overabundant and eating habits are excessive. A handful of psychologists and academics have pointed to this combination of factors as an explanation for eating disorders. "While each case involves a mix of individual biology, psychology, and culture, eating disorders flourish whenever affluence combines with the idealization of a slim female body," Joan Jacobs Brumberg, author of *Fasting Girls: A History of Anorexia Nervosa,* writes in her excellent introduction to *Thin,* the companion book to Lauren Greenfield's much-praised documentary of the same name. I believe, however, that this idea also goes a long way toward explaining the widespread female fascination with weight.

When I watched *Thin,* which follows four young women receiving treatment at a clinic for eating disorders, I was struck by the shots of the food the girls are expected to eat as part of their "refeeding" process. Much of it was junk: chips, cookies, pizza. The young women are taught that it's unwise to "restrict," and that paying attention to nutritional content is a form of restricting. In one photograph in the companion book, an enormous box of Pop-Tarts looms ominously in the foreground; the girls sitting nearby anxiously eye the box in anticipation of having to partake of its contents. "In a Mindful Eating therapy session, residents have to eat a 'fear food' such as Pop-Tarts, doughnuts, or candy bars and then discuss their feelings," the caption reads. The irony—that consuming Pop-Tarts and doughnuts is considered "mindful eating"—is difficult to miss. Then there are the nurses who direct the girls' treatment: They are not just overweight; they are, to be blunt, obese. The contrast between these corpulent women and their tiny, birdlike charges is shocking. One group is thin to the point of disease, the other fat to the point of disease. Even as they repeatedly remind the girls that counting a single caloric is verboten, the nurses are several times shown discussing their own diets and methods for shedding pounds.

All of this serves to highlight how truly dysfunctional our collective attitudes toward food and weight are. The uncomfortable truth is that anyone who eats a diet consisting predominantly of the sort of processed foods so prevalent in the film, without restriction, without regulation, will likely end up struggling with his or her weight. We live in a culture of excess that teaches us we *must* "restrict" what we eat to a greater or lesser degree. We obsess about dieting and calories because there is no other way to remain healthy. Women with eating disorders have simply taken our universal preoccupation to its frightening extreme. Emaciation has become a status symbol— a sign of discipline, a willful shunning of the temptations most people cannot resist. You might say our morbid curiosity about anorexia and bulimia is a logical extension of our morbid relationship to food.

———

After a time, the scrutiny began to wear on me. I grew paranoid. I fretted that my friends and colleagues thought I was willfully ravaging my body, and I tried to demonstrate otherwise every chance I got. At restaurants, I ate heartily regardless of whether I felt hungry. If sweets were offered during meetings, I made a show of devouring some. Once, after I had grown gaunt enough to prompt a remark that I looked "like Anne Frank," I bought a giant, gooey cinnamon roll, the sort consumed primarily by travelers in Midwestern airports, and polished it off during an editorial meeting. I'm sure my colleagues thought I was bulimic. The absurdity of my behavior was not lost on me: In my quest to make clear that I did not have an eating disorder, I was acting like someone who did.

Why not simply admit I was sick? That, too, seemed a delicate personal matter, and not one for interoffice parsing. In any case, I wouldn't have known what to say; after numerous visits to my internist, I still didn't know what was wrong with me. When I typed "unexplained weight loss" into Google, the scary possibilities floated up: thyroid malfunction, pituitary tumor, lupus, cancer, HIV. If the world was going to believe I was ailing—and who could blame them, as it was disturbingly evident I was—perhaps anorexia was the best of the many bad disorders to have. The truth is, the other maladies so terrified me that I didn't want to think about them. And so you might say that in my unwillingness to speak of my mysterious illness, I perpetuated my coworkers' misguided assumption.

Meanwhile, my body pressed on with its death march toward cadaverous. I stopped getting my period. At some point, I started to avoid mirrors as actively as I had once sought them out. My face looked so drawn that whenever I caught a glimpse of it, the Bob Dylan lyric "the ghost of electricity howls in the bones of her face," came to mind. Indeed, I felt ghostlike, invisible. If I pulled my hair back, my ears looked enormous. I thought I resembled a hobbit, some kind of wood nymph or elf.

Every couple of weeks, as I grew increasingly ill, I'd visit Dr. F. And here is where the knee-jerk cultural assumption I'd been facing—bony young woman equals practicing anorexic—ceased to be merely annoying and became potentially dangerous. When his initial exploratory measures didn't lead to a diagnosis, Dr. F. neither ordered more tests nor sent me to a specialist, even as I continued to drop several pounds a week.

Instead, he decided that I had an eating disorder and, if I was interpreting his forbearing tone correctly, that I was a hypochondriac as well. I was causing my problems. I might be imagining things. I needed to *eat.*

I can almost understand his failure to listen to me. Anorexics are known to be duplicitous, and I'm sure he assumed I was lying. Eating disorders can also create a host of physical symptoms not unlike my complaints (nausea, abdominal pain, fatigue). But why not entertain other possibilities? Why discount weight loss as one of the surest signs of illness? Why not consider that deranged digestion, rather than being the self-induced consequence of some aberrant dietary practice, might itself be a serious problem, a signal flare sent out by a body gone astray? Would he have treated me so cavalierly had I been a man?

And what if I *had* been anorexic? The irony, of course, is that although he may have diagnosed the disorder, I still would not have received proper treatment. Some Victorian-era rest cure consisting of fatty foods (the sort of therapy Virginia Woolf was forced to submit to) can hardly be the answer for a young woman with a crushing fear of gaining weight. Nor is telling the patient to *just eat, just get over it,* as though the disease were a question of a quick change of mind rather than a problem of disordered brain chemistry.

———

Eventually, six months after I first fell ill, I left Dr. F. and found myself a specialist.

Months after that, I received a diagnosis. I'd acquired a parasite called *Entamoeba histolytica,* more commonly known as an amoeba, in Belize. Since I'd had it for so long, multiple courses of drugs over several years (megadoses of Flagyl, Humatin, combinations of the two) were required to treat it. When I think back on the experience, I can't help but mentally shake an angry fist at Dr. F. for refusing to see beyond his prejudice. Parasites are notoriously difficult to diagnose, and multiple tests are often required to pinpoint one, but had he taken my clamoring more seriously, I doubt so many months would have passed before the problem was uncovered.

When I got the diagnosis, I finally enlightened my boss and several of my coworkers. In truth, I had no choice in the matter; the Flagyl left me so dizzy and disoriented for several hours after each dose (a very high seven hundred and fifty milligrams several times a day) that I had to use vacation days to take it. "A parasite!" an editor exclaimed when I told her. "So that's it! We were wondering what was wrong." And with her comment, the nagging suspicion that my weight loss had been gossiped about over after-work drinks and midday cigarette breaks was confirmed. A few colleagues, upon hearing the story, asked, half-jokingly, where they could get a parasite of their own.

EARNING LIFE

Clara Elliot

———

We lived in a small New England town, at the edge of the woods; the forest was part of our home. My mother and father are professors, my sister and I strong of mind. I have a half brother, too—my father's son from his first marriage—but for most of my childhood he lived in the South with his mother. We were brought up to live respecting nature and the quiet introspection that nature provides. I loved both nudity and fine clothes. I dried off after baths by running naked up and down the hall; I swam naked, danced naked, played in the dirt naked. Conversely, I would go to the barbershop or a Girl Scouts meeting in a princess costume or a wedding gown. Bodies were glamorous and triumphant to me. They were also curious things. My stomach, for instance, was elastic. I could roll it like dough in my hands, but it would glide back, smooth and cool, as soon as I let it go. And let us not forget the belly button: the original mystery. Why it could not turn outside-in was beyond me. I never stopped trying.

We gathered together for family dinners with minnows of reflected pool-light swimming on our ceiling and the noise of my father's printer pounding out his night's work down the hall. My mother put her excessive pile of work aside to cook; she functions best on the adrenaline of too much to do. In a vegetarian household, such as ours, the cook must practice variety and creativity with meals to keep everybody both healthy and interested (especially my father, who is not a willing vegetarian). My mother was up to this challenge. I remember in particular her root phase. It all started with the yucca root. Once she had discovered these hairy, edible beasts, she would come home with what looked like a football-size potato and a packet of papers under her arm. As she sliced us slabs of root like Christmas ham or ladled us a grayish root puree, she read to us of its exotic tropical origin and the benefits of eating its vitamin-rich skin. For Christmas that year she received roots of all shapes and sizes. I remember her beating them with mallets in the kitchen as the chairs and china rattled throughout the downstairs.

It wasn't until middle school that I realized your body's appearance could cause you pain, or considered the connection between what you eat and how you look. My physical gripes had always been with my red, fuzzy hair, which I thought made me look like a pumpkin. But my sister, Elizabeth, was two years older than I, so the insecurities of puberty hit her first. She refused to eat anything cooked in oil. Then she stopped eating dinner with the family, though my parents still forced her to sit with us. Occasionally, when I gazed in Elizabeth's direction, she would look uncomfortable and demand, "Stop looking at my fat!" I had never seen anything like it before, and I swore I would never become trapped like that. If I kept my body thin, I decided, I would be safe.

———

For the tenth grade, my sister was accepted into an elite private school. One day that summer, I heard retching noises coming from the bathroom next to mine. I laughed and called over, "It sounds like someone is throwing up in there!" Later, Elizabeth came and sat on my bed. Speaking nervously, with tight, flickering smiles, she confessed that she had started throwing up her food. She said that she had wanted to tell me for weeks. When I asked her why, she explained that she didn't want to enter her new school fat.

I was worried and wanted Elizabeth to tell our mom. When she refused, I came up with an easy subterfuge: I realized the only way to make her expose herself was to say I'd decided to start throwing up myself. Cruel as she was being to herself, I knew she wouldn't be able to watch me suffer that same cruelty. She was horrified and brought her concerns to our mother, who handled the situation with uncharacteristic calm, coaxing my sister to discuss her fears and address them with less hysteria. Elizabeth maintained a punitive relationship with her body for years, but she stopped purging shortly after this intervention.

Unfortunately, the idea of punishing your body to soothe your anxious soul had registered in my mind.

Two years passed, and I entered high school myself—a much more liberal school than Elizabeth's, but no less rigorous. In our family, academic success was a measure of your worth. It wasn't grades themselves that were important, but something more abstract, which my mother referred to as "intellectual integrity." Since that is hard to judge, I figured if I studied to the limit of my capacity, I would be forgiven my human shortcomings. So at least once a week I would be hunched over my textbooks at 3:00 a.m., my intestines twisted and acidy with fear, my eyes burning, mouthing facts as I read. My mother complained that I wore myself out, but she also brought me coffee at midnight, and it was hard not to think she secretly approved of my rigor.

In many ways, I emulated her. She pushed herself with equal want of mercy, as if dogged by ceaseless fears of being exposed as a fraud. Her parents had left enormous academic and artistic footprints, and she followed in their path, becoming a teacher and poet. Obscure mediocrity was to her, I believe, not worth calling life. It was an ethos she'd inherited from her own mother, who was as imperiously dismissive of the foolish and lazy masses as she was fiercely loyal to those whom she admired and loved. Diligence was assumed in that family, brilliance expected. But my mother never trusted herself to succeed naturally, so she drove herself all the more. Teaching, writing, judging literary prizes, manning literary boards—she continually accepted more work than she could comfortably handle. Part of her was frozen as the child I was myself: contorting beautiful, intuitive passions into self-flagellation, trying to earn her mother's and the world's approval. Success was survival. Success was security and love.

My mother resembled as much as feared my grandmother, though she couldn't recognize how much she did either. My grandmother had been notorious for her tyrannical fits of fury, condemnation, and contempt. In my mother's outbursts, she would say things I later discovered echoed her own mother's words.

———

I was the good child. My half brother moved in with us that year after dropping out of college and disappearing for several months. He was strange: withdrawn, filthy, and protective like a miser of his mildewed and bundled possessions. He seemed to watch the world from a stormy, unreachable place. As for Elizabeth, she felt tormented and devalued by the social priorities at her school. She dimmed her natural creative, artistic, and intellectual self, abandoning her books for expensive clothes and becoming fiercely critical of our family's eccentricity. Our parents were vocally worried about how both she and her schoolwork suffered. I didn't want to cause them any additional worry, so I studied all the harder.

Because scholastic success was uncertain (there would always be another test, another chance to fail), I found that I needed something more reliable to control. That became my stomach. As part of my evening study routine, I started doing crunches, and the practice became religious. I did more and more. Even after I had finished studying at 4:00 or 5:00 a.m., I would lie down in the bathroom and do my crunches on the hard tile floor. As my academic stress increased, I started eating less, too. Whenever I felt out of control, I went to the mirror and lifted up my shirt, to remind myself that my stomach was small and flat.

My father used to infuriate me by gently insisting that everybody, consciously and unconsciously, makes the life they fundamentally want. I had never had a boyfriend and wouldn't until I was almost seventeen. My father saw what I didn't: More than loneliness, I feared intimacy. I trusted only the veneer I could present, not my core. My anxious study habits and my boniness kept the world at arm's length, where I felt secure.

———

We spent my sophomore year in Italy, where my parents had been offered a grant to live and study by the American Academy in Rome. My sister and I rented Italian-language tapes and

eagerly prepared for the trip. My brother, who was withdraw-
ing deeper into the shadows of his mind, stayed behind. Later
that year he would be diagnosed with schizophrenia.

Rome enchanted me with its combination of grandeur and
ruin. I was infected with Roman ease and sensuality. The celebration of food was everywhere. How could I not respond? The
gelato was smoother, and more subtly flavored, than regular ice
cream. In pastry shops I found apricot tarts, sticky pastry curls,
chocolate-cream-filled puffs spiraling into minarets in the windows. Pizza came in long, flat strips that were snipped with
scissors to order: pizza with salt and rosemary, pizza with
potato and garlic, pizza with baby tomato, pizza with zucchini
flower and cheese. As a restaurateur friend of ours said, people
in Europe eat less because the food tastes better. Elizabeth and
I wanted to try everything, and we did. I still avoided eating
with my parents and rarely sat down for a real meal. But along
with the ease of the environment, the freedom of the city,
and the feeling of possibilities before me, my love of the food
there soothed away a good deal of my fear. The schoolwork at
the American school Elizabeth and I attended for the year was
less demanding, too. I stopped burning the midnight oil and
adopted a more natural rhythm.

The beauty of Italy offered a kind of sensuality that enticed
rather than threatened me. In Rome, for the first time, I took
my hair down from its rigorous bun and let it flow. I often forgot to do my crunches and didn't care. Looking in the mirror, I
felt like a bundle of flowers, and I longed to give myself away.
I realized how much wealth I had in me, how much I had to
give.

When I returned to Boston, I was determined to worry less
about schoolwork and concentrate on enjoying my friends. I

fell in love with my first boyfriend, Christopher. I gained weight, and loved that, too, for it was squeezed in the smooth-fingered hands of a lover who treated it like a gift he was privileged to hold.

But at home, my parents, instead of being happy with my new, more relaxed approach to life, were concerned that I was losing focus. After all, college applications were just around the corner. When I procrastinated on an important paper for over a month in the spring, my mother became hysterical. I told her, "I used to study until I got physically ill." "Yes!" she wailed, "but you got better!" She said she no longer respected me, that I had no more "intellectual integrity." I felt betrayed, and also ashamed. I feared that she would stop loving me, as I know she feared her own mother would stop loving her if she faltered.

If my mother was harsher than she intended, it may have been because, at the same time, my parents' marriage was unraveling. My brother had moved back in with us as soon as we returned from Rome, and his illness was worse than ever. My parents couldn't understand each other's needs: My mother wanted stability and freedom to live without the fetters of illness around her. My father wanted to save his son.

Living there, I often doubted my own sanity. My brother seemed to identify me as a kind of connection to the world. Almost daily, he would creep up behind me and, with lizardlike alacrity, slip his freezing, filth-caked hands down the back of my shirt, or dart his tongue across my neck. It was heartbreaking, fragile, and desperate, but it was also revolting, terrifying, and obscene. I never felt safe. Everything in our house was infected by his madness.

Since there was no one to blame, I didn't allow myself to express anger. I just avoided spending time at home, now a place of sorrow and disease. Toward the end of my junior year, my brother finally moved into a group home. But already his illness had shaken apart the trust that bound our family together. I was angry and confused. Most of all, I felt like I was a horrible person, because I lacked the compassion to forgive my brother, who was, I reminded myself, the one who suffered most.

While I thrived in school and the outside world, at home I had lost everything I knew myself by. I was no longer a good person, because I was angry with my brother. I was no longer a respectable student, because my mother told me so. So while I appeared to mature and grow, my foundations dissolved.

———

Sensing my own frailty, I tried to rebuild my foundations— but with borrowed material because I did not trust my own. I was constantly getting messages about what I needed to improve about myself. I thought if I could just write them all down, make some master list, I could figure out how to survive.

That summer I lived alone with my sister while my parents spent time working in the country. Elizabeth was also seeking to transform herself. She had gained some weight in college and had a strict plan of diet and exercise laid out. She was working at a schizophrenia lab (her way of coping with our brother's illness), as well as reading and painting; she'd decided too much socializing and insecurity in high school had stifled her creative outlets. My parents praised her for all of this.

My own list of activities for self-improvement was long. I was to read at least one science or nonfiction book a month, study for the math section of the SAT for one or two hours each day, donate at least $200 in charity a month, do at least four hours of community service a week when school started, sign up for posture lessons, eat only a certain number of calories with no sweets or fats, watch no television, read at least a novel a week, write my college essay, wash my face with all those weird bottles of ointment my mom got me, get a job, take up yoga, learn Italian, get straight As.

Obviously, I could not do everything, so I felt I was constantly failing. The deadline for early college applications was fast approaching, and I was terrified of being thrust out into the world. My mother always intervened to protect me, as she saw it, from my perilous ignorance. Away from her vigilance, I wouldn't know how I was failing, or how to rectify my life. Though I didn't need to lose any weight, I followed my sister's diet with her. And without knowing why, I also started to binge and purge.

The purging became compulsive. I was frightened. By October I managed to stop, and running every day helped compensate. While my other goals were more elusive, running on my treadmill in the sunken basement was a concrete thing to focus on, and it became the prime source of my security each day. My schoolwork came in second, as did my friendships and my relationship with Christopher. Not only did I sacrifice time with them to stay home and run, but I also felt I had to hide my growing obsession, because I knew it looked insane.

As I lay in bed in Elizabeth's dorm room that fall on an overnight visit from home, I asked her if she ever felt chased by a shadow, a nameless fear. It lived in the darkness behind my eyes and harried me wherever I went. It twisted its hands around my spine, squeezed my heart, and slowed my breath. I asked her across the sleepy darkness if she knew that fear at all.

"No," she said. "Honey, that's the first sign of going crazy."

"Shut up, it's not like that," I said, and curled my head into my sleeping bag. I was alone with my shadow. Not even my sister could understand my isolation, or see me for who I was. Where had I lost myself? I closed my eyes and went to sleep.

Of course, I lost weight—lots of it. And I looked terrible, which I knew. But I couldn't make myself give up running. I lost so much weight that I could see all the bones on my back when I turned around in the mirror. My shoulder blades jutted out so that I looked like a fossilized pterodactyl. I felt lost and frantic, but still I couldn't stop.

During Christmas break I started to binge and purge again. In the dark weeks of winter, isolated from my friends and unable to study for exams because of my anxiety, I grew depressed and stopped trying to keep myself from vomiting. By the time exams arrived, I cared even less. I felt like throwing myself away.

On the morning of my last exam, not having slept in two nights or eaten in God knows how long, I decided to have breakfast. Once I started, I couldn't stop. I ate so much that I couldn't purge, no matter how I scalded my throat trying, no matter how I squeezed my head in my hands crying, because I had no time, no time at all, and I could not go on, and I was sorry sorry sorry. I got in the shower and started to scream. I did not know how to stop. I heard myself cry, *"I am sorry! I am sorry!"* though there was no one there. Finally I managed to cower out of the shower, still wet, and shivered into my bed. Somehow I got the phone and called my dad. "I'm sorry, I'm sorry. . . ." It was all I could say. Finally I asked him to please help me, please never let this happen again. He calmed me down as I huddled and cried. He was at work, as was my mother. My test was in an hour. I'm still amazed that I made it there, and that I passed.

After the test, I sat in the bathroom with one of my best friends and told her about the lists, the fear, that I was out of control. She wanted to put me in a hospital that day, and I wasn't diametrically opposed to it. But I had another exam to take, so I sat through that, too. Finally my father came to retrieve me from school. I relaxed into the hard embrace of his arm.

That night, I lay in my mother's lap. I wanted nothing more than to be cared for like a small child. I told her, though I could barely shape the words, that I thought I had an "eating . . . disorder." They were words I could hardly understand. She stroked my head, and said, with great sadness, "I'm afraid I have something to do with this."

———

The final months of my senior year were a haze. I felt as if I was living in a glass coffin; my obsession, shame, and self-disgust cut me off from life. I could see the world moving, but I was no longer a part of it. Bulimia is a means of dissociation: When the world becomes too much, it allows you to detach. It's a means of flirting with death. Crouched over the toilet, immersed in filth of my own making, I felt death hovering over me. I looked out the window where our frozen garden lay and cried. There was a life out there I longed for, but the glass seemed impenetrable.

I was skinnier now than ever. I was pale. I had bags under my eyes. I wouldn't let my boyfriend touch me. My friends asked me what was wrong, but I wouldn't talk to them. I wouldn't talk to anyone except my parents and the therapist they found for me, the incisive and compassionate Dr. Lieberman. I saw her every week and forced my parents to stay home with me at night. They canceled their calendars for me, had

meeting after meeting with my therapist, and tried to figure
out why this had happened to us all.

It was a terrible time for them. One Sunday, my mother
planned to take me into Boston to the Museum of Fine Arts, to
see a movie of great interest to her. When she was ready to go,
she opened the bathroom door to find me naked next to the
bathtub, my skeletal back hunched over the toilet, which was
filled with vomit, my face smeared with blood from my gush-
ing nose. I was like a mammoth insect with the bloody and terrified face of her dying child. She screamed, and I screamed.
She covered her face with her hands. She was also furious with
me. She wanted to go to the movie, but she couldn't leave me
there.

The prom was in May. I had broken up with Christopher
about a month before. My parents planned to go out to a fancy
dinner, which they had not been able to do since January. I had
a knee-length gown, black taffeta over pink satin, sequined,
and layered to look like a giant bell. But the farce was too great;
I did not want to go. I felt weak and wanted only to rest. My
parents were already dressed. My mother looked beautiful: She
wore a black-and-gold embroidered cape over a black lace shirt
and black slacks. Her face was lightly brushed with makeup,
which she never wears. They stood on the stairs. "Why are you
not in your dress?" my mother asked, already afraid. When I
said I would not go, she said, her voice breaking, "But we can't
leave you here! This just isn't fair! You've ruined my winter!
You're ruining my life! Oh, you just can't do this to me! You're
not going to ruin my night!"

In the cab, on the way to the prom, I could not stop crying. I entered the ballroom and stood by the door. People and
lights swirled by me, and one of my friends spun off the rest to

come and greet me. "Hey! Nice dress! The music's not so great but . . ." and she swirled away. I ate some fruit. I sat on the floor. A dessert table threatened me from across the room. A friend came to sit by me and asked me what was wrong. I told him my mother didn't love me anymore.

"Let's go get some cheesecake," I said. It didn't seem worth it to protect myself. My mother didn't love me, so why should I? Once again, I ate so much that I couldn't throw up. From the stall, I heard people clicking and clacking in and out of the bathroom, exchanging gossip. I found an empty ballroom and hid there, trying to breathe. All I had in my purse was a phone, a paper clip, and gum. Nothing here to die with. I could go to CVS for ipecac or sleeping pills, but moving was difficult. A teacher opened a door and asked me if I was okay. "No," I said, smiling. "Could I please be alone right now?" He slowly retreated and shut the door. I picked up the phone and called my parents. "If you don't come take me to the hospital, I am going to die," I said. I didn't allow my mother her one night of peace after all.

The hospital wouldn't take me that night, because they said I was not sick enough. They held me until about 3:00 a.m. I kept guzzling water. My stomach ached from so much food; it hurt to move. My mom and dad made light talk and tried to distract me. Occasionally one of them would take a heavy breath, and my mom would put her hands in her lap and look down as my father ran his fingers through his hair, and one of them would excuse him- or herself to get some air. My mother sat by me, our party clothes glittering in the hospital-room light. As she stroked my hand, she explained how proud she was of me, how much a part of her own body I was. "I know you can't believe me now, but I will say it again and again that my love is not conditional. We all say crazy things when we suffer. We will work this out together. This will all get better. It has to." She looked around with her drawn and beautiful eyes, silvered from the party and colored, too, with grief. "It has to," she repeated. "It can't go on like this."

That weekend, my doctor forced the hospital to admit me. For a week, I lay in bed and ate. I wasn't allowed to get out of bed except to pee or take a ten-minute shower, and this I was only allowed to do at least an hour after meals, so that I couldn't purge. Christopher came to visit and took me on a piggyback ride around the floor. I got yelled at by the nurses but it was worth it: It was the only time I left the room all week. None of my other friends knew the full extent of my eating disorder. I told the few who knew I was in the hospital that I simply needed to gain some weight. I told them to tell everyone else at school that I had SARS, which was all over the news at the time.

One night I told my parents not to come. I was angry with the doctors, who I felt treated me like a mental patient and a liar. I didn't want my parents to see me feeling so pessimistic and bitter, so down on myself and on life. But they came anyway, and when they arrived, my father told me he was proud of me. "And I wanted to say it now, when you're feeling like you don't want to be here. When you feel that you aren't doing a good job because you're upset. I know this is very difficult for you, and I am proud of you."

Being in the hospital was an enormous relief. But aside from nourishing my body, it accomplished little else. When the week was up, I wanted to stay: I hoped that in that safe environment I could begin to regain the mental clarity I needed to recover. But I'd gained weight and my insurance had expired, so I had to leave.

There was less then a month left of senior year. I wanted to graduate, and the hospital promised me that as soon as I did, I could enter an inpatient program specifically for eating disorders. I kept myself together until after the ceremony; at home, afterward, I threw up while all of my relatives toasted my success downstairs.

But then the insurance company decided that, because I had been able to graduate, I must be well and no longer need inpatient treatment. When I heard this, I was distraught. I threw up all night. At 4:00 a.m., my mother heard my sobbing and found me in the living room. Unfinished food was scattered around like carnage after a battle. She took me upstairs to her bed and read to me from a book of short stories by Faulkner, whose long sentences calmed us. For an evening, we were true to our love of literature and each other. We were humbled by our pain, and words brought us closer together, and to ourselves.

Though I don't think I would ever have gone through with it, I started thinking about killing myself. My sister, home for the summer from college, found me weeping one night on my bed. She came up from behind, placed her arms around me, and pressed her face against my back. What she did not know was that there was a bottle of sleeping pills under the pillow in my hand. Without help, which my insurance denied me, I couldn't help myself. And I could not go on living as I was. I thought that my family would be better off if I were gone where my trauma could no longer torment them. After my sister left, I put the bottle of pills back on the bureau and cried until I slept.

A few days later, my mother came home to find me slouched in the living room, wrapped in a blanket, with an empty gallon of ice cream and a spoon in my lap. She decided to take me to the hospital.

When we got there I told a half-truth: that I had been considering suicide, and that if they did not let me in, I would do it. They put me in a room with no electrical outlets, no pictures behind glass, no stethoscopes, nothing except a cot. They put a guard in front of the door to watch. We stayed there all night, my mother sleeping fitfully, until an ambulance came to pick me up to take me to another hospital with a psychiatric ward. All these formalities were because of what I'd said, but I wasn't sorry at all. I was finally getting help.

At 6:00 a.m. I was taken to Waltham Hospital's General Psychiatric Ward. My mother described it as "more depressing than a bus stop on Christmas." Middle-aged alcoholics and drug addicts roamed the halls. No one monitored my meals or made sure I ate. I threw up in my bathroom just to prove I could. After three days of pestering, I was finally moved to the eating disorders unit downstairs.

My progress always followed a pattern during treatment. When I first arrived I was Miss Gung-ho Recovery, ready to be the best at what I do yet again. Then, after a few days, I crashed. I had been holding my emotions back for too long, and once I stopped my addictive behaviors, there was a flood. I was bowled over. But finally I calmed down, and then the real work could begin, the deeper work, which had nothing to with food or weight at all.

The problem was, once I reached that point, my insurance usually cut me off, so there wasn't time to do more than begin that hard work.

After two and a half weeks in Waltham, I went home. I felt a glimmering of life return. I no longer looked at the growing life of trees, of people on the street, and thought with hatred how separate from them I was. I had hope. My mother said she felt there was healing coming from me.

One night I went to a concert with some friends. A swooping, waltzing song began to play, so I grabbed a boy, a friend of a friend I barely knew. He had black eyes and curly black hair. He had an energy inside that seemed to spark in his eyes. We'd seen each other at parties during the year, but we'd never really spoken. Suddenly his arm seemed very warm behind my back. His neck was bent so that his smooth skin tightened and glowed in the clubhouse light.

We spent the night at my friend's house, and the next morning when we woke up, I put my head in Nick's lap. He stroked my corduroy legs and asked if I had lost some weight since we were first introduced. Yes, I said. It was a question, not a compliment. I felt again how much of myself had been lost, and hoped that I would get it back someday.

———

I saw Nick frequently over the next few weeks, spending nights in the humidity of his closet-size room. The summer was blossoming and redolent with heat. I brought protein bars and liquid supplements with me to concerts and friends' houses. I tried to follow my meal plan and keep my appointments with doctors and nutritionists all over the city. On the morning of my eighteenth birthday, I made love for the first time to Nick and then went to the circus with him, my mother, and all my friends.

It was clear, however, that I couldn't go to college in the fall. I was still struggling with bingeing and purging, and I was drained of emotional strength. I decided to devote the coming year to the task of recovery, and to find ways to give myself the time and space to do it.

I attended some day programs that my insurance provided. In the first one, the patients were let out after groups for a half hour, during which they would frequent the Dunkin' Donuts next door and its bathroom. I left that group after one day. Another program mixed kids ages seven to eighteen, with problems ranging from anger control to social phobia, from self-mutilation to drug addiction, and, of course, eating disorders. Discussions were necessarily broad-ranging, and therefore disappointingly superficial. Clearly, my insurance was not going to provide the structures I needed for support. I had to build them on my own.

I got a job at a bookstore, scheduled appointments with one of my doctors each day, filled my time with Nick and friends, and tried to keep my behaviors under control. I signed up for fiction, Italian, and life-drawing classes for the fall. My parents heard about a support group that met once a week in Newton, so I signed up for that, too.

Unfortunately, my bookstore turned out to be more of a candy shop. My coworkers ripped open bags of candy and left them under the counter where I stood. It was too easy to binge at the vacant register and then take a fifteen-minute break to the bathroom. From another woman in the support group, I learned about a residential center called Laurel Hill Inn, a small shingled house that looked like it belonged to the kind of grandmother we all ought to have, who makes Sunday dinners, crochets her own pot holders, and decorates in floral chintz. I stayed there for three months. My mother and father visited me at least once a week, trying to be cheerful but often leaving in tears. We had family therapy there once a week, as well. Neither they nor I had been able to comprehend the severity of my illness or the damage wrought by my brother's schizophrenia while we were still all together in the same house. Laurel Hill put the brakes on life and allowed us to look at what was happening. "These are watering tears," my mother said. "They will help us grow."

———

The most important step in recovery is regaining the ability to think clearly. The process of winning my mind back has taken almost four years and is not over yet. Some people say it is never over, no matter how long you've been free of symptoms.

Eventually, I moved out of the center of trauma—my parents' house—and in with Nick. I was diagnosed with posttraumatic stress disorder and received medication for anxiety and depression in conjunction with extensive therapy. Later on, I underwent a radical method of treatment with Dr. Pamela Cantor, where I spent a large portion of my days at her house receiving treatment: casually chatting, eating meals, grocery shopping, reading, writing, taking naps or walks.

This treatment was the most effective of any, helping me learn healthy ways to fill unstructured time and requiring that I go most of the day without throwing up. Still, my behavior plateaued at a level far below true recovery, and I remained in this semifunctional state for several years. I felt that I just couldn't concentrate enough to make the right day-to-day choices. I could not battle my anxiety when it came. I could not focus on tasks and deadlines. I could not stick to plans I made with my doctors or even get to my appointments on time. I couldn't keep up a fulfilling life, and I saw myself going to waste. I was horribly depressed.

I went to college one year later than I'd planned. I kept bingeing and purging, and my spirits dropped. Being a part-time student and a part-time addict is exhausting. After two years, I took a semester off. I got a job selling dresses and attended therapy twice a week. At the end of my time off, though, I felt that I was still dissociated from life, and that this was the obstacle inhibiting me from recovery and my true self. I asked my new therapist, the keen yet optimistic Dr. Woolston, to prescribe Adderall. Every student knows it helps you focus for exams, but I was interested in how it could clarify my thoughts in daily life. This medication isn't traditionally used to treat eating disorders, but I felt that it would address the root of what held me back. Trauma-induced dissociation is an inability to focus; lack of focus caused my depression, anxiety, and powerlessness to follow through on treatment strategies. I hoped Adderall could give me the wherewithal to combat my disease, earn back my mind and my life. We discussed it, and Dr. Woolston consented.

The drug has produced astonishing results. Not only do I function more normally, finishing tasks and meeting deadlines without the paralysis of anxiety, but I no longer feel helpless against my illness. I now have the power to make choices, rather than feeling victimized by forces beyond my control. The relief is incredible. I used to think that the best I could hope for was a strained truce between me and my disease. For the first time in years, I feel I have a chance at reclaiming my mind.

One unlikely benefit of my illness has been coming to know my father well, and realizing how well he always knew me. When my parents' marriage finally fell apart, he forced me to express my anger. He understood how much I needed to stop trying to protect my family from my fury and pain. With his insistence and guidance, I found a way to rebuild a relationship of intimacy and trust with my mother, which had been threatened in the development of my illness and the disintegration of my parents' marriage. After all, it was from love that her destructive anxieties sprung. Without my father's bravery, insight, and deep compassion, I could never have earned the strength I have today.

Things didn't ultimately work out with Nick, although I'll be grateful to him for the rest of my life. My current boyfriend is similarly contemplative and artistic. There is, however, a subtle and important difference between this relationship and any that has come before. He serves no function in my recovery; I do not *need* him to fulfill any role in my life. He enriches me, and I hope to do so for him. This affection is not fundamentally based on ego, and because of that, it is authentic and precious to me. I see in it a crystallization of the great gift of recovery: the integrity of what I can give, receive, and make when I am free to be whole.

MODELING SCHOOL

Elizabeth Kadetsky

New York circa 1980—era of fiscal crisis, draught, garbage
strikes, and "Nothing comes between me and my Calvins"—
was where my mother, then newly divorced, relocated us to
pick up her modeling career. At her peak as a model before the
birth of my older sister, my mother specialized in sixties haute
couture, a niche that required a small waist and chest, straight
lines from shoulder to hips and all the way down to thighs.
Because she was Quebecoise and because it was the era of the
Kennedys, her marketers promoted her as like Jackie but better,
elongated and more exotic.

Now, once again, my mother's hipless, breastless, exotic
brand of beauty aligned with the tastes of the times. Though
she was well into her thirties, she easily gained reentry.

And so at first, my mother, my sister, and I rode Checker
cabs. We all seemed too wispy to fill the capacious backseats,
and yet I very quickly came to understand it was exactly that—
our *weightlessness*—that made us capable of taking our place in
those cars, of participating in the kind of airborne flight New
York City seemed to be offering us.

Upon our arrival, we stayed with my mother's best friend,

Marty, a model and a divorcée, who lived in a great art deco skyscraper overlooking Central Park, with leaded windows and embossed tiling. I remember how, upstairs, we lived luxuriously amid Aubusson carpets and brass furniture, our sleeping bags laid out on parquet floors. On the ground floor, the building had its very own Gristedes; meanwhile, garbage stacked up because of a building employees' strike.

I also remember the omnipresence of Brooke Shields, the Calvin Klein model, on subway ads and bus kiosks. When we moved to an apartment on the Upper East Side, I started to see her on the street and in shops around my school and hers, a private one, also in the neighborhood. Shields was almost exactly my age, and thin, like me. It seemed to me that she and I occupied the same New York City universe, one whose essential ingredients were models, taxicabs, and glamour.

With Marty, my mother hatched a business scheme borrowed from the subway and park-bench ads: *Barbazon Modeling School: Three months to beauty and a new career.* Marty and my mother believed they could do a modeling institute better. They were the real thing, after all: towering beauties, barely a half-pound each, and graduates of the Carol Nash School of Charm in Boston. Their institute, offered by Marty in her apartment to me, my sister, and a friend from school, did not survive for long. But like the presence of Shields, it left a lasting impression on me.

As a student in Marty's modeling sessions, I dutifully imbibed such tricks of the trade as the runway pivot; the skipped meal; the single-sweet-a-day rule; the shoulders-back-and-down rule; the plumb line dropped from the ceiling pulling up the crown of the head; the runway sashay in which legs kick out from hips in apparent isolation from all other movement; the gaze fixed on a single point in the distance, slightly above parallel; the mechanics of holding one's center of gravity very high up in the rib cage.

But the real purpose of our studies was to learn about something deeper than these techniques, something ineffable and nearly holy: beauty. "Beauty is a form of Genius," Marty would say, quoting Oscar Wilde. "It is only shallow people who do not judge by appearances. The true mystery of the world is the visible, not the invisible."

Marty was thin like our mother, most often dressed in neatly pressed trousers and lacy camisole tops that failed to hide her boniness. She was flat in the chest and angular in the joints, and when she hugged me, I could feel her every bone. Her elegance came across better in photos—eyelids painted a dusky black, lips sculpted to sharp and full, cheekbones that took up the largest portion of her face.

Marty talked a lot about beauty—*"la beauté,"* she liked to call it—but often what she referred to as beauty was really just thinness. Each of those lessons in poise, I was coming to understand, either required thinness or enabled it. If beauty was the grail, thinness played an important part.

Perilous developments in fashion, for instance, struck Marty as assaults on svelte elegance. The papers were celebrating a trend toward "antifashion"—Yves Saint Laurent had called for "the end of haute couture"—and Marty perceived a conspiracy of all things frumpy and unflattering. "The peasant skirt will make you ugly," she opined, with a pause and a shudder. "The midi skirt. Oh, ban the midi! Please ban it."

She was especially undone by a recent innovation in *The New York Times* to use, as she scoffed, "models from *real life,* real people, not models."

Meanwhile, Marty instructed us in how to eat. Dole out a modest portion and tuck away the remainder safely in the fridge before you sit down, she advised us, so you eat less: "Large tummies result from a lack of self-control." After a session in her apartment, she'd hand us each an Entenmann's oatmeal cookie and repeat the rule, "One sweet a day. If you have a cookie in the afternoon, no dessert at night."

———

My mother actually hewed closer to Marty's hated ideology of antifashion, so we internalized certain contradictions and mixed messages. What I was to be, and how I was to be it, seemed clear, and yet not clear. The nature of the dichotomy—fashion versus antifashion—masked the existence of greater complexities. It seemed unquestionable, for instance, that what was available to my mother through her looks was not only available to me, but worth wanting.

My sister, who was two years older than I, injected the occasional note of skepticism. If the whole project seemed unworthy, by voicing this doubt she also scotched discussion about whom this project pertained to. Her own looks, quite striking, were less in keeping with the style of the times. Sometimes she criticized our mother for being vain or "acting like a queen."

"If I am a queen, you are a princess," my mother whispered to me in private. In defending herself against the charge of narcissism, my mother thus planted another hardy seed—I was her chosen heir. And I *was* her natural ally: I wanted to be like her—leggy, gorgeous, and charming in the lens of a camera. Who wouldn't?

One scene comes to mind in particular as illustrating the

choices—and privileges—before me. The three of us sat on one of the floor mattresses in my sister's and my bedroom, my mother's favorite plus-size crystal ashtray, a pack of Winston Longs, and matches laid out on the ground. My mother wore slim men's blue jeans belted near the hip, a man's white undershirt, and a pair of Geoffrey Beene tennis shoes—she'd acquired matching pairs for each of us on a modeling shoot. She'd left her thick hair unstyled so it swept around her cheekbones and accentuated their size, and as was her habit off the job, she wore no makeup or jewelry. "This is my new uniform," she explained with great seriousness. "All my life I've been trying to fit into women's clothes that are too short in the waist and too round in the ass." She patted her butt, or lack of one. "*Men's jeans!* Who knew? No one ever told me."

My sister mixed us each a cup of powdered café au lait from a tin, and I lit our mother a cigarette using a finger trick I was fond of. Her cigarette gave her fingers an appearance of exaggerated elegance. She inhaled and then exhaled long, swirled her powdered coffee to a foam. An empty Entenmann's box and bag of Stella D'oro anisette toast spilled crumbs onto the top of our bureau. It was well past dark, the dinner hour having come and gone.

I remember this as the moment my sister revealed the news she'd gotten into Stuyvesant, the celebrated public school in New York City that sent more grads to Harvard and MIT than any prep school. "You're my genius girl," I recall my mother saying, embracing her. It was a welcome victory for my sister, who for too long had to tolerate frequent comments from our relatives about how I resembled our mother. It wasn't so much that I was prettier, though it came across this way; what struck them was that I was tall, like our mother, and thin. On my father's side especially, they wouldn't let up about it. They rued that day a model left their clan, felt nostalgia for her glamour and exotic graces.

Nevertheless, my sister was generous about her moment of triumph. "You'll get in, too," she said to me.

Later, I did—and went to Stuyvesant as well. Still, somehow, that evening, when we sat on the floor with our mother, the world cleaved for my sister and me, leaving brains on one side of the chasm, beauty on the other. I was left the mantle of that exalted undefinable, Beauty. After that, my sister dropped out of our modeling classes and developed her own adolescent chic, involving boxy men's clothing that hid the contours of her newly voluptuous body. Her model's walk gave way to the impatient, eye-rolling shamble of an adolescent; mine remained driven from the rib cage. On visits with our father and his relatives in Boston, they began to call her "the smart one" while indulging her with extra dessert. Me they referred to as "the picky eater" who took after our mother—a backhanded compliment in its own way.

———

It was, paradoxically, my grooming in my mother's ideology of antifashion that led me to yoga. By the time I was in college, my mother, sister, and I were once again in solidarity, rejecting the materialist imperatives of our eighties culture.

Together, if at a distance now, we three cultivated a distaste for makeup and fancy clothes, a certainty that shaving one's legs or underarms or even keeping a mirror by one's closet were pointless vanities as well as a waste of time. I still wanted to be beautiful, but I took up antifashion and the "natural look" as personal crusades. I didn't wear makeup again until I was twenty-five.

Yet I believed I was beautiful, and believed this to be important. Without giving much thought to it, I remained thin. It wasn't hard, because I still ate the way I'd learned from my mother. This meant eating not meals, but just a sweet here and there to keep the blood sugar pumping. "Normal" eating seemed to me to involve a certain amount of denial, accompanied by midafternoon hunger crashes in which the world got slippery and objects took on a silvery shine. This seemed commonplace for others around me, too. "You girls," a friend observed one time when I turned up to a nighttime movie starry-eyed from a day without food. "You starve yourselves all day and then you come out at night ready to pass out." He shrugged.

So in college and after, living with roommates or a boyfriend, I rarely ate a meal that wasn't prepared for me by someone else. I took from yoga the idea that things came to you without your actively seeking them—and I applied this both to food and to looks.

In my years after college, the messages I took from yoga came to underlie my worldview as fundamentally as did those teachings from Marty. As Marty extolled the aesthetic as numinous, so, too, did the physical postures of yoga seem to embody a nameless and pure form of beauty. The body in the postures rang with the universal harmonies of their perfect shapes.

Pursuit of beauty did not vanish from my consciousness; it simply took another form. As I became more dedicated to yoga, I found the postures were aesthetic in themselves, and that myself in those postures could be beautiful as well—an expression of the divine. I struggled to locate grace in the pleasurable way the postures felt, and to suppress the self-consciousness that caused me to imagine how they looked to others. I tried to shift the gaze from *on* me to *in* me. This seemed an avenue toward achieving the oneness and loss of self we strived for in practice. Bliss was characterized by, above all, a lack of self-awareness, while self-awareness was the greatest obstacle to achieving that bliss. At times, the postures came to inhabit me so completely I felt that bliss.

But it was still difficult to separate the physical expression from the wish to be admired for it. My thinness, and the poise I'd acquired through my mother's training, gave me a natural facility, and people often praised this. One time I was in a class with Annette Bening, at a studio in West Hollywood that we both attended. I held a difficult posture, unmoving, and lost myself in the moment. Then I heard Bening gasp and exclaim to the room, "That is absolutely incredible." Her spotlight had shined on me. I felt the old, familiar rush. I was once again fashionable, once more *belonged.*

———

In many ways yoga seemed to support my habit of nursing a hunger, and pursuing a thinness. It seemed in keeping with yoga's denial of the physical self, while the dizzy, tingly sensation of hunger seemed a path to the ineffability and egolessness we sought through practice. For instance, my teacher at the time, an Indian guru, wrote:

> When all the eight disciplines of Yoga are combined and practiced, the yogi experiences oneness with the Creator and loses his identity of body, mind and self.

The haze of a skipped meal—that sensation of being empty, transparent inside—was an altered and euphoric state of consciousness. In yoga, this euphoria was achieved in a moment of instant awareness, called *samadhi,* when ego dissolved and you became a part of the large and holy "universal One."

Wrote the guru about *samadhi:*

> All thoughts and emotions are emptied. The seeker has no feeling of his own separate identity; nothing exists for him. He has crossed all barriers and becomes an emancipated soul *(siddha).* This is the State of the Void *(Sunya Desa).*

There were other ways yoga and hunger seemed to complement each other. Just as the yogi in euphoric *samadhi* experienced a loosening and ultimately a dissolving of the boundary between self and universe, my thinness—which was becoming more and more extreme in this period—seemed to make my physical boundaries fluid. It was as if my skin were becoming a thinner and thinner membrane between the outline of my physical body and the space around it. As I lost more weight, I came to envision a ghostly sheath around me tracing the contours of my old, larger self. It was a kind of force field, keeping me both protected and separated from those around me, and a reminder that physical boundaries were permeable and capable of shifting. Someday they could disappear entirely.

My vision was influenced by my reading of classical yoga texts. They spoke of *kosas,* or sheaths, fitting in nested layers within the outline of a mystical, or "subtle," body that was superimposed upon one's physical form. Each person's subtle body contained five sheaths nested one inside the other. The sheath closest to the center was closest to the "true" self, the self that was detached from the ego and therefore joined with the Universe. Peeling away the layers of my physical self, it seemed to me, would get me closer to that core. The thinner me would be the truer, more essential me.

I might also reach that core through a pursuit of purity, physical as well as metaphorical. In the medieval Hatha yoga texts, purity (called *saucha* in Sanskrit) was conceived as a kind of a mental state with a physical basis:

"*Saucha,*" wrote the guru, was

> the rooting out of the six evils: passion *(kama)*, anger *(krodha)*, greed *(lobha)*, infatuation *(moha)*, pride *(mada)*, and malice and envy *(matsayra)*.

In the conception of the medieval yogis, those "evils," like all things metaphysical, resided in the physical body. Monitoring what went into one's body was therefore one way to expunge them. This also held true because notions of purity in yoga accompanied deep-seated Indian beliefs that certain foods, behaviors, and kinds of physical contact could be polluting in a metaphysical, or even spiritual, sense.

"Both the quantity and quality of food should be moderated," the guru counseled.

> Chosen food might appear to be dainty and delicious, but it may not be good for the seeker. It may have high nutritive value and yet it may develop toxins affecting progress in pranayama.

Meanwhile, eating to satiety interfered with the emptiness one sought before physical practice in order to enable the ultimate experience of *samadhi.* Therefore, the seeker

> should fill half his stomach with solid food, one-fourth with fluids, and keep one-fourth empty for the free flow of breath.

I took to these guidelines naturally. I practiced strenuous physical forms, flipping in and out of seemingly impossible shapes, my brain wired and lacy from hunger.

———

My euphoria, and my conviction in the rightness of my habits of self-denial, were interrupted by a crisis. I came down with Montezuma's revenge in Mexico and dropped another five pounds. Afterward, the food poisoning lingered, and triggered a further diminishment in my diet. Five more pounds sloughed away, then another five pounds. There was something thrilling to me about this accelerated process of paring down. My feeling of dazed lightness edged into a state of mania, while my thinness edged into a state of malnutrition. I went to see a doctor at the campus medical clinic of the university where I was then in graduate school. She called it "morbid weight loss," and then uttered the phrase "anorexia nervosa," like a slur.

I believed she meant it that way, and I rejected it. *Anorexia:* the word to me was ugly, counter to everything I felt I was. It was harshly medical, clumsy, and impersonal. I'd observed anorexics in college, basketball-eyed triathletes on their bicycles seeking out whole grains at the health food store. I was not like them. I was congenitally thin, like my mother. If my emaciation made me less than beautiful in conventional terms right now, it still gave me the beauty that was based not on looks but on that most profound experience of life—an essential connection with one's own authentic self, a pure, unmediated interaction with the world. Beauty was thinness, and this state was godly.

A battle of wills ensued with my doctor and her team of

medical experts, who, nonetheless, through medical tests and steady pounding, ultimately convinced me there was no other cause for my stomach trouble, weight loss, and now-constant fatigue than my own willful self-starvation.

Like a scene from George Orwell, the doctor drubbed me over and over: "So, do you accept the diagnosis?"

I agonized about it endlessly, until I fell into doubt about everything. My mind spun into chaos. I wrote in my journal:

I hate my thinness and my fatness at once. I hate the pound I gained this week and the pounds I lost last month. The whole way home I am seized by hunger, but when I get there I can't eat. My stomach knots. What do I want? What can I afford? What should I eat? What time should I eat? I think-about-it, think-about-it, think-about-it and then discard all options and think-about-it more. Eventually I never wind up eating.

If I did eat, I continued in my journal, there was "panic. Panic all over. Cells bursting with too much inside them."

A nutritionist I'd been sent to believed that punctilious record keeping would reveal to me I was ingesting far less than I imagined and induce a *Eureka!* moment: I would be instantly cured of my resistance to the doctors' advice that I "supplement." So in compliance with orders, in my journal I also kept food and weight charts. I wrote down every morsel that passed my lips, and with niggling accuracy measured out every portion to the ounce, annotated it according to when I ate it and how much time had elapsed since I'd eaten before, and calculated how this contributed to my overall daily intake of calories and fat and protein—meanwhile categorizing my charts by the few foods I'd determined did not make me nauseous or bloated or gassy or sick all over.

It is a startling experience today to read through that document, a study in rigidity and obsession:

"There are twelve foods I can eat," I wrote. "Apple, quinoa, banana, polenta, yam, papaya, rice milk, soy milk, mango, amaranth, peach, zucchini."

In fact, these notations were helping me keep the numbers at a steady idle. I wasn't going to break the pattern and, indeed, three weeks after I first saw the doctor, those numbers hadn't budged a decimal point—pounds, calories, protein. This was because I truly believed beauty was thinness. Even while I knew my own was "morbid" and grotesque—ugly as the girls' on the bikes—I was addicted to it, just as I was addicted to afternoon hallucinations, feelings of mental tingly-ness, feeling wired, feeling like I could fly, *weightlessness*. These, I thought, were beauty as well.

———

I was indeed irrational. For their part, the doctors were infantilizing—I was thirty, not a teenager sulking behind a locked door in my room, rebelling against my parents' *rules;* not a reader of fashion magazines; not a proponent of the myth that thin was voguish or *in;* not eating one pea at a time off my plate strictly in the hope someone would notice and tell me to stop.

We became locked in combat. Such was my stubbornness at this time, I sought to document the ins and outs of our skirmishes, and so procured and filed away, among other things, my medical record. Their stance toward me, I see in looking it over now, was needlessly alienating. I never had a name, only "client," "patient," or its abbreviation, "Pt." The standard medical terminology—*Hx* for history, *Sx* for symptoms—seemed to hold me at even further distance.

I also see that I was an intransigent opponent:

> Pt admits that she's underweight . . . denies Hx eating disorder/depression. . . . She is a vegetarian with an alleged allergy to wheat . . . claims Sx parasitic GI infection. . . . Pt refuses to eat dairy products. . . . Client adamant. . . . Client hesitant and resistant. . . . Pt flatly refuses. . . . Client cried several times. . . . Patient very reluctant to accept probable diagnosis of anorexia nervosa. . . .

In spite of our mutual antagonism, through a chain of referrals originating with those doctors, I eventually found a therapist who helped me understand the illogic that lay at the foundation of my beliefs about beauty, and the damaging effect this was having on my body. Getting better required recognizing that beauty, whatever this really was, was less important than basic survival. Only once my weight was closer to normal could I take a step back and, with the help of several years' therapy, reassess those lessons from childhood.

All leads pointed to that indissoluble structure that was my family threesome—a triangle, that most sturdy of shapes.

Ironically, through a skeptical pestering of my original doctors in which I demanded they justify their methodology, I came to learn not only about the basis for their authoritarian therapy model, but some deeper and more insightful strains in the teachings on anorexia. These helped me identify this cause.

One theorist in particular influenced my treatment team in manners both nefarious and helpful. He was Salvador Minuchin, a 1980s-era child psychologist from Argentina who endorsed forced hospitalization—accompanied at times by what my doctors referred to euphemistically as "hyper-alimentation techniques," or tube feeding.

Originally, such humiliations were not necessarily intended to break the subject's will; now, Minuchin stated this as their goal. Curtailing the intransigent and stubborn behavior of an anorexic adolescent, he argued, required engaging her in a parent-versus-child-like battle for power in which she must ultimately succumb to the greater power of her superiors—be they parents or their stand-in, the therapist. This was without doubt a model doomed to breed resistance in any patient who happened to be a grown-up.

Minuchin, however, took this approach one step further by identifying a symbiotic role of parents and other family members. Hailing, thus, from the "family systems" school of psychology, Minuchin coined the term *anorexic* (or *enmeshed*) *family*. This lay on one extreme of a continuum of family types in which interpersonal boundaries ranged from enmeshed to permeable to rigid. In a 1978 study of anorexic girls, Minuchin determined that each came from a family characterized by an enmeshment; as he described it, "Each member of the family was overly involved with the others' feelings and thoughts." Anorexia, he theorized, was an attempt to escape from this—an expression of the sufferer's desire for identity and autonomy.

I read Minuchin, as well as other theorists, and began to consider the ways the clinical picture reflected my life. The context of my upbringing—New York City in its Fiorucci moment—had not in itself caused my anorexia, nor had my intimate contact with the world of fashion. Likewise, yoga could not be blamed. These environmental factors had only exacerbated something deeper and preexisting.

———

This struck me with the force of revelation as I drove to my therapist's office on Orange County's 5 freeway one day: My mother, my sister and I had all struggled over the years with individual problems and crises. Until now, I'd perceived them as isolated expressions of our distinct personalities. Now, however, I saw how our behaviors interlocked. It didn't seem a coincidence anymore, for instance, that my period of anorexia overlapped exactly with a different crisis of my sister's. Nor was it accidental that my mother had an almost micromanagerial involvement in both our recoveries.

Among the many random pages and documents I salvaged from this time, I have notes scribbled on the backs of everything—envelopes, sales receipts, one on the back of a slip from a hardware store documenting the purchase of a bathroom scale. On one scrap of paper, I took notes from a phone call in which my mother gave me an update on this crisis of my sister's. My mother then asked about the course of my treatment. I dutifully reported my own numbers, and heard my mother scribble them on her own envelope scraps that I would later find stacked on her desk beside her notes on my sister.

"I hate the clinicians," I told my mother.

My mother echoed my outrage: "They are so condescending." She recommended a supplement that I could purchase at the health food store to replace the doctors' sugary one. She asked for copies and references of academic texts I was reading on eating disorders.

My mother was so helpful, so sympathetic.

She said a counselor recommended she attend a meeting for codependents. Someone told her, she said, "that I'm suffering a codependency hangover from when I was a kid."

Soon after that conversation, she and my sister came to visit me in California. My mother started touching my hair, going through my cupboards. I felt revulsion. My sister asked what I weighed. "What gives them the right?" I wrote in my journal bitterly.

My mother hovered over my shoulder as I cut a papaya. She stared at it with a look, her look, *the look.* "My God, it looks alive," she whispered.

It did. I saw flesh red, obscenely slick, like the inner thighs after a warm bath. The seeds were a forbidden black, taut and alive, like breasts jiggling in beach Spandex. "A gaping maw," I said to my mother angrily, making a dark little joke to myself, because in spite of her thinness, she'd always been an enthusiastic eater—an eater, it just then occurred to me, of *other people's food.* My sister and I had an expression when we were kids, "a Mommy bite"—a sandwich-size deletion from your food that you'd prepared for yourself. My mother was a devourer.

I'd recently read something in a book about anorexia, *Hunger Strike,* by Susie Orbach, suggesting that fatness, for the anorexic, "represents folds and folds of uncontrollable needs." A gaping maw was how I saw myself, it was true. As in the clinical picture, I felt shame at my desires, large and fleshy. On the other hand, thinness, I was coming to understand from my readings on enmeshment, represented a lack of privacy. If becoming healthier meant making a separation from my mother, being thin meant inviting her to absorb me.

"Is this what I want?" I asked myself in a journal entry narrating that scene.

An obliteration of boundaries, my mother in the space where the rest of my body is supposed to be, my mother looking in, close, closer, come closer. See me.

"You look like a skeleton," people say this. "You look

like an X-ray," they say this too. I have nowhere to hide. Anorexia makes me bright, sparkly, sharp. But it gives me no extra room, no folds of fat, no place to go. There's nothing extra, only the bones. No place private.

———

If I am a queen, then you are a princess. Our matching tennis shoes, the way my mother encouraged all that commentary so wounding to my sister about our likeness; other things, too—how she became a vegetarian when I did, took a hitchhiking trip after I did, took to meditation, yoga. We had a lot in common. Or did she, in fact, want to *be* me, and for me to be her—a total collapse of boundaries?

I understood that this revelation held some truth when I reflected that my sister had desperately wanted to be a part of us and had felt often she wasn't. We were indeed a triangle, envy's favorite shape. There had been many clues that my sister believed us to be an unbalanced tripod.

One was an evening when the three of us were eating at a diner in New York while my sister and I were on breaks from college. There were mirrors on the walls both in front of and behind us, creating a disorienting tunnel of repeating images. I saw my mother in the reflections: olive-skinned; cat-eyed; a headband in her thick, dark, long hair. I saw my sister, her hair also thick and long and in a headband, her eyes dark and moody, her lips full, her cheekbones wide, her eyebrows strong and full. I saw myself. More hair like theirs. More eyebrows like theirs.

Sitting across from my sister, I lifted my fork. Watching me, she started and coughed. "I saw you in the mirror, and I thought you were Mommy. Then your fork moved, and hers didn't!"

She instantly got a pained expression, and just as instantly my mother and I assured her that we'd seen her reflection, too, and thought it ours, and not only that, but we'd gotten confused about one another's reflections, and wasn't it just a gas being three beautiful brunettes in a restaurant who all looked alike?

"We could all be sisters," my sister uttered with a smirk.

The therapist who finally helped me climb from my crisis said to me, "If you refuse to participate in the structures of a codependent family, you will make everyone very, very angry. The structure can't hold if you're not willing to be a part of it. In order for *them* to be them, *you* have to be you." We needed one another, it was true, each of us hoisting our equilateral beam. "They will do anything to keep you in it."

———

He made my family sound like a cult, which, funny enough, was sort of an apt description for that part of my life involving my yoga school. *Cult* was perhaps too strong a word, but around this time I also came to notice that the same lack of privacy that characterized my relations with my mother and sister also characterized those among the students at the school, who, after all, eagerly received the guiding patriarchal embrace of our guru in India. He spoke of a vast international spiderweb of followers as his "family." His relationship to his students was in the beginning, he wrote, like "a mother cat holding a blind and helpless kitten in her mouth." As the student progressed, the teacher became more like "a mother monkey when her baby first releases its grip on her fur, [who] keeps it close to her." Finally the student would develop the independence and fortitude of "the fish with unwinking eyes."

During my crisis, I continued to participate in a teacher's course at the yoga institute in West Hollywood. In the rest of my life, a don't-ask-don't-tell policy communicated what I took to be disgust from the people around me. Here, on the contrary, I submitted to frank questioning and proffering of advice.

During a workshop, someone I barely knew passed me a note: "I was bulimic once. I'm better now. But it's where I go, when things get bad. If you ever want to talk . . ."

"You are so thin," said another, during a break. As she spoke she touched my hair, *just like my mother.*

"You need to eat more," cooed another. "I wish I could cook."

"You look better," said a stranger. "I didn't want to say anything last time, but you were looking terrible." She held me by the shoulder. I didn't even know her name. *And what is your most intimate problem?* I said/didn't say/wish I'd said.

Though I didn't see the connection at the time, I began to break from this yoga community at the exact same time that I also resolved to cut off contact with my mother and sister. My therapist's predictions had been correct. Fury descended from everywhere. There were angry exchanges of letters, fights on the phone. "I used to think we were in everything together," my sister burst out at me. "Now it's like you're not on my team."

"I'm not," I lashed back at her. "Just because I'm related to you doesn't mean I'm your ally."

For nearly a year, I disappeared without an address or a phone number—a year, not so coincidentally, during which I lived in India and became disillusioned with my yoga community.

———

My break from that "family" involved going to study at a rival Indian yoga school and eventually adopting this school's methods: a small shift, in real-world terms, but in the eyes of a clan built upon codes of loyalty, a betrayal. The reaction among my former peers was swift and fierce. Because I'd become something of a public figure in this subculture, I learned about the anger directed at me from reading online discussion groups. I was asked not to appear again at the guru's studios in America.

I regretted the pain I caused my family. When I came back from India I moved to New York. My mother came to meet me immediately, and embraced me and started to cry. After that, our relationship changed dramatically. It no longer bothered me when she touched my hair, and she no longer drew parallels between herself or my sister and me.

Today I live across town from my mother and sister and see them often. They live together, enmeshed as lace, in a walk-up whose state of bohemian clutter closely resembles that in my own apartment. They bicker like an old married couple and light each other's cigarettes and dote on me and touch my hair. They regard me as the lucky one, the one who got away. Only I know how much I had to work for it, and how unlucky I was, too. But when I'm with them, I feel lucky because I have them, and also lucky that I got away.

I also know I'll never have back what I had with them—the feeling we could fly, together, a great three-headed creature of beauty circling the glittering city for all the world to gaze up at.

THIRTY YEARS LATER,
STILL WATCHING THE SCALE

Joyce Maynard

There was a pair of schlock artists popular in the sixties, Walter and Margaret Keane, who made their reputation by painting images of young girls with huge eyes and skinny bodies, looking sad. All through my growing-up, people would comment that I looked like a Keane painting—and it's true, I did: Skinny. Large-eyed. Hungry. *Love me* is the message those girls in the paintings conveyed, and I guess what my own waiflike countenance suggested. Though my parents were alive and well, in certain ways, it could be said, I was up for adoption. Calling out to be protected, rescued. And maybe it was in those early years that the lesson came to me: To be adored, a person should be thin.

It was not a look I consciously cultivated at first. A picky eater, I was underweight from the start. When I think of them now, the words my mother used to describe me seem odd, even bizarre—all the more so because she was the daughter of Russian immigrant Jews, and a woman for whom the Holocaust stood as a daily presence of oppression and tragedy. Still, what she said to me, when I left my plate untouched at dinner, was "You look like a concentration camp victim." Although her comment was an overstatement, this part remained true: There was little meat on my bones. I might not live on bread and water, but a bag of Fritos and a glass of water was plenty for me.

My mother—a voluptuous beauty and lifelong dieter—may have taken a certain pride and pleasure in that. Certainly my weight, and the issue of how to get me to eat, was a constant topic of conversation in our family. But as much as I heard about eating more, trying new foods, drinking my milk, I got another message, too: It was a good thing to be skinny. Looking that way inspired people to pay attention to me, worry about me, take care of me. I liked that, I think.

For the first fourteen years of my life, my waifish Keane look came naturally and without effort. Then (hardly a unique story here), sometime around the beginning of high school, my body began to change and fill out. I didn't have those little-match-girl legs anymore, or the flat, almost hollow chest. And maybe because so much had always been made of how thin I'd been, and maybe in part because my mother had taken a certain vicarious pleasure in my skinniness, I registered the womanliness of my body with increasing concern. If I didn't look fragile and hungry, who would feel a need to protect me or lavish me with tender care? If I didn't look like a child anymore, would I have to act like an adult?

In the fall of my senior year of high school, when I was seventeen years old, my weight reached a hundred and twenty pounds. Not really heavy, but curvy. I stopped eating and joined a gym. All that winter and into the spring, I continued to do my schoolwork, but my most passionate and obsessed energy went into making my flesh disappear. All those months, I executed sit-ups and counted calories. There weren't many to count. By my graduation that June, my weight had dropped to eighty-eight. And still, I thought I wasn't skinny enough.

This is the old story, of course. We know what it looks like now, and even, to a certain degree, where it comes from. It comes from the desire to hold off on womanhood and remain, as long as possible, in the safer territory of childhood. It's about the need to control one's life, perfectionism, depression, possibly, rejection of sexuality, the longing to please a highly critical parent, or the urge to punish that parent, or both.

In my case, just about all of those stories played a part in the radical transformation my body went through that year. Not just my body, either. Denying hunger also requires a rewiring of the brain.

———

In the fall and winter of 1970, when I was seventeen years old, I trained my mind to view self-denial as a good thing. I programmed my thinking in such a way that no bite of food entering my mouth went unnoticed or unmonitored. I taught myself to associate an empty stomach with a sense of pride and accomplishment, and a full one with shame. Nights alone in my bed, I ran my hand over my stomach and ribs. If I let myself slip and ate a piece of bread, or a piece of chocolate, what followed was a wave of self-hatred and disgust so great that after a while, I would no sooner have eaten bread than I would lick the floor of the subway at Times Square. For months, I had been telling myself that food was my enemy, and hunger my friend. There came a time—I am not sure anymore when it arrived—that I believed those things.

At the point when I stopped eating normally, I was a student at a prestigious boarding school that had only that year begun admitting women. The summer after my graduation—a summer during which my daily food intake consisted of a container of Dannon yogurt, an apple, and an ice cream cone—I maintained my low weight, though doing so required almost total concentration and dedication to the task. By this time, I had ceased menstruating. My breasts had virtually disappeared.

That fall, I entered Yale. Once again, I found myself surrounded by brilliant students and professors, inspiring courses, a world-class library, gym, theater, and more. And still, my greatest energy was spent on staying thin. Looking back on this now, I am appalled at the waste, but there you have it. I cared more about being able to trace every rib than I did about Faulkner or Chaucer or the history of postwar America, the play I was acting in, or—this is saddest of all—the friends I had come to know and like, but with whom I could not share a meal in the dining hall because if I did, I might have to consume food.

By this time, age eighteen, I had embarked on a writing career that opened all kinds of doors for me: job prospects in New York City, magazine assignments, even a book contract. Among the magazine stories I pitched that year was one about a disease called anorexia. The magazine turned it down. "Too way out and unusual," the editor told me. "The kinds of stories we want are the ones readers can identify with."

I attracted the attention of a man who liked that I was skinny and, in fact, taught me new tricks to stay that way. Over the year that followed, the relationship grew increasingly difficult for many reasons, but I suspect his policing of my body and my eating was one of them. I had liked it when I held the control myself. But the experience of having another person— even one I loved—telling me what to eat and forbidding certain foods filled me with frustration and anger, though I never acknowledged that at the time.

I started to sneak food. I borrowed the car and went to the

supermarket, and then—in the parking lot, with the heater on because it was winter—ate three yogurts in a row, followed by a bag of popcorn or half a pack of Fig Newtons. And, though I knew by this time how to make myself throw up (a skill the man had taught me), I couldn't get rid of everything I took in. I ceased to be so thin. Maybe I was a normal weight, but I felt gross, unlovable, and ashamed. And when the relationship ended, and grief overwhelmed me, and no one was there watching what I ate anymore, my appetite felt bottomless.

The years of self-starvation had removed all memory of how to eat like a normal person. I knew only two conditions: total denial, total indulgence. I binged often enough that I remained unhappy with my body. And I starved myself enough afterward that to eyes other than mine, I continued to look normal. Inside my head, it was as if a radio remained permanently tuned to my food and body concerns. I monitored my weight and the feeling of my stomach—bloated or flat—sometimes on an hourly basis. Wherever I went, whatever I did, I considered the calories I was burning, the foods I could or could not eat.

When I was twenty-three, having lived for more than five years in a state of constant vigilance and anxiety about my weight and eating, I fell in love again. Not right away, but after a while, I revealed my problem to the man who would become my husband. A naturally lean person, with healthy eating habits, an athletic lifestyle, and a disinclination to explore emotional complexities, he offered a single piece of advice in what would be our only conversation on the topic during our twelve years of marriage: "Eat what I eat," he told me. "Do what I do. You won't have a problem."

It was a little more difficult than that. Within months of our getting together, I was pregnant. The midwife instructed me that a thirty- to forty-pound weight gain was standard and appropriate. For a woman who could be thrown into despair by a fluctuation of more than a pound on the scale, this was a challenge, but oddly, also a relief. There was no way of looking thin anymore. It was unthinkable to starve myself, because to do that would starve my baby, too. The brain I'd taught to send off alarms and shut down all food consumption anytime I could feel a pinch of fat on my belly had to be reprogrammed again.

A person might expect someone like me, with my history of eating disorders, to enter into pregnancy with disgust and horror. No doubt the biggest reason I didn't had to do with my excitement over our baby and my lifelong anticipation of motherhood. Also, there was something that consumed my attention more than monitoring myself and my body. That is one fundamental gift of parenthood: how it takes you out of yourself and teaches you to consider another person first, as you may never have done before. I would like to think love of one's partner would do this, but in my case, it took love of my child.

For the first time in years, I ate. Not knowing how to do it very well, I ate too much, and the wrong things, and by the time I went into labor, I had gained more than fifty pounds. My face—pinched and sallow for so long—was now round and full. So were my legs, my arms, my ankles. A few years before, seeing myself this way, I would have felt shock and dismay, but pregnancy had obliterated my old standards. Where once I lay in bed at night feeling my ribs, now I ran my hand over my belly and felt a foot kicking, and I was happy.

In February 1978, our daughter was born, weighing seven and a half pounds. I was the first one among my friends to have a baby, so I was unfamiliar with the next part. Maybe I actually imagined that once she was delivered, the rest of the pounds would vanish.

They didn't. I don't know if what overtook me then was postpartum depression or the panic any person with eating disorders would experience in finding herself suddenly carrying an extra forty pounds. I know that the first time I stood naked in front of the mirror after my daughter's birth, I wept. Childbirth was not as painful as confronting my body afterward.

My husband had become a parent the same day I did, but—unfairly, it struck me—he bore none of pregnancy's ravages on his flat stomach, his perfectly defined abdominal muscles. *Eat what I eat, do what I do* felt like a bad joke. Now, indeed, there was an adorable, large-eyed girl living at our house, but she was my daughter, and as much as I delighted in every single thing about her, I mourned, too, for the girl I had been once, who seemed no longer to exist.

When I was seventeen, and feeling a need to trim down, I cut myself down to starvation eating levels and gave hours of my day over to exercising. When I was twenty-three, with a nursing baby, that wasn't possible. I covered myself in loose shirts instead. I had what I wanted more than anything: my daughter. But it also felt to me, at the time, as though what was required to get her had been nothing less than the loss of myself.

Much has been written and said about the condition of anorexia. The signs are obvious. The problem, in its most extreme form, is terrifying to witness, and the stakes—the risk of death—very clear. Less dramatic is the story that comes later—after the weight is gained, the body no longer skeletal or at risk of organ failure, or other medical crises.

In my case, the period of my life during which my weight remained dangerously low was relatively brief—a year and a half, maybe two at most. For me, it may be that far more suffering and pain occurred later, when I reentered the world of normal eating, or tried to. For me, it was making peace with no longer inhabiting the body of a waif that proved the hardest.

This is the other half of the story, the story of coming back. The body returns to normal weight, or maybe, as was the case for me, above the old normal. The shape fills out. And still, the brain of that person holds to the old set of ideas: that there is a kind of virtue in extreme thinness, and on the other side, that failing to be thin, and watching bones recede and disappear beneath flesh, is evidence of far greater failures—of will, of fortitude, of character.

Twenty-nine years have passed since, one day after my daughter's birth, I stepped onto my well-used bathroom scale and saw the number 158. Even all these years later, I can still remember how it felt, and the long painful months that followed, in which I slowly worked to regain some semblance of my old self.

Eventually, I lost the rest of those fifty pounds. I was never again the possessor of a flat stomach, and nobody again compared me to a girl in a Keane painting. Or a girl, period. I was a woman, clearly—with a baby in her arms, and nursing breasts, and widened hips, and stretch marks. It is evidence of my ability to embrace motherhood and womanhood over waifdom that I went on to bear two more babies. (Never again did I gain fifty pounds during pregnancy, though. The next time I knew better how to take care of myself.)

I am fifty-four now. Most people would describe me as normal weight. Now and then—generally during the summer, when I have time and energy to devote to the project—I apply myself to getting slimmer than normal. Never skinny, however, and I'm glad to say I no longer want to be that way. Still, certain aspects of the disease are with me, and always will be.

When I told someone recently that I had suffered from eating disorders as a young person, he looked surprised. "I would never have guessed," he said.

So it no longer shows on the outside, but in my brain, it's always there: the vigilance, the old anxiety if I see the numbers creeping up, or run my hand over my belly and feel too much flesh there. The wiring in the brain never quite gets ripped out. In the same way that an alcoholic, thirty years sober, still speaks of herself as "recovering," so do I.

All these years later, in bed at night, I sometimes still run my hand over my ribs, to make sure I can feel them. I can tell you the exact number of calories in a cashew. And then there is this: Suppose I get the flu. I feel miserable, lose my appetite, and throw up for a couple of days. And from some deep place, that internal radio signal I can't tune out completely, the old Keane girl in me still whispers in my ear, "Oh good, I bet I'll drop four pounds."

I no longer expect this voice will ever be silenced entirely. All I can do is take it in, and change the station.

CONTRIBUTORS

Priscilla Becker is a writer living in Brooklyn. Her first book of poetry, *Internal West*, won *The Paris Review* Book Prize, and her second, *Stories That Listen*, has just been completed.

Francesca Lia Block is the award-winning author of many books, including *Dangerous Angels: The Weetzie Bat Books*, *Necklace of Kisses*, *The Hanged Man*, and *Psyche in a Dress*. She lives in Los Angeles.

Maya Browne was the Development Executive for *Ray*, starring Jamie Foxx, Kerry Washington, and Terrence Howard, and last year she financed and produced *American Fork*, starring Billy Baldwin, Bruce McGill, and Kathleen Quinlan. She is also a writer and producer. She currently lives in New York City.

Jennifer Egan is the author of *Look at Me*, *The Invisible Circus*, and the story collection *Emerald City*. Her stories have been published in *The New Yorker*, *Harper's*, *GQ*, *Zoetrope*, and *Ploughshares*, and her nonfiction appears frequently in *The*

New York Times Magazine. She lives with her husband and sons in Brooklyn.

Clara Elliot (a pseudonym) is a senior at Yale University. Her poetry has been published in the *Seneca Review*.

Amanda Fortini is a contributing editor at *Slate*. She has also written for *The New Yorker*, *The New Republic*, *The New York Times Magazine*, *The New York Times Book Review*, *New York*, *The Forward*, *I.D.*, and *Elle*, among other publications. She lives in Los Angeles.

Louise Glück has won the Pulitzer Prize, the National Book Critics Circle Award, and, most recently, Yale's esteemed Bollingen Prize. Glück teaches at Yale University and lives in Cambridge, Massachusetts. Her next poetry collection, *A Village Life*, will be published by FSG.

Latria Graham is currently a student at Dartmouth College, studying English and Theater. She spends her vacation time with her family in Spartanburg, South Carolina, collecting stories for her senior thesis.

Francine du Plessix Gray has written twelve books, most recently *Madame de Staël: The First Modern Woman* and *Them: A Memoir of Parents*. She lives in Warren, Connecticut, in the house she shared for half a century with her late husband, the painter Cleve Gray.

Trisha Gura is the author of *Lying in Weight: The Hidden Epidemic of Eating Disorders in Adult Women*, and a journalist for such publications as *Science, Nature, Scientific American, Child, Yoga Journal,* and *Health.* She is a Knight Science Journalism Fellow and a Resident Scholar at Brandeis University.

Sarah Haight is a fashion writer for *W* magazine and *Women's Wear Daily.* Her writing has appeared in *Vogue, Teen Vogue, Nylon,* and *The New York Times Book Review.* She received her Master's in Social Work from NYU and lives in Brooklyn.

Lisa Halliday lives in New York and London and is working on a novel.

Elizabeth Kadetsky is the author of a memoir, *First There Is a Mountain,* about her year as a Fulbright scholar in India. Her short stories have appeared or are forthcoming in *Best New American Voices,* the *Pushcart Prizes, TriQuarterly,* and the *Gettysburg Review.*

Maura Kelly has published personal essays in *The New York Observer, Glamour, Salon, The Washington Post,* and other publications. A dating columnist for *AM New York,* she is working on a novel about a teenager who is losing her mind.

Ilana Kurshan lives in Jerusalem, where she studies Talmud and works in book publishing.

Joyce Maynard is the author of nine books, including the memoir *At Home in the World,* which has been translated into fourteen languages, and the novel *To Die For.* She lives in Northern California and runs the Lake Atitlan Writers' Workshop in Guatemala.

John Nolan (a pseudonym) is a journalist who has been published in *The Washington Post* and *The New York Times*, among many other newspapers and magazines.

Rudy Ruiz is a published author, entrepreneur, and frequent public speaker. A two-time Harvard graduate, he is an expert and advocate on Latino and Multicultural issues. He serves as CEO of Interlex, one of the nation's Top 20 Hispanic Ad Agencies, focusing on advocacy and social marketing.

———

Although they were written thirty years ago, Hilde Bruch's *Eating Disorders* and *The Golden Cage* remain among the most insightful and compassionate books about anorexia by a medical professional. *Eating Disorders*, which is the earlier (as well as the longer and denser) of the two, also offers an interesting perspective on the relationship between anorexia and obesity.

For further historical reading, Joan Jacobs Brumberg's *Fasting Girls: The History of Anorexia Nervosa* presents a detailed narrative of how anorexia has been understood from the late nineteenth century to the present. *From Fasting Saints to Anorexic Girls: The History of Self-Starvation*, by Walter Vandereycken and Ron van Deth, covers some of the same material but offers a broader scope, beginning in the early modern period and analyzing how self-starvation went from being primarily a religious concern (interpreted as a mark of either divine blessing or demonic possession) to being a medical one.

If you were interested by what you read here, have questions, or want to share your own story, please visit the book's Web site, www.goinghungry.com. However, I am not a qualified professional and can't offer medical advice. If you or someone you know is suffering from an eating disorder, you should seek help as soon as possible. The Web site of the Academy for Eating Disorders, the professional organization devoted to research and treatment of eating disorders (www.aedweb.org), allows you to search for treatment professionals in your area.

K.T.